Economic Crisis
and
Crisis Theory

Paul Mattick

Economic Crisis
and
Crisis Theory

M.E. Sharpe INC.

WHITE PLAINS, N.Y.

Copyright © 1981 by M. E. Sharpe, Inc.,
901 North Broadway, White Plains, New York 10603

Translated from the German by Paul Mattick Jr.

German texts: *Krisen und Krisentheorien* © 1974 by Paul Mattick.
Ernest Mandels 'Spätkapitalismus' © 1973 by Paul Mattick.

Library of Congress Cataloging in Publication Data

Mattick, Paul, 1904-
        Economic crisis and crisis theory.

        Translation of Krisen und Krisentheorien.
        Includes bibliographical references.
        1. Depressions. 2. Bussiness cycles.
I. Title.
HB3716.M3413   338.5′4   80-5459
ISBN 0-87332-179-0

Printed in the United States of America

Contents

Preface

It was not so long ago that Keynesian economics seemed to offer instrumentalities not only to overcome depressions but to avoid them altogether. This is no longer true, as we find ourselves in a post-Keynesian world in which neither the equilibrium tendencies of supply and demand nor Keynesian interventions in the economic processes are able to prevent the steady deterioration of the economy through rising inflation and growing unemployment. Due to the long postwar prosperity in the leading capitalist nations, this has come to many people as an unpleasant surprise and has led to a new concern with the problem of the capitalist crisis. Although largely ignored by bourgeois economists before 1929, crises accompanied the whole of capitalistic development as the decisive "regulator" of the capital accumulation process. It is thus worthwhile to take an overall look at the crisis cycle both as it has asserted itself historically and with respect to the responses it evoked in economic theory.

As regards bourgeois economics, however, there is very little to say, as its general equilibrium theory has no room for the dynamics of the disequilibrating process of capital expansion. Accumulation appears here as a matter of "saving," or as a phenomenon of "growth," for which an equilibrium path must be found in order to escape the persistent "business cycle." That the problem is considered at all reflects the inescapable recognition that many, or all, of the categories of bourgeois economic theory have no more bearing on long-run capitalistic development than on the everyday production and exchange relations of the capitalist market. There is a strong tendency to look back to classical political economy, or even to Marx, in search for a more useful theoretical approach for solutions to the problems of capital production. In this connection it is interesting to note that the questions raised by present-day economists merely repeat, but in a shallower form, the discussions around the crisis problem carried on in the Marxist camp around the turn of the century. These controversies, too, concerned the possibility of an "equilibrium path" leading to a crisis-free, harmonious development.

The different and contradictory interpretations of Marx's crisis theory may provide some comfort to its opponents, but they indicate no more than the infiltration of bourgeois economic concepts into Marxian doctrine as the theoretical complement to the practical integration of the socialist movement into the capitalist system. There was, and is, a two-pronged endeavor to reconcile, at least to some extent, the historical antagonism between Marxism and bourgeois economic theory, which finds its reflection in an increasing eclecticism in both quarters. That the crisis of Marxism is still deepening may be surmised from the article on Ernest Mandel's book on "late capitalism," which brings the discussion, so to speak, up to date and confronts it with undiluted Marxist crisis theory.

P.M.

Part I

But a great period of world history never expires as quickly as its heirs would hope, and perhaps must hope, if they are to be able to attack it with the necessary force.

Franz Mehring

1

Bourgeois Economics

The progressive development of the capitalist economy was from the start a process punctuated by setbacks. There were good and bad times, and for this an explanation was sought. That social production was at first still dominated by agriculture made it possible to find the cause of economic distress in the inconstancy of nature. Bad harvests could be blamed for the general scarcity of goods. In addition, the low productivity of agricultural labor, in the context of a growing population, awakened the fear that the development of capitalist production would run up against natural limits, indicating the inevitability of a stationary state. Bourgeois political economy was colored by a deep pessimism, which was overcome only with the accelerating growth of capital.

Although in classical economics social relations were regarded as "natural," this did not stop the classical theorists from explaining the distribution of income specifically in terms of these relations. And, while in classical theory the equilibrium of different interests was guaranteed by the exchange process, because the latter was regulated by the quantities of labor contained in the commodities exchanged, this character of exchange was called into question by the theory of distribution, and with it the equilibrium based on it. A purely formal consideration of exchange relationships, that is, together with the assumption of free competition, makes individual interests appear to coincide with that of society as a whole, and the economic law of the exchange of equivalents appears to ensure the system's justice. But recognition of the class-defined distribution of the social product between rent, wages, and profit implied that the formal model of the exchange process was not a legitimate abstraction from reality.

The labor theory of value propounded by the classical economists examined the conditions of the time and their future development from the standpoint of capital and, therefore, from the
standpoint of capital accumulation. With few exceptions, although
with different arguments, the classical theorists hypothesized that
capitalist accumulation would have definite limits that would manifest themselves in a decline of profits. According to David Ricardo,
accumulation would inevitably be limited by the decreasing productivity with which the soil could be cultivated. An increasing
difference between the returns from industry and agriculture would
raise wage costs and lower profit rates to the benefit of rents.

This theory obviously reflected the relationship between the
landowners and capitalists of Ricardo's time and had nothing to
do with developmental tendencies inherent in value production.
As Marx put it, it was Ricardo's inability to explain the developmental laws of capital on the basis of the nature of capitalism
itself that caused him to flee "from economics into organic chem-
istry."[1] Nevertheless, Marx saw in the English economists' concern
over the decline of the rate of profit a "profound understanding of
the conditions of capitalist production." What worried Ricardo,
for example, was

> that the rate of profit, the stimulating principle of capitalist production,
> the fundamental premise and driving force of accumulation, should be
> endangered by the development of production itself. . . . It comes to
> the surface here in a purely economic way—i.e., from the bourgeois
> point of view, within the limitations of capitalist understanding, from
> the standpoint of capitalist production itself—that it has its barrier,
> that it is relative, that it is not an absolute, but only an historical mode
> of production corresponding to a definite limited epoch in the devel-
> opment of the material requirements of production.[2]

If the tendency of profits to fall was first explained by
increasing competition and by increasing rents (in connection
with population growth), it was not long before wages were
also seen as conflicting with the profit requirements of accumulation. On the other hand, the extension of wage labor
as a social institution suggested, to those who analyzed value in
terms of labor time, questions about the origin of profit—ques-

tions answered by the producers' demand for the full proceeds of their labor. Like profit itself, accumulated capital came to be understood to be accumulated unpaid labor. To refute the accusation of capitalist exploitation thus demanded abandonment of the labor theory of value. Moreover, the problem of accumulation could simply be forgotten, as earlier apprehensions appeared to be false. Accumulation did not decline but increased, and capital unmistakeably dominated the whole society. Wage labor and capital now represented the fundamental antagonistic classes that determined the further metamorphoses of bourgeois economics.

The increasingly apologetic nature of economics did not, to be sure, require a conscious effort on the part of the bourgeois economists. For them, convinced as they were that the capitalist economy was the only possible one, every criticism of it was an unjustified and subjective distortion of the real facts of the matter. Apologetics appeared as objective, scientific knowledge, which no demonstrable shortcoming of the system could shake. Of course, the generalization of the capitalist economy as a model for all social systems required an ahistorical approach and the conversion of the categories of political economy into general laws of human behavior.

As the past can only be conceptualized in terms derived from the present, for Marx also the bourgeois economy provided a key to the understanding of earlier forms of society, "but not at all in the manner of the economists, who smudge over all historical differences and see bourgeois relations in all forms of society."[3] There are general, abstract categories applicable more or less to all forms of society, but for the analysis of any particular system they must be given a content corresponding to that system alone. Money as a means of exchange and money as capital express different social relationships, and the means of production utilized in the past are not to be equated with capital or self-expanding value. The capitalist economy cannot be explained on the basis of abstract general categories of human behavior; the attempt to do so arises either from ignorance of real social interrelations or from the wish to escape the problems they involve.

According to Marx, the classical theory of value rested on a confusion between the natural and the economic senses of production. Taking labor as a starting point, it thought of capital as a thing, not as a social relationship. However, "to develop the concept of capital it is necessary to begin not with labor but with value and, precisely, with exchange value already developed in the movement of circulation."[4] It is on the difference between the exchange value and the use value of labor power that the existence and the development of capitalist society depend, a distinction that presupposes the separation of the worker from the means of production. Labor itself has no value, but the commodity labor power generates, when consumed, a surplus value in addition to its own value. This surplus value divides into the various economic categories of the market economy, like price, profit, interest, and rent—categories that at the same time conceal their origin as shares of surplus value.

The Marxian critique of bourgeois economics was therefore a double one. On the one hand, it consisted in the rigorous application of the labor theory of value to the study of capitalist development, which it analyzed in terms of the system's own fetishistic economic categories. On the other hand, it exposed these categories as expressions of the class and exploitation relations specific to capitalist commodity production. Marx achieved what the classical economists could not—namely, an explanation of capital's growing difficulties by the contradiction, specific to capitalism, between exchange-value and use-value production. In this way he succeeded in showing that the limits of capital are set by capital itself. And since the economic categories mask real class relations, the economic contradictions characteristic of capitalism are at the same time real antagonisms of interest, which can therefore be abolished only by revolution.

Because it refused to observe the class conflict between labor and capital to which capitalism gave birth, classical economics saw itself as an unbiased science. It did not, however, fall into pure positivism, since at the same time, from its normative side it indulged itself in proposals for the redress of persisting or newly emerging grievances. The harmony of interests expected to characterize market society was held to be delayed by the retrograde efforts of mercantilist monopoly and monetary policy. At the same time, however, doubts arose that universal competition would be a cure-all for economic injustice. The obvious pauperization of the workers led John Stuart Mill, for instance, to suggest a modification of the economic consequences of capitalist production by a more just distribution of income, to be achieved by political means. For Marx the relation of production to distribution was determined by the class relations of production. From this point of view Mill only shows his "fatuity" when he "considers the bourgeois relations of production as eternal, but their forms of distribution as historical, [and thereby] shows that he understands neither the one nor the other."[5] The normative elements of classical economics expressed only an insufficient understanding of the capitalist economy.

In general the political economy that arose along with capitalism was still the idealized representation, from the bourgeois point of view, of commodity production in which exchange enabled the possessors of the means of production to realize profits. The practical critique of political economy represented by the workers' struggle for better living conditions remained within the same conceptual framework, seen from the workers' side. The content of political economy was thus the struggle between labor and capital disguised in economic categories. So long as the bourgeoisie adhered to the labor theory of value, in its own way it recognized objective realities, even if it passed over in silence the fact of exploitation. By abandoning this theory it deprived itself of the possibility of objective knowledge of economic relations and relinquished to its Marxian critique the scientific investigation of bourgeois society.

It would be incorrect, however, to explain the bourgeoisie's abandonment of the labor theory of value solely by the desire to deny the fact of exploitation. To begin with, the real significance of this theory—the dual character of labor power, at once an exchange value and a use value—was not correctly understood. In addition, the labor theory had no practical importance for the bourgeoisie. In the business world we encounter not labor-time values but the prices derived from them and established through competition. This need not have prevented the classical theorists from establishing the validity of the value theory, since their starting point was the society as a whole, and indeed they put a great

7

deal of effort into the matter. But the solution of the theoretical difficulties connected with the labor theory of value was left to Marx. Their inability to overcome them thus surely had a role in the economists' abandonment of the law of value.

Be that as it may, to account for profit, interest, and rent on the basis of the law of value could only make it clear that the workers produce a surplus value, in addition to the value of their labor power, which the nonproducing layers of society appropriate. The idea that labor alone creates value had to be dropped if income in the form of profit, interest, and rent was to be justified. This move was not only necessary but also plausible, for under capitalist conditions the workers can no more produce without capital than capital without workers. As the workers' lack of property is the presupposition of capitalist production, so capitalist possession of property is the presupposition of the existence of a proletariat. Since labor is as necessary as capital, and people do live on the earth, we can speak of three factors of production— land, labor, and capital—that play equal parts in production. Thus the labor theory of value gave way, to begin with, to a theory of the determination of production costs by these three factors.

Although incompatible with the law of value, the cost-of-production theory remained an "objective" conception of value (in contrast with the later derivation of value from the subjective evaluations of consumers) in that it acknowledged the role of various putative contributions to social production and represented their value. In this theory the value of commodities was determined not only by the labor directly expended in their production but also by the conditions of production without which this labor would be impossible. Interest, often not distinguished from profit, was explained as arising from the "productivity of capital." "Pure" profit (distinguished from interest) was explained as the payment to the entrepreneur on whose activity another portion of the total social value was supposed to depend. The cost-of-production approach, however, was unsatisfactory both from the theoretical and from the practical point of view. Moreover, the idea of property ownership as *per se* creative of value also was rather questionable. But the identification of the market price of labor power with its value (so that the worker seemed to be paid the full value of his labor) permitted the illusion that the gains obtained on the market were not based on exploitation. The problems of bourgeois economics seemed to disappear as soon as one ignored production and attended only to the market. This exclusive concentration on the market led to the transformation of the objective concept of value into a subjective one.

The plausible idea that the value of a commodity derives from its utility for the purchaser had also not been foreign to the classical economists. Thus Jean-Baptiste Say had already tried to explain value on the basis of utility only to come to the conclusion that the latter could not be measured. It was measurable only by the quantity of labor which a person would be willing to perform in order to purchase a commodity. For Marx, too, the exchange value of commodities presupposed their having a use value. But capitalism is based not on the exchange of products of labor for the satisfaction of individual needs but on the exchange of some use value, playing a role as exchange value, for a greater quantity of exchange value in its gold or commodity form. For such an exchange to be possible as an exchange of labor-time equivalents, there must be a commodity whose use value is greater than its exchange value in an objectively measurable sense—i.e., in value terms. The commodity labor power—whose use value is labor itself—fulfills this condition. But if, like the economists, we disregard this real basis of capitalism, exchange indeed appears to serve the satisfaction of individual needs, and the valuation of commodities seems to be determined by the multiplicity of subjective human preferences.

Viewed apart from production, the price problem can be dealt with purely in terms of the market. If the supply of commodities exceeds the demand for them, their price falls; in the opposite case it rises. The movement of prices, however, cannot explain the phenomenon of price itself, as a property of products. Even if the objective concept of value is given up, some other concept of value must be maintained to say more than that prices determine prices. The "solution" to this problem was found in a move from economics to psychology. Prices, economists began to claim, are based on consumers' individual evaluations as represented by their demand for goods. Prices are then explained by the scarcity of the goods in question relative to the demand for them. It did not take long for this subjective treatment of value, in the form of "marginal utility theory," to become almost universally accepted within bourgeois economics.

With the marginal utility theory the idea of political economy lost its sense and was abandoned for that of "pure" economics. Marginalism was not different in method from classical economics, but it applied this method no longer to social problems but to the behavior of individuals with respect to the goods available to them and to the consequences of this behavior for the exchange process. Naturally, classical economics also concerned itself with the individual who, as *homo economicus*, competed with other individuals for the greatest possible gain. But this competition was thought to be a process of equilibration and ordering that adjusted production and distribution to social requirements. While this process took place—as if directed by an invisible hand—behind the backs of the producers, it nevertheless took place, effecting the necessary unity of private and general interest. Conversely, it could obviously not occur to the marginalists to deny the existence of society. But for them social conditions were only a means to the end of establishing the "economic relation" of the individual to the things he finds of use. They saw this relation as holding for individuals outside society as well as for each person in any and every society, so that the nature of any particular society was irrelevant.

Marginalism rested on the application to the economy of the not overly profound discovery that there can be too many good things as well as too many bad ones. In Germany it was Hermann Heinrich Gossen[6] who first argued for this principle. At first unappreciated, it later won recognition through the popularity of the Englishman William Stanley Jevons's independently developed concept of marginal utility.[7] At the same time, Karl Menger[8] founded the "Austrian School" of theoretical economics, based on the subjective value concept, to which, among others, Friedrich von Wieser[9] and Eugen von Böhm-Bawerk[10] belonged. Although these economists differ among themselves on details, they can be lumped together as joint founders of marginal utility theory.

Marginalism takes its departure from the needs of individuals.

The evaluation of these needs is an affair of human consciousness and thus is subjective. Exchange value and use value, which take account of the scarcity or superfluity of consumer goods, are only different forms of the general phenomenon of subjective evaluation. The desire for any particular good is limited. The point, on an individual's scale of satisfaction, at which the desire for a good is satisfied determines that good's marginal utility and thereby its value. Since an individual's needs are multiple, he chooses between the various goods available in such a way as to realize the maximum of marginal utility. Since some pleasures of the moment have painful consequences, he measures present satisfactions against future privations in order to minimize dissatisfaction. In the market everyone measures the value of a commodity by its marginal utility, total utility reaching its maximum when the marginal utilities of all the commodities purchased are equal.

Who does not know that human life is attended by pleasure and pain and that everyone seeks to diminish the latter and increase the former? Just like the utilitarian philosopher and social reformer Jeremy Bentham, Jevons held pleasure and its opposite to be quantifiable and calculable, thanks to which economics can be mathematically conceived and algebraically represented. But what Say had already failed to do Jevons and the other marginalists did not achieve, and the attempt to measure subjective utilities was soon abandoned. It was agreed that utilities could be compared but not measured exactly.

Bourgeois apologetics had taken on two tasks. On the one hand, it was thought essential to represent the winning of profit, interest, and rent as participation in the creation of wealth. On the other, it was thought desirable to found the authority of economics on the procedures of natural science. This second desire prompted a search for general economic laws independent of time and circumstances. If such laws could be proven, the existing society would thereby be legitimated and every idea of changing it refuted. Subjective value theory promised to accomplish both tasks at once. Disregarding the exchange relation peculiar to capitalism —that between the sellers and buyers of labor power—it could explain the division of the social product, under whatever forms, as resulting from the needs of the exchangers themselves.

This attempt had already been anticipated in Nassau W. Senior's[11] view that interest and profit should be considered as recompense for the sacrifice undergone by the capitalist in his abstention from consumption in favor of capital formation. Thus the cost of capital, like the cost of labor—in the sense of the pain of work—could be seen as an abstention from pleasure, and profit could be put on a par with wages. Apart from these abstentions the goal of exchange was the satisfaction of the needs of the exchangers, so that everyone could only gain in exchange, since everyone obviously valued the goods or services that he received more highly than those he gave in return. The capitalist buys labor power because it means more to him than the sum of wages paid for it, and the worker sells his labor power because it means less to him than the wage received in exchange. Thus the exchange benefits both, and there can be no talk of exploitation.

Since subjective value cannot be measured, the psychological foundation of marginal utility was soon given up, of course without abandoning the theory itself. "Utility" now referred not to the subjective evaluations themselves but to their manifestations in market demand. Utility, it was now held, concerned not so much a particular commodity as the number of commodities among which the buyer would be pleased to choose. This ordering or preference scale of the consumer's was represented graphically by so-called indifference curves. Thus economists now distinguished between the absolute (cardinal) magnitude of utility and the relative (ordinal) utility, which was represented in the preference scale. The concept of marginal utility metamorphosed into that of the marginal rate of substitution, the rate at which the quantity of one good must increase to compensate for the diminishing quantity of another. Maximal want satisfaction could then be defined in terms of the marginal rates of substitution between all pairs of goods. In other words, the buyer would so distribute his money that all the goods he purchased were equally valuable to him, at which point his choice behavior would come to a satisfactory conclusion.

Not all marginalists were ready to give up the concept of cardinal utility, and for others the concept of ordinal utility did not go far enough, as it still referred to subjective value. Since the marginal utility could be observed only in the price, this group preferred a pure price theory which kept its distance from all value problems. Marginalism ran into another difficulty, that it was impossible to regard price as determined by the demand side alone. Without a doubt there must be production as well as consumption and supply prices as well as demand prices. In meeting this problem they moved to unite the subjective value theory with its precursor, the cost-of-production theory. This gave rise to the so-called neoclassical theory, which found its most important representative in Alfred Marshall.[12]

Of course, in this approach production costs were defined in subjective terms, as capitalist abstention and workers' disinclination to work. Just as marginal utility was supposed to determine demand, so behind supply was discovered the marginal propensity to work more or to defer consumption in favor of capital formation. At the same time, it was clear to Marshall that these factors determining supply and demand were not observable as such, and that the only clue to these "real" factors would be found in the actual price relations. The monetary system converted subjective valuations into prices that thus reflected "real" needs and abstentions. In the form of price the nonquantifiable subjective value would become a measurable value. Since prices were regulated by the tendency of supply and demand toward equilibrium, the relation of supply and demand would determine commodity values in the long run, if not at every moment.

For another variant of the marginal utility theory, production, as an obvious prerequisite of exchange, required no particular investigation. For Leon Walras,[13] the founder of the "Lausanne School," economics as a whole was nothing but a theory of commodity exchange and price determination. For him, too, value arose from the scarcity of goods in relation to wants, with marginal utility explaining the variations in the intensity of felt needs. But exactly as the individual through his choices on the market would bring his various needs into an equilibrium of want satisfaction, so exchange on the level of society as a whole would tend to a "general equilibrium" in which the total value of demanded goods and services would correspond to the total value supplied.

To be sure, the assumption of a tendency to equilibrium of supply and demand effected by exchange lay at the basis of all market theories. Walras, however, attempted to prove the validity of this assumption in the manner of the exact sciences. According to him marginal utility was not only self-evident but also measurable by the application of the principle of substitution to the commodity market as a whole, where all prices inextricably intertwined. Prices seemed to him to be inversely proportional to the quantities of commodities exchanged. Production costs were formed, in his eyes, by the wages, interest, and rents entering into them, which he considered alike as payments for productive services. All persons exchanged their productive services for consumer goods of equal value. The "reality" of the subjective values manifested in equilibrium prices was here visible in the equilibrium of the economy, and this equilibrium in turn demonstrated the validity of the subjective value concept. As value and equilibrium defined each other, the theory of value was equated to that of general equilibrium, and it sufficed to prove the theoretical possibility of the latter to prove the validity of the subjective theory of value.

Despite its dependence on circular reasoning, the idea of equilibrium—applied to the economy as a whole, to parts of it, or to particular cases—remains one of the methodological principles of bourgeois economics, if only because from this discipline's point of view, all movement in the world—not only that of the economy—tends toward equilibrium states. Of course, the Walrasian system of general equilibrium—represented by a system of simultaneous equations—was only a model and not a picture of concrete conditions. It claimed, however, the status of scientific knowledge on the ground that though the economy might depart from equilibrium, it would always tend to return to this condition. On account of the involution and complexity of the manifold intertwined economic processes, theoretical proof of the possibility of equilibrium could be furnished only by means of mathematics on a level of abstraction which, while corresponding to the theory, had lost all connection with reality.

The hypothesis that in the last analysis the consumers determine the value of commodities took no account of the social distribution of income. John Bates Clark[14] attempted to remedy this situation through the application of marginal analysis to the factors of production. Just as in consumption the degree of saturation determined marginal utility, so a steady increase in the supply of labor implied its decreasing marginal productivity. This marginal productivity was represented by the wage paid at the time. The identity, or equilibrium, between wage and marginal productivity could of course be disturbed, but only to reestablish itself. For example, if the marginal productivity exceeded the wage, the demand for labor would increase until marginal productivity and wage again balanced. If the wage exceeded the marginal productivity, the demand for labor would go down until the identity of marginal productivity and wage was reestablished. What held for wage labor would hold for all the other factors of production, so that in equilibrium all factors would share in the total income in proportion to their marginal productivity. In this way not only supply and demand but also the distribution of the social product were explained in terms of marginal utility (or disutility). And since every factor of production received the share of the social product corresponding to its contribution to social production, the existing distribution of income was not only economically determined but also just.

To some adepts of marginalism the inclusion of social production in the subjective value theory seemed uncalled for. To Böhm-Bawerk,[15] for whom all production in the last analysis was only for the sake of consumption, it made no sense to make a special study of production or to speak of a dependence of income distribution on the marginal productivity of the factors of production. The production of capital was for him "indirect" production, by contrast with "direct" production, or production carried on essentially without the use of means of production. From this point of view, every production process that involved means of production would be a capitalist production process, even in a socialist economy. For Böhm-Bawerk there were only two factors of production, labor and land; he considered capital as a purely theoretical concept, not a historical one. All present goods represented means of consumption, and future goods—including means of consumption—appeared in the intervening time as capital goods and products of labor. Profit, of which he took account only as interest, arose not from production but from the exchange of present goods for future goods. Marginal utility decided the relative valuation of present and future goods.

According to Böhm-Bawerk interest was thus not only inevitable but also justified, as all production depended directly on the capitalists' propensity to save, and workers, like landed proprietors, depended on capitalist credit. Neither could live directly from their production, as this would require various periods of manufacture. While they were producing they had to live on products made at an earlier time. Anyone not willing or able to restrain his consumption and to save would have no claim to the interest due to the time factor. Although interest was the form in which the revenue from capital goods was paid or collected, it was a product neither of labor nor of capital but a gain due simply to the passage of time —so to speak, a gift from heaven. Interest was all the more a heavenly gift as it was equally the instrument of economic equilibrium and progress. It established the necessary equilibrium between current and future production by regulating the extension or contraction of capital investments in reference to the consumption requirements given at any time. As indirect production increased, moreover, the mass of consumption goods would grow, thereby decreasing the need for new saving for additional means of production. In this way social progress would manifest itself in a declining rate of interest.

It would not be worthwhile, however, to spend time on other exponents of the subjective value theory, just as it was hardly wrong to ignore it completely in its heyday. Marx had nothing to say about it,[16] and for Friedrich Engels it was only a bad joke,[17] although he thought it quite possible "that it is just as easy to build up . . . [a] plausible vulgar socialism . . . on the foundation of Jevons's and Menger's theory of use value and marginal utility."[18] In fact, a section of the reformist Social Democracy did turn toward the marginal utility theory out of the conviction that Marx's alleged neglect of demand and its role in price formation had kept him from grasping the real interconnections of the economy. But even while the subjective value theory was gaining ground in the Social Democratic camp, it had already lost its persuasive power in the bourgeois camp and would soon be completely abandoned. Indeed, it is the rejection of the psychological conception of value by the bourgeoisie itself which renders superfluous a detailed critique of this theory.

The subjective value theory was discredited, first, by a theoretical refinement so excessive that it lost any visible connection with reality, and second, by the frank renunciation of the attempt to explain price by value. Joseph A. Schumpeter[19] may be mentioned in connection with the first of these endeavors. From the standpoint of the Austrian School, from which he came, the value of final products, or consumer goods, depends on their marginal utility for the consumer, while the marginal utility of intermediate products, such as raw materials and machinery, is derived by a process of imputation from the marginal utilities of the final goods. For the consumer the various raw materials, means of production, and semifinished goods have no direct but only an indirect use value, but this is represented, through the process of imputation, in the prices of the consumer goods. The same analysis was offered for commodity circulation. A distinction was made between first-order and second-order goods, the latter being those which have not yet entered into consumption and whose utility must be imputed to the marginal utility of the consumer goods. Schumpeter concluded from this that, seen theoretically, supply and demand are one and the same, so that the demand side is sufficient to state the conditions of equilibrium.

In Schumpeter's conception of equilibrium not only were supply prices superfluous, since they could be understood in the form of demand prices, but profit and interest can be omitted as separate categories by including them under the rubric of wages. Equating production with exchange, Schumpeter saw no need to deal with utility or its opposite. He replaced the psychological concept of value with a logic of choices, since even the subjective concept allowed one to say no more than that a person, with given tastes and income, is guided in his purchases by the given prices. Schumpeter had no interest in investigating the fundamental factors which determine consumer choices but took them as the given starting point for economic analysis. The logic of choice was sufficient for the mathematics of equilibrium, which on this abstract level admittedly had no real significance. Nevertheless, the "pure theory" was supposed to be a means to the understanding of reality and to stand in the same relation to it as theoretical mechanics to practical engineering. In any case, "pure theory" was a valuable pursuit in itself because it was interesting in its own right and satisfied human curiosity.

Among others it was notably Gustav Cassel[20] who strove for the abolition of the marginal utility theory because of its vicious circularity. Although the theory was supposed to explain prices, prices were made use of in the explanation of marginal utilities. As business is transacted in terms of measurable quantities, money and prices, in Cassel's view the analysis of those transactions required nothing but price concepts, so that economics had no need of any theory of value. On the assumption that economic relationships are determined by a general "scarcity," Cassel saw the task of economics as the optimal adaptation of people's various wants to the insufficient means available for their satisfaction.

The derivation of prices from the scarcity of goods can of course only explain one price by another and leaves the question of what lies behind prices unanswered. Bourgeois economics, however, sees no need to pose this question. It has therefore abandoned the original doctrine of marginal utility, as it can make do without it and is able to return to it, when necessary, with the assertion that in the final analysis prices express consumers' subjective evaluations. Indeed, it came to be said that modern economic theory became an objective science just because it is based on the subjective. According to Ludwig von Mises,[21] people's needs are observable in their behavior, which requires no deeper investigation; they are to be taken as they are given. Since the marginal utility theory was finally boiled down to an identification of the economic realm with the domain of the price mechanism, the various attempts to substitute psychologically grounded marginal utilities for the objective value theory must be considered to have failed. They led only to the elimination of the value problem from bourgeois economics.

Although the concept of marginal utility was abandoned, marginal analysis remained generally accepted by bourgeois economists. According to Joan Robinson, this showed that even "metaphysical concepts, which are strictly speaking nonsense, have made a contribution to science."[22] As an instrument of analysis the principle of the "margin" is no more than a generalization of Ricardo's idea of differential rent. Ricardo believed the price of agricultural products to depend on the yield of the least fertile soil; *mutatis mutandis*, the Ricardian law of diminishing returns is supposed to hold for industry just as for every other sort of economic activity and to determine prices and their fluctuations. The individual arranges his purchases, on the basis of the given prices, in such a way as to obtain the maximum satisfaction available with his income; in the same way, since all individuals follow this "rational" or "economic" principle, the interdependence of prices produces a general price configuration in which supply and demand are balanced. When the total demand is equal to the total supply, all prices are equilibrium prices; conversely, application of the economic principle (or marginal principle) leads to prices which represent a general equilibrium. Thus "pure theory" was anchored by the all-embracing marginal principle, on which the price theory in all its detail was built.

It is not worth the consumer's effort in daily life to "optimize" the distribution of his expenditures by the application of marginal calculation—apart from the question of whether he is in a position to do so. In the behavior of the capitalist entrepreneur as well, marginal calculation does not play the role assigned to it by the economists. To be sure, the latter admit that their theoretical reflections do not picture the world as it really is. But they are supposed to be close enough to reality to have practical validity over and above their value as scientific knowledge. The fact that entrepreneurs transact their affairs without troubling themselves about the calculation procedures of theoretical economics does not prevent the theorists from finding confirmation of their theories in practical economic life.

Of course, this requires translation of "ideas from the businessman's language into that of the economists, and vice versa." This would reveal that the theoretical "explanation of an action must often include steps of reasoning which the acting individual himself does not *consciously* perform. . . . [T]he construction of a pattern for the analytical description of a process is not the same thing as the actual process in daily life; and we should not expect to find in daily life the definite numerical estimates that are part of the scientific pattern."[23] While it is conceded that the behavior of consumers and businessmen also displays "uneconomic" elements, both must on the whole operate rationally, that is, strive for maximum gain at minimum cost. Entrepreneurs must consider the proportional relations between their production and the existing demand, and between their production and the capital invested and the wages paid out, as well as make choices with respect to means of production and raw materials. In brief, they must proceed in accordance with the principle of the marginal rate of substitution. According to this principle the economic optimum is reached at the point where further alterations in the combinations of the multiple factors of production would yield no additional profit, the marginal rate of costs then coinciding with that of benefits.

What we have here is thus not so much a matter of economics as a more precise than normal calculation of expenses and receipts. But at the same time, this method of calculation is viewed as the basic principle of all economic phenomena, since it establishes a common denominator for all exchange relations by means of the simple identification of value and price. In this way it eliminates a major defect of the classical theory of value. Although they founded their theory on an explanation of the phenomenon of value in terms of social labor time, the classical economists had nonetheless spoken in the same breath of individual market prices. Since they saw the true content of political economy as lying in the question of the class distribution of the social product, they struggled to show how individual prices are determined by social value relations. With the appearance of subjective value and "pure price theory," the realm of economic questions was reduced to that of exchange, and the problems posed by the classical theory, like those of the relation between value and price and of distribution, could thereby be ignored. Now the marginalists saw distribution, just as the classical economists had seen production, as regulated—whatever the outcome of the process—by the price system. The problem of distribution ceased to exist as a topic for theoretical economics. It was integrated into the general problem of price formation, since the different forms of revenue were treated as prices of factors of production. Since all prices are functionally related to each other, the solution of the general price problem already includes the solution of the problem of distribution.

In this way all questions about the economy were to be dealt with in terms of one principle. This principle had the form of a calculus that could pass for neutral with respect to any particular economic viewpoint. In the eyes of its advocates, marginal analysis and the concept of equilibrium derived from it gave economics, for the first time, a positive, scientific character. The marginalist calculus, however, rested on no more than the old illusion, inherited from the classical theorists, of the possibility of an equilibrium of supply and demand and the possibility of price formation as governed by this equilibrium. The very nature of the mathematization of economics on the basis of marginal analysis led to the conception of equilibrium in terms of a static model. Since the capitalist economy in fact knows no steady state, static equilibrium models could not be confirmed by reality; and the mathematical expressions, while undeniably exact, "related not to the content of economic knowledge but to the technique of mathematical operations."[24]

In contrast to Marx, for whom the assumption of a static condition (in his terminology, simple reproduction) was only a methodological device to exhibit the necessary dynamic of the capitalist system, bourgeois economics saw its static model of the economy as furnishing "scientific" support for the hypothesis of a tendency toward equilibrium. The endless playing around with such equilibrium models gave rise to the conviction among theoretical economists that this mental expedient is a prerequisite for economic analysis, even though they admit that the actual economy is never in perfect equilibrium. Just as every machine can be in need of repair, the equilibrium of the economic system can be disturbed by internal or external shocks. In either case only equilibrium analysis permits identification of the reasons for the disturbances and allows for the discovery of the factors needed to re-establish equilibrium.

The idea of the equilibrium of supply and demand, imposed on the market through competition, has thus remained a common theme of bourgeois economics from the time of Adam Smith and Jean-Baptiste Say to the present, however the foundations of this hypothesis have been transformed and however unrealistic they have meanwhile become. The question that neoclassical theory set itself was not how the price system really functions, but how it would function if the world were as the economists have imagined it. This theory required the equilibrium principle in order to see the price system as the regulator of the economy, and it required the amalgam of the pure price system in order to be able to pass off the actual state of affairs as rational and therefore immune to attack. But this all added up to no more than a new version of Adam Smith's "invisible hand" in mathematical formulas, together with Say's conviction that every supply brings with it an equivalent demand.

Neoclassical theory not only remained at the level of bourgeois economic science's first results but fell far short of it, since the equilibrium approach makes it impossible to investigate the real dynamic of capital, the accumulation process. The freeze-frame image of static equilibrium did not allow predictions about the process of development. While the fact of economic change of course could not be overlooked, it was treated as self-explanatory. Since they could not abandon the static equilibrium conception without declaring their own theoretical bankruptcy, the market theorists limited themselves, in dealing with development, to "comparative statics": the features of one nonexistent equilibrium were compared with those of a later nonexistent equilibrium, in the hope thereby of registering economic changes in the actual world. But since there is no profit or any other sort of surplus in the neoclassical equilibrium, there can be no expanded reproduction of the system. To the extent that it nonetheless occurs, it falls outside the framework of theoretical economics.

In contrast, the classical economists had directed their attention to the accumulation of capital, the growth of national wealth. Their theories of distribution started from the necessity of accumulation and inquired what factors would favor or hinder accumulation. The profit economy was for them the condition *sine qua non* of accumulation. The pursuit of profit thereby served the community because on it depended the improvement of living conditions through increasing production and productivity. Market problems were subordinated to those of accumulation and governed by the law of supply and demand. Under the conditions of general competition, exchange was considered to be a process regulating the economy in the framework of continuous social development.

This self-regulating and therefore crisis-free economy of classical theory confronted a refractory reality. The accumulation of capital took place not as a smoothly continuing process but as one interrupted periodically, since the beginning of the nineteenth century, by profound crises. How were these crises, clearly contradicting the dominant economic theory, to be explained? Although the classical economists, especially Ricardo, concentrated on the accumulation of capital, at the same time, they shared Say's conviction[25] that the market economy is a self-equilibrating system in which every supply will find an equivalent demand. According to Say every person produces with the intention either to consume his product or to sell it in order to acquire other commodities for his own consumption. As this holds for all producers, production must naturally be balanced by consumption. If all individual supplies and demands match, social equilibrium results. This state can of course be disturbed from time to time by an oversupply of a particular commodity or an insufficient demand for another. But the price changes produced by such partial disequilibration lead to the restoration of equilibrium. Apart from such disturbances in particular markets there can be no general overproduction, any more than accumulation can overstep society's propensity to consume.

Thus the classical economists' theories of accumulation were combined with a static conception of equilibrium that obliged them to explain disturbances of the system's equilibrium by reference to factors outside the system. The fact of crises of general overproduction led J. C. L. Sismonde de Sismondi[26] to renounce classical theory and soon to reject the laissez-faire system as a whole. In his opinion it was exactly the general competition, based on nothing but prices, which, instead of resulting in equilibrium and general welfare, opened the way to the misery of overproduction. The anarchy of capitalist production, the passion for exchange value without consideration of social needs, gave rise to production in excess of effective demand and therefore to periodic crises. The underconsumption resulting from the unequal distribution of income was the cause of overproduction and the accompanying drive toward foreign markets. Sismondi was thus the founder of the theory, still widespread today, of underconsumption as the cause of capitalist crisis.

Among many others it was notably John A. Hobson[27] who applied Sismondi's theory to developed capitalism and related it to imperialism. In Hobson's view, anticipating that later elaborated by Keynes, the demand for consumer goods, and with it the rate of capital expansion, falls as a result of unequal distribution and the increasing accumulation of capital. Since consumption cannot keep step with production, there are periodic crises, since part of the accumulating profits can no longer be profitably invested and therefore lies fallow. Only the reduction of overproduction in depression makes possible a new beginning of the expansion process, which will lead again in time to overproduction and idle capital. Overproduction resulting from insufficient consumption also explains the need for foreign markets that characterizes imperialism and imperialistic competition. Hobson, however, was of the opinion that this state of affairs could be remedied by reformist government interventions in the economic mechanism to strengthen consumer demand; in this respect he remained an ideological prisoner of the capitalist economy.

What should be clear here is that it was necessary to abandon the classical and then the neoclassical theories in order to come to grips with the reality of the economy. Viewed from a perspective defined by the allegedly self-regulating market mechanism, the actual economic processes were incomprehensible; this pushed Sismondi and Hobson to renounce the market-oriented theory. To deal with the capitalist crisis, as with social conditions generally, was also to reject traditional economic conceptions, to develop theories closer to reality, though without questioning capitalist property relations this is possible only to a limited degree. Attempts in this direction were conditioned not only by the dominant theory's flagrant conflict with reality but also by the impact of capitalist competition on the development opportunities of backward countries. This accounts, on the one hand, for the empiricism of the historical school and, on the other, for the evolutionary perspective of institutionalism, both of which opposed the theories developed by the classical economists. In the process of capitalist accumulation, the advantage of those who come first represents the disadvantage of those they have left behind. Thus free trade appeared as an English privilege and monopoly that made the industrialization of less developed lands more difficult and the misery of their "take-off" appear unbearable. In the struggle against monopolistic competition, the principle of laissez-faire had to be abandoned and with it the theories of classical economics. This was not, as Rosa Luxemburg supposed, a "protest of bourgeois society against the knowledge of its own laws"[28] but an attempt to use political means to reach a stage of development to which the ideology of free trade would be appropriate. It was only after they experienced the effects of the international competitive struggle that the economically weaker countries escaped the influence of English political economy and developed an ideology suited to state intervention and protective tariffs. That the historical school which flowered briefly in Germany only expressed the particular needs of competitively weak countries was already visible in the contradiction implicit in its doctrine: that it recommended in the national context what it condemned in the international.

To be sure, the adherents of the historical school of political economy endeavored to demonstrate that a distribution of income regulated exclusively by the market would lead to the pauperization of the workers and would thereby call the existence of bourgeois society itself into question—an apprehension seemingly corroborated by the rise of an independent labor movement. The remedy for pauperization was simply a more rapid and more orderly development of capitalism. In this way the historical school combined a nationally oriented economic policy with the social policy known as *Kathedersozialismus* (academic socialism), an ideology which rejected the abstractions of classical theory with the aim not of transcending them completely but of adapting them through historical criticism to particular national interests.

In the eyes of the historical school, economic knowledge was much more than a deductively established understanding of the market mechanism. It included also the inductive discovery of the historically determined, nationally specific, and extraeconomic aspects of the social totality and its development, so that assertions about the content of political economy were held to presuppose extensive historical research. Things did not progress beyond the level of research, however, since the continuing homogenization of the economies of the West, which accompanied the capitalization of this part of the world, also dedifferentiated economic theory, and the historical school lost its influence. It left behind the need it had awakened for an unprejudiced investigation of the empirically given phenomena of the economy, which finally precipitated in business-cycle research.

Although the economy remained afflicted by crisis and cyclical fluctuations, bourgeois economics still had no theory of crisis as an inherent aspect of the capitalist system but explained economic fluctuations in terms of events external to the economy. Jevons went so far as to connect crisis with extraterrestrial natural phenomena. He discovered that the periodic appearance of sunspots coincided with the outbreak of economic crisis. Supposedly the sunspots adversely affected the weather and with it agricultural production, whose decline led to a general crisis. Of course, this theory did not win many supporters. Although the weather certainly has some influence on the economy, crises have begun in periods of good weather, and a significant correlation between the weather and sunspots cannot be established.

Schumpeter,[29] in contrast, attempted to explain the economic development resulting from the trade cycle and the cycle itself by reference to the nature of the capitalist system. Familiar with Marx's theory, he was aware that all fundamental progress depends on the development of the social forces of production. But for Schumpeter the agents of new productive forces were the particularly energetic entrepreneurs who by their genius broke through custom-bound, monotonously repeated economic processes. He developed a kind of heroic theory of business fluctuations, seeing in them the dynamic of the capitalist system.

To this end, however, he made use of two different theories corresponding to two psychologically differentiated types of people. In the general equilibrium of "pure theory" there was no development. This corresponded to the fact that in the real world the majority of mankind was too sluggish and lazy in spirit to oppose the monotony of the static state. As we have already seen, in equilibrium there is no profit, the appearance of which indicates a perturbation of the system, which will again be overcome by the countermovements it provokes. So the problem is posed: how can a situation that knows no development give rise to development?

Here Schumpeter had the advantage that he, as earlier an adept of the historical school, had not forgotten that economics did not need to be confined to the abstractions of supply-demand equilibrium. To account for its dynamic the capitalist system must also be considered from the historical and sociological points of view. But in the framework of economic theory he would consider only the special mechanism that would transform the static to a dynamic model. This mechanism he embodied in a type of person who, tormented or blessed by creative unrest, breaks by self-willed activity through the cycle of static equilibrium. This type, the innovative entrepreneur, always on the lookout for new industrial, scientific, business, and organizational projects that would quantitatively and qualitatively alter existing productivity and production, destroys the consumer-governed economic equilibrium in such a way that it can be reestablished only on a new, higher level. This spontaneous, accidental, but ever recurring process produces the business cycle, at once creative and destructive, in which the dynamic of the capitalist system is played out. While certainly regrettable, it is unavoidable that adaptation to changing circumstances involves costs and misery. These disadvantages, however, Schumpeter thought could be mitigated with better economic forecasts and government interventions. In any case, in his view the inherent dynamic of the capitalist system was of greater importance than the problem of economic equilibrium with which bourgeois economics had almost exclusively occupied itself.

Even if it was only in his imagination that Schumpeter's theory was relevant to the laws of capitalist development, this theory was nonetheless symptomatic of the profound uneasiness of bourgeois theoreticians about cyclical fluctuations and crisis periods, which were becoming more serious as accumulation progressed. The theory of a self-regulating price mechanism made the crisis phenomenon an unsolvable riddle. Schumpeter's attempt to find a solution in the repeated violation of equilibrium conditions by a special kind of person was no explanation but only a confession that the equilibrium tendency attributed to the market was not to be found in the real world. As we have seen, this had already been recognized by the earliest economic critics of capitalism, like Sismondi and Hobson. But the simple statement that the theoretical harmony of supply and demand, production and consumption, was refuted by reality was in the end reduced to a mere description of obvious states of affairs, which in itself provides no explanation of the laws of motion peculiar to capital.

Unsolvable by the dominant economic theory, the problem of the nature of capitalist crisis could nevertheless not be ignored. Attempts were made to deal with it by empirical methods. This approach had been anticipated by the establishment of private institutions for the study of the business cycle with the aim of turning cyclical fluctuations to commercial account. From this arose a special branch of economic science, concerned exclusively with business-cycle research, which grew with the systematic multiplication of private and public data collection. Wishing to describe the course of economic events as it unfolds in reality, cycle research "made use of 'pure theory' only as an elementary theory."[30]

This rather minor concession to neoclassical economics was already an exaggeration, as business-cycle research could develop only in direct opposition to "elementary" economic theory. This theory dealt, as we have seen, only with the static equilibrium state, in which the course of economic events brings no change in the data. Such a stationary equilibrium was precisely excluded from the domain of cycle theory, as the latter dealt with the continuous transformation of the economy. While in the "elementary theory" deviations from equilibrium only led to the reestablishment of equilibrium, business-cycle theory did not deal with transient irregularities but attempted to lay bare the laws of motion of capital and to explain the phenomena of crisis. Success in this attempt would mean the construction of a dynamic theory of capitalist development transcending the static conception.

It goes without saying that the theory of capitalist development and its laws of motion long since formulated by Marx was intentionally neglected. The "unbiased" methods of the historical school were supposed to confer on business-cycle research the "objectivity" indispensable for knowledge of the actual process of economic events. In historical surveys of the changing market conditions and their oscillations, researchers attempted, on the basis of relevant statistics and with the aid of mathematical methods such as correlation coefficients, to trace the rhythm of economic life in order to determine its driving forces and internal relations. Of course, purely empirical research can yield no more than data; the facts, once determined, still require an explanation. For this a theory is required that would not only describe the business cycle but would also make it intelligible. But none of what seem to be dynamic theories of the business cycle[31] investigates the causes of cyclical changes; instead, these changes form their point of departure and are taken as given. In these circumstances the business-cycle theories remain mere descriptions of the economic dynamic without exposing the nature of the dynamic itself.

The diversity of economic phenomena seemingly indicated a plurality of causes for the cyclical fluctuations and prompted the construction of various theories which, though confronting the same facts, distinguished themselves from each other by the emphasis laid particularly on one or another aspect of the whole process. Distinctions were made between economic and noneconomic, endogenous and exogenous factors responsible for the business cycle, while some opted for a combination of both to elucidate the rhythm of the economy. Sometimes money and credit questions, at other times technical matters, market discrepancies, investment problems, or psychological factors were pushed into the foreground and declared the decisive element of the whole movement. Starting from these various viewpoints, people sought the causes of crisis and depression in the events of the preceding period of prosperity and its decline or looked for means and ways to move from crisis to a new upswing.

The aim of business-cycle research was not a methodical and more exact description of the cyclical fluctuations observable in any case but the discovery of some way to intervene for the alleviation of crisis situations and for the "normalization" of the changing economic processes with the aim of evening out the harsh alternation of boom and crisis. Cycle diagnosis was to lead, on the one hand, to the formulation of a prognosis facilitating the adaptation of economic activity to a given trend of economic development and, on the other, to the attempt to stabilize the economy over the longer term through a cyclical policy counteracting the automatic course of the cycle. Business-cycle theory thus saw itself as an applied science whose forecasts, even if they remained abstract, still permitted the drawing of analogical conclusions of possibly practical significance.

Of course, cycle theory did not call the social order into question and therefore remained from the start limited to the investigation of market phenomena. Not the essence of capitalism but its world of appearance formed the domain of business-cycle research and served as the basis for the various theories in which it clothed itself. According to the cycle theorists it is the obscurity of the developed market economy and the ignorance or misunderstanding of economic conditions that are the causes of the disproportional economic development in which the business cycle manifests itself. Consumption lags behind production, credit expansion leads to overinvestment, profits decline due to an unjustified expansion of production, so that at a certain point, the point of crisis, the economy swings in the other direction. Then investments lag behind savings, the saturated market finds no effective demand, capital values are destroyed, production decreases rapidly, and unemployment gains ground. The crisis and the period of depression that develops out of it make a clean sweep of the excesses of the period of expansion until the requisite economic proportions are restored, making possible a new upswing, which of course will in its turn meet its high point and collapse into a new crisis.

This represented an accurate picture of the economic events produced by capitalism's tendency to crisis, but it did not explain this tendency itself. The cyclical movements appeared in this view to be departures from a normal course of affairs which without them would run smoothly. We see here the presence, in the minds of the business-cycle theorists, of the equilibrium mechanism of "pure theory," a mechanism which to be sure can work only by way of irregularities, so that the proportionalities necessary for the "normal" course of the economy must be established through the ups and downs of the cycle. The business cycle was seen as the actual form of the equilibrium tendency of the market mechanism. It evidently followed that an exact knowledge of the factors responsible for the deviations from the norm could open the way to the conscious use of economic instruments to alleviate or eliminate the harmful sides of the cycle.

According to this view the capitalist economy is characterized by both static and dynamic tendencies, of which the latter condition the former. It follows from this that "pure theory," the static equilibrium approach, ought to be subordinated to the business-cycle theories, since it applies to a situation that arises only momentarily, as a point of transition toward the perpetually changing conditions, and that could therefore yield no information about the real position of the economy and the direction in which it was moving. Although the partisans of the theory of general equilibrium claimed only that it was an abstract representation of the price system without direct correspondence to real economic processes, they nevertheless insisted on its heuristic value for the study of economic relationships. From their point of view even business-cycle movements could be considered as proof of the factual existence of equilibrium tendencies, since the departure from an equilibrium state taken as a norm is finally followed by a restoration of equilibrium. Whatever brings them about, these deviations will in turn be annulled through the system's own equilibrium mechanism, so that equilibrium theory cannot be denied the front rank among economic theories.

Some bourgeois economists went so far as to deny the very existence of the business cycle. For example, Irving Fisher[32] found no justification for speaking of a business cycle, as the term referred to nothing but the record of economic activity at a level above or below the average. The supposition that these phenomena were characterized by a definite periodicity and that this opened a way to the making of economic predictions was untenable so long as the economy was governed by changing price relations. In Fisher's view it was more important to show how the economy would function if there were no cyclical deviations so as to understand the character of these disturbances and to counteract them where possible. In the end a division of labor developed within economic science that preserved the equilibrium approach for the "pure" theorists and left the field of business-cycle analysis to the more empirically oriented economists.

Aside from the fact that there exists no unbiased empirical

research, it is also worth noting, as W. C. Mitchell[33] was led to see by his own experience, that two observers can interpret and utilize the same empirical material quite differently. Accordingly, all statistical investigations must be looked at with a skeptical eye, a requirement that of course is often forgotten, since simply as a result of being published, numbers and tables acquire an authority that in reality they do not deserve. Oscar Morgenstern[34] has pointed out that the statistics relevant to the amplitude, the interactions, and the historical correspondences of cyclical waves are completely uncertain, although this flaw is for the most part ignored. The accepted data are not free from error, and the judgments made on their basis are open to doubt.

Despite the acknowledged deficiencies of statistical techniques and the conflicting interpretations of the data, the results obtained by this kind of research do reveal the cyclical movement of capitalist development. But this only confirmed what was already obvious from the qualitative side. The series of crisis years—1815, 1825, 1936, 1847, 1857, 1866—suggested the existence of a ten-year cycle, although it could not be established why the industrial cycle had this particular rhythm. Later crises and the data worked up from past crises pointed to a less pronounced regularity in the onset of crisis periods, which in any case had different effects in different countries. Of course, it could also be shown that with the passage of time the phenomena of crisis took on an evermore international and uniform character. The more exact analysis of statistical time series yielded both smaller cyclical movements within the two phases of the business cycle and so-called long waves encompassing shorter wave movements. The second of these put business-cycle fluctuations into the context of an underlying trend—the "long wave" or "secular trend," with a wavelength estimated, depending on the calculation, at either twenty-five or fifty years.

All these cases represented different uses and interpretations of statistical time series, which by themselves could lead only to provisional statements of probability. The "long wave" theory has nevertheless maintained its power to fascinate until today,[35] since on the one hand it allows the bourgeoisie to sink the irrefutable Marxian law of crisis in a mysterious, epochal wave motion of economic life, and on the other hand it gives the critics of bourgeois society an opportunity to adhere to the inevitability of crises despite their changing periodicity. But the statistical data themselves offer no explanation for the "long waves," since the hypotheses are lacking that alone could lead to their interpretation.

From these bewildering descriptions of various types of cycles neither can short-run predictions be made nor long-range policy be defined, as every cycle has its particular character and accordingly calls for measures tailored to it, and hence not decidable in advance, with equally incalculable consequences. Although a cycle policy in the broad sense is a practical impossibility simply because of the private interests that govern society, it was nonetheless attempted to make the overall trend of business perceptible to the general public by means of so-called business barometers, in the hope thereby of influencing the economy in a beneficial way. The disappointing results of this attempt soon put an end to it, and business-cycle research remained a field within economic history.

Various theories of capitalist crisis, aiming in their results at the confirmation of preconceived ideas, had already been suggested without reference to cycle research. Some took the hypothetical equilibrium as their point of departure, only to show how it was violated in reality. The economy could expand free of crisis only if all its elements develop at the same time, something which, unfortunately, is never the case. The balancing mechanism does not operate directly but manifests itself only when the various deviations from the necessary proportionality reach their limits. The demand for commodities cannot be discovered in advance, for example, and production and its volume therefore cannot be adjusted to it. So production exceeds demand, which leads to declining profits, bringing the expansion process to a halt and releasing the crisis. This process is accentuated by the credit system, since low discount rates stimulate new investments, which then affect the whole economy to a point at which the extension of credit comes up against the limits of bank reserves and with this comes to an end. The resulting rise in interest rates leads to deflation, which also grips the whole economy and introduces a period of depression. The reduction of demand relative to production and capital accumulation arises either subjectively, from the decreasing marginal utility of the increasing quantity of consumer goods, or objectively, from the shrinking consumption of the working population as determined by the wage system.

In opposition to such views the adherents of "pure theory," who not only started in their reasoning from equilibrium but remained there, insisted that the crisis situation should be blamed not on the system but on arbitrary disregard for or interference with its regulatory functions. They took their stand on the absolute validity of Say's law of the market and consequently found it self-evident that when more is consumed, less will be invested, and when more is invested, less can be consumed. In either case the equilibrium of production and consumption remains intact. Of course, to err is human and can lead to bad investments; the consequences of such errors, however, disappear of themselves as entrepreneurs adapt to the changed market conditions. There is no point in racking one's brain over the crisis, since the price mechanism also makes it possible to overcome whatever distortions of the economy may appear. That these distortions can end up having very far-reaching effects in one or another phase of the cycle is a reflection less of the nature of the system than of the psychological properties of human beings. Although objective changes engender cyclical movement in the economy, saying this leaves unanswered the question:

> why is this movement first pushed so far in one direction, only to be later reversed? Why does it lead to an incorrect relationship between consumption and production over time, instead of a permanent, one-time change in this relationship? This question can only be answered in a nonartificial way by a "psychological" theory.[36]

The course of economic affairs can only be said to be dynamic "when we find, on the highest level of theoretical abstraction as well as in reality, no tendency toward the establishment of a static equilibrium."[37] The assumption that there is such a tendency in the construction of theories, whether they denied or recognized the tendency to crisis as well, ruled out from the start any real insight into the dynamic of the capitalist system. Such theories must always be in contradiction with reality, despite the greatest efforts to escape this. The futility of trying to comprehend capitalist development with the methods of classical and neoclassical theory led in the bourgeois camp itself to a sharp critique of these theories and to new attempts to approach the laws of development by other paths.

According to Smith and Ricardo, the ultimate basis of economics was human nature, particularly the propensity to exchange, by which man is differentiated from animals. The division of labor, classes, the market, and the accumulation of capital were seen as natural phenomena that neither could be nor should be changed. Moreover, the political economy developed in England took up the ideas of the French physiocrats, notably the assumption that a smooth-running economy is in the nature of things, and that everything will turn out for the best if this natural order of things is undisturbed. The physiocrats' theme song, laissez faire, became a moral element in the classical theory. While this moral principle was exchanged—to some extent already by Ricardo and after him even more widely—for conceptions borrowed from Malthus and Darwin, the capitalist mode of production nevertheless continued to pass for a nature-given order.

With Social Darwinism we see the bourgeoisie at the high point of its self-understanding. It had no more need of illusions about the character of society. The class struggle was confused with the general struggle for existence, with which all progress is patently connected. For the Social Darwinists every individual person is in competition with every other person, and this competitive struggle has nothing to do with the particular social relations of capitalism but expresses the operation within the economic realm of a law of nature. If one person is more successful than another, this is not because they have had different social opportunities but because of their differing individual aptitudes. If one can abstract from class divisions, one might as well abstract from the relations of production in which they manifest themselves.

As a theory of evolution Darwinism implied a slow but continuous transformation of nature, society, and mankind. Accordingly, the present state of society must also be regarded as transitory and hence as a process that could not be comprehended by means of the statics of "pure" or orthodox theory. According to

Thorstein Veblen,[38] the founder of the American "institutionalist" school, orthodox theory's neglect of development and its treatment of social relationships in isolation from any but abstract economic aspects prohibited any real insight into socioeconomic reality. The transformations of society are to be seen, according to Veblen, in the changes of its institutions, by which he meant the culturally developed customs or habits of thought and feeling that he thought determine the way and manner in which people satisfy their vital needs. Cultural development is a slow but uninterrupted process of small but cumulative changes that results in new customs and new social relations.

The current result of this general process of development and the accumulation of experience is, according to Veblen, a set of customs or institutions whose expression we see in the machine process of production and in capitalist entrepreneurship. Although they developed simultaneously, these institutions are in conflict: the aim of the first is goods production, that of the second, money making. While industry represents the material basis of modern civilization, this civilization is controlled not by industry but by businessmen. From this arises all the absurdities of the economy and its crises.

The profit motive that dominates the economy conditions both its rise and its decline. Profits arise from the difference between the cost prices and the market prices realized. The value of an enterprise, however, is estimated by reference not to the profits it actually earns but to expected future profits. The nominal capital value differs from the actual capital value, but it is the former that determines the credit worthiness of the enterprise. Competition compels the increase of productivity, the expansion of the enterprises, and therefore of their borrowings, which affect future profitability. So long as there is enough money to be borrowed and the prosperity engendered by expansion holds, the growing sum of capital value represents no problem. Otherwise, however, a divergence arises between the inflated capital values and their actual profits that leads to a process of liquidation and the depression to which this gives rise.

Thus prosperity bears the seeds of its own demise. Productivity and production increase as profits grow in tandem along with credit and the accompanying price increases, until the extension of credit comes up against its own limits and those imposed by the contraction of profits. As loan capital becomes scarce and interest rates rise, the earlier relationship between the profits expected and the capital invested on this basis changes, compelling a deflationary revision of capital values. To this are added the causes of sinking profitability resulting from production itself, such as rising wages, a decreasing intensity of labor, and the spreading disorganization of the enterprises, which arises from the hectic character of the boom.

Though Veblen's description of the course of the business cycle does not differ from those given by others, he does however relate it to the conflict between *production* and *capitalist production*. He sees that it is only because the aim of production is the increase of capital rather than the satisfaction of human needs that the lamentable conditions of capitalist society, and the crises characterized by overproduction and underconsumption, arise. Unlike other observers, Veblen saw crises not as phenomena determined by equilibrium relations and representing nothing but temporary deviations from the norm, but as the normal condition of capitalist society as soon as it has attained a certain maturity. From the crisis cycle of an earlier period arose the chronic crisis of developed capitalism, which could be eliminated only by a transformation of the social system.

Since there exist no static state and no economic equilibrium, it cannot be expected, according to Veblen, that the capitalist system will develop continuously despite or by means of its cyclical fluctuations. The system as such contains no equilibration mechanism. During the money-and-credit society's period of ascendance, the periodicity of crisis had nothing to do with the system itself but was most likely due to external circumstances. The divergence between capitalism and profitability could still for a while be controlled by extrasystemic means, such as monetary inflation or an enlarged and cheapened gold production and the price increases bound up with this. The crises that periodically arose were for the most part commercial crises, quite different from the crises of industrial society. With the development of the latter, the contradiction between the exigencies of capital and the profits attainable cannot be even momentarily overcome. From this arises the chronic crisis condition.

According to Veblen it is of the essence of machine production, and the continually increasing productivity that goes with it, that under competitive conditions prices fall and the profit of a given capital declines. The maintenance of profits requires the enlargement of the individual capitals. Thus a sort of race begins between capital expansion and the tendency of profits to fall, which of course only the latter can win. As capital values and the attainable profits increasingly diverge, an attempt to combat this is first made through trustification and monopolization. Monopolization, however, gives rise to monopolistic competition and a new start to the race. The need for profitable prices is then met by an extraordinary growth of unprofitable consumption, a production of waste; but this encounters impassable barriers. The end result is a situation that can only be described as one of chronic crisis. Veblen believed that this no longer surmountable crisis already existed and, accordingly, that a general breakdown of society could be avoided only by the replacement of the economic system (as a money-and-credit system) by another system of production.

This new system would be the existing system of production without its capitalist perversions. It was for Veblen already anticipated in the widening split between ownership and management and in a growing consciousness that industrial production can progress without the capitalist institutions parasitic on it. The increasing sabotage of industrial development by the decay of profit production (together with the growing significance of technology and machine production) would destroy antiquated customs and allow new ones to arise that were better suited to industrial production and to further social development.

As it became a branch of bourgeois economics, institutionalism, despite its critical moments, lost much of the consistency to be found in Veblen's work. If Veblen (like Adam Smith) could in the last analysis only trace the ruin of capital back to the effects of increasing competition, his aversion to capitalist civilization extended to all its aspects. The critique made by his followers, in contrast, arose more from anxiety about the threatening end of capitalist society than from a desire for new social relations. For them the irresponsible behavior of the powerful "profit hyaenas" drove the system to collapse; thus "Institutionalism is a call to action, an SOS to save a sinking world."[39] Conscious intervention in economic processes was necessary if a way out of the spreading misery was to be found. Orthodox theory offered no handle on a solution to the mounting social problems and conflicts. Here institutionalism wished to be of help by suggesting a set of reform measures, pointing in the direction of a planned economy, that would overcome the defects of competitive capitalism.

With this to offer, institutionalism could win no extensive or lasting influence and was seen as a curiosity, capable only of serving, in a modified form, as an ideological foundation for temporary government interventions in crisis situations. It played all the greater role in various reform movements, particularly in the English Fabian Society.[40] Orthodox theory—subdivided into numerous specialities subordinated to "pure theory"—controlled the field of theoretical economics, offering a rapidly growing number of academics the opportunity to make a relatively good living. The purely ideological function of theoretical economics was also evidenced by the growth of business schools, dedicated to the practical life of business, which remained undisturbed by theoretical economics.

As an ideological apologia for the capitalist system, theoretical economics found itself more and more embarassed thanks to its increasingly obvious irrelevance to real economic affairs. Since it could not approach this reality without renouncing itself, it took the opposite road to greater abstraction in order to be able to escape every confrontation with reality. It now no longer investigated merely the economy but a principle of rationality, purportedly relevant to all human action, which adapts scarce means to alternative ends in order to achieve the best possible result. Economics concentrated, in this conception,

on a particular aspect of behavior, the form imposed by the influence of scarcity. It follows from this, therefore, that insofar as it presents this aspect, any kind of human behavior falls within the scope of economic generalizations. We do not say that the production of potatoes is economic activity and the production of philosophy is not. We say rather that, insofar as either kind of activity involves the relinquishment of other desired alternatives, it has its economic aspect. There are no limitations on the subject-matter of Economic Science save this.[41]

This extension of economics to every subject matter as a principle of rationality was at the same time its reduction to a purely analytical procedure, which prohibited it from saying anything at all about the economic system itself. Thus economic crisis, too, lay outside the sphere of interest of economics, and it required a worldwide crisis, shaking the globe for years, to overcome this lack of interest.

Notes

1. *Grundrisse*, Harmondsworth, 1973, p. 754 [translation corrected].
2. *Capital*, vol. 3, Moscow, 1962, p. 254.
3. *Grundrisse*, p. 105 [translation altered].
4. Ibid., p. 259 [translation altered].
5. Ibid., pp. 758-59.
6. *Entwicklungsgesetze des Menschlichen Verkehrs, und der daraus fliessenden Regeln für Menschliches Verhalten*, 1854.
7. *Theory of Political Economy*, 1871.
8. *Grundsätze der Volkwirtschaftslehre*, 1871.
9. *Über den Ursprung und die Hauptgesetze des wirtschaftlichen Wertes*, 1884.
10. *Kapital und Kapitalzins*, 1884.
11. *Outline of the Science of Political Economy*, 1836.
12. *Principles of Economics*, 1890.
13. *Éléments d'économie politique pure ou théorie de la richesse sociale*, 1874.
14. *The Distribution of Wealth*, 1899.
15. See Note 10.
16. That Marx was most likely familiar with the line of reasoning of the subjective value theory can be seen from his study of the English economist W. F. Lloyd, to which W. Pieper has referred in a postscript to a letter from Marx to Engels (see Marx-Engels, *Werke* [MEW], vol. 27, p. 169). Although Lloyd, even more than Gossen in Germany and A. J. Etienne-Juvenal Dupuit in France, has fallen into oblivion, he must be numbered among the first exponents of the subjective approach to value (see W. F. Lloyd, *A Lecture on the Notion of Value as Distinguishable not only from Utility, but also from Value in Exchange*, London, 1834). In addition Marx dealt thoroughly, both in *Cap-*

ital and in *Theories of Surplus Value*, with S. Bailey's subjective value theory (see Bailey, *A Critical Dissertation on the Nature, Measures and Causes of Value: Chiefly in Reference to the Writings of Mr. Ricardo and His Followers*, 1825). Similarly, he wrote on the theory of use value in the *Marginal Notes on A. Wagner's "Lehrbuch der Politischen Ökonomie"* (MEW, vol. 19, pp. 355-83).

17. On January 5, 1888, Engels wrote to N. F. Danielson, "Just now the fashion is the theory of Stanley Jevons, according to whom value is determined by *utility*, i.e., exchange value = use value, and on the other hand by the extent of the demand (i.e., by the costs of production), which is only a confused, ass-backwards manner of saying that value is determined by supply and demand" (NEW, vol. 37, p. 8).

18. *Capital*, vol. 3, p. 10.

19. *Das Wesen und der Hauptinhalt der theoretischen Nationalökonomie*, 1908.

20. *Theoretische Nationalökonomie*, 1918.

21. *Nationalökonomie, Theorie des Handels und Wirtschaftens*, 1940.

22. *Economic Philosophy*, 1964, p. 67.

23. Fritz Machlup, "Marginal Analysis and Empirical Research," in *American Economic Review* (1946) 44, pp. 537, 535, 547.

24. Henryk Grossman, *Marx, die classische Nationalökonomie, und das Problem der Dynamik*, 1969, p. 53.

25. *Traité d'économie politique*, 1803.

26. *Nouveaux Principes d'Économie Politique*, 1819.

27. *The Industrial System*, 1909; *Imperialism*, 1902.

28. *Gesammelte Werke*, vol. 1, part 1, p. 731.

29. *Theorie der Wirtschaftlichen Entwicklung*, 1911.

30. E. Wagemann, in *Vierteljahrshelfte zum Konjunkturforschung*, 1937, no. 3, p. 243.

31. Among others, see Juglar, *Des crises commerciales et de leur retour périodique*, 1889; Veblen, *The Theory of Business Enterprise*, 1904; Karmin, *Zur Lehre von der Wirtschaftskrise*, 1905; Lecue, *Des crises générales et périodiques de Surproduction*, 1907; Bouniatan, *Studien zur Theorie und Geschichte der Wirtschaftskrisen*, 1908; Mitchell, *Business Cycles and Their Causes*, 1913; Hartrey, *Good and Bad Trade: An Inquiry into the Causes of Trade Fluctuations*, 1913; Sombart, *Der Moderne Kapitalismus*, 1917; Vogel, *Die Theorie des volkswirtschaftlichen Entwicklungsprozesses und das Krisenproblem*, 1917; Aftalion, *Les Crises périodiques de Surproduction*, 1913; Mombert, *Einführung in das Studium der Konjunktur*, 1921; Liefman, *Grundsätze der Volkswirtschaftslehre*, 1922; Hobson, *Economics of Unemployment*; Kuznets, *Cyclical Fluctuations*, 1926; Spiethoff, "Krisen," in *Handwörterbuch der Staatswissenschaften*, 1925; Löwe, "Der gegenwartige Stand der Konjunkturforschung in Deutschland," in *Festgabe für Lujo Brentano*, 1925; Cassel, *Theoretische Nationalökonomie*, 1918.

32. In "Our Unstable Dollar and the So-Called Business Cycle," *Journal of the American Statistical Association*, 20, p. 192.

33. *Business Cycles: The Problem and Its Setting*, 1927, p. 364.

34. *On the Accuracy of Economic Observations*, 1963, p. 60.

35. Parvus was one of the first to call attention to the longer upswing and depression periods overlapping the seven-to-ten-year cycle (*Handelskrisen und Gewerkschaften*, 1902). The Dutch economist J. van Gelderen spoke of a sixty-year cycle (*De Nieuwe Tijd*, 1913). De Wolff followed him and Parvus ("Prosperitäts- und Depressionsperioden," in *Der Lebendige Marxismus*, 1924). Particular attention was paid to the Russian economist N. D. Kondratiev's theory of "long waves" witha duration of fifty years (see *Archiv für Sozialwissenschaft und Sozialpolitik*, vol. 56, no. 3, 1926). Ernest Mandel has adapted this theory for his description of the present-day state of the economy (*Der Spätkapitalismus*, 1972; *Late Capitalism*, 1975). J. B. Shuman and D. Rosenau base their prognosis for the future development of the American economy, to the year 1984, on Kondratiev's "long waves" (*The Kondratieff Wave*, 1972).

36. L. A. Hahn, *Wirtschaftswissenschaft des gesunden Menschenverstandes*, 1955, p. 157.

37. A. Löwe, "Der Gegenwärtige Stand der Kunjunkturforschung in Deutschland," in *Festgabe für Lujo Brentano*, 1925, p. 359.

38. *The Theory of Business Enterprise*, 1904.

39. J. A. Estey, "Orthodox Economic Theory: A Defense," *Journal of Political Economy*, December 1936, p. 798.

40. See S. and B. Webb, *The Decay of Capitalist Civilization*, 1923.

41. L. C. Robbins, *An Essay on the Nature and Significance of Economic Science*, 1945, p. 17.

2

Marx's Crisis Theory

The stagnation of bourgeois economics with respect to its content was for Marx a foregone conclusion. "Classical political economy," he wrote,

> belongs to a period in which the class struggle was as yet undeveloped. Its last great representative, Ricardo, ultimately (and consciously) made the antagonism of class interests, of wages and profits, of profits and rent, the starting-point of his investigations, naively taking this antagonism for a social law of nature. But with this contradiction the bourgeois science of economics had reached the limits beyond which it could not pass....
>
> In France and England the bourgeoisie had conquered political power. From this time on, the class struggle took on more and more explicit and threatening forms, both in practice and in theory. It sounded the knell of scientific bourgeois economics. It was thenceforth no longer a question whether this or that theorem was true, but whether it was useful to capital or harmful, expedient or inexpedient, in accordance with police regulations or contrary to them. In place of disinterested inquirers there stepped hired prizefighters; in place of genuine scientific research, the bad conscience and evil intent of apologetics.[1]

Marx's critique of political economy is based on his theory of value and surplus value. It differs methodologically from classical economics due to Marx's understanding of the social dialectic, which "includes in its positive understanding of what exists a simultaneous recognition of its negation, its inevitable destruction; regards every historically developed form as being in a fluid state, in motion, and therefore grasps its transient aspect as well; and because it does not let itself be impressed by anything, being in its essence critical and revolutionary."[2] Of course, as Marx prefaced these observations,

> The method of presentation must differ in form from that of inquiry. The latter has to appropriate the material in detail, to analyze its different forms of development and to track down their inner connection. Only after this work has been done can the real movement be appropriately presented. If this is done successfully, if the life of the subject matter is now reflected back in the ideas, then it may appear as if we have before us an *a priori* construction.[3]

His works show that in the course of time Marx increasingly freed himself from the philosophical interpretation of social development with which he had begun. It is therefore inappropriate to regard the formal dialectical method as fundamental for the understanding of capitalist reality and to maintain with Lenin that a real understanding of Marx's *Capital* presupposes comprehension of Hegel's *Logic*.[4] While for Hegel philosophy was the age grasped by thought, for Marx the dialectic was the expression of the actual development of capitalism, which yielded in bourgeois philosophy only a false ideological precipitate. According to Marx it was not that Hegel's philosophy led to a correct perception of the capitalist world but that an understanding of capitalism would make it possible to grasp the "rational kernel" of the Hegelian system.

Of course, Hegelian philosophy constituted Marx's starting point, but it was soon overshadowed by his knowledge of the concrete capitalist social relations out of which the idealist dialectic had arisen. "What appeared to be only an object of philosophy became the object of political economy; what in the conceptual analysis appeared to be only a phantom had to be shown to be a real phenomenon of the external world."[5] Independent of the Hegelian logic in principle if not in fact, Marx's economic and historical investigations revealed the dialectical nature of capitalist development. Thus the dialectic is to be found in *Capital* just because it is the law of motion of capitalist society, which alone justifies the dialectical method as a means to discovery of the truth.

Thanks to the inherent dynamic of the capitalist relations of production, namely the unity of the opposites capital and labor, the relatively static process of production and development characteristic of European feudalism gave way to a process of social development of previously unknown rapidity and impetuousity, a process with worldwide effects. This engendered the theories of political economy, the bourgeois revolution, and its reflection in philosophy. Every revolutionary development of society is based on the creation of new productive forces, which require corresponding relations of production for their full unfolding and utilization. Inversely, the creation of new production relations generates new productive forces, which of themselves operate on the existing production relations. Whatever stands in the way of these productive forces and remains bound to the old relations of production leads through conflicts between social classes to the political struggles that transform one social order into another. The process of development is thus at the same time a process of revolution that comprises more or less all aspects of human social existence.

The capitalist mode of production arose with the development of commodity production under the conditions of private property and presupposed the historical separation of the producers from the means of production. Labor power became a commodity and formed the basis of the conditions of the market economy. Capitalist production is social production only in the sense that commodities are produced not for personal use but for sale to other consumers. This type of social production must at the same time satisfy the profit requirements of the private owners of capital. The social division of labor is thus equally a class division. Social production serves society only insofar as it can serve the capitalists; it is social production subordinated to private interests. It can therefore be social production not directly but only indirectly, and this only when the needs of capital accidentally coincide with social needs.

The social character that capitalist production may in this sense be said to have appears in the relation between buyers and sellers on the market. The production carried out by individual firms must conform to social needs as they are defined by capitalism. In bourgeois economics the market mechanism appears as the regulator of the relationship that must obtain between production and consumption and of the proportional distribution of social labor that underlies it. In this conception the dual character of production as the production of commodities and of profits is ignored, as the second of these is accomplished by means of commodity production and so is already covered by its laws. Although as a result of the commodity character of labor power this is actually the case, it in no way alters the circumstance that the production of commodities presupposes the making of profits and that it is this, in the first place, that determines the market and price relations. The symmetry of supply and demand found in bourgeois economics thus excludes insight into the true market relations and into the dynamic of capital they make possible and that arises from the drive for profit.

The limits of bourgeois economics are the starting point of the Marxian critique. For Marx economic relationships are the form assumed by class relationships under the conditions of capitalist production. Value and price are equally fetishistic categories for the real class relations that lie beneath them. While the classical theory of value speaks of exchange value and use value, Marx asks why the concept of value exists at all. His answer is that under the conditions of capitalist property relations, the social labor process is necessarily represented in terms of value relations. Since in such a system the class relations of exploitation have the form of exchange relations (since capitalists buy labor power from workers), the division of social production into labor and surplus labor must take on the character of value relations and appear as value and surplus value. Were society not a class society resting on exchange, there would be no exchange between the owners of the conditions of production and the propertyless workers, and the social production relations would not be value relations.

The difficulties which the classical economists had with the theory of value were due to the fact that although they considered commodities as combining exchange value and use value, they did not discover this double character in the commodity labor power. This discovery was reserved for Marx, who was thus the first to account for exchange relations as they actually exist without abandoning the law of value. The exchange of commodities on the basis of labor-time equivalence can yield no profit. The double character of the commodity labor power creates the possibility of profit. While according to the law of value the purchaser of labor power pays its exchange value, he acquires at the same time its use value, which is able to produce a value greater than its true exchange value. This is as much as to say that the price relations of the market can be understood only with reference to the value relations on which, as relations of production, they are based.

The essence of the value-governed system is not the exchange of labor-time equivalents but the capitalist appropriation of unpaid surplus labor. The owners of capital do not exchange labor-time equivalents among themselves. The law of value governs the capitalist economy only in the sense that the forces of social production that exist at any moment set definite limits to the production of surplus value, and that the distribution of the surplus value among capitals must be more or less adapted to social requirements if the existence and development of capital is to be secured. Because of this the exchange relations must appear not as value relations determined by labor time but as price relations deviating from them, without this negating the regulation of capitalist production by the law of value.

The deviation of price from value excluded the consistent utilization of the labor theory of value by classical economics, which was principally concerned with distribution. If the law of value is to be maintained, it must be shown that the actual price relations, although different from value relations, are nonetheless determined by the latter. While this determination of price by value cannot be read off from the prices given in the market, it can be seen in the changing prices of production, which are formed from cost prices and the average rate of profit. In the capitalist's consciousness, as also in the reality of the market, only the prices of commodities exist. For the individual entrepreneur even production presents itself as a problem of buying and selling. He purchases means of production, raw materials, and labor power in order to produce commodities whose price on the market brings him a profit from which he can live and which preserves his invested capital and increases it. Not value and surplus value but only the costs of production and the gains obtained, expressed in prices, are meaningful for him. But this indifference to value relations, shared by all capitalists, in no way alters the fact that production costs, like profits, are only other expressions for definite quantities of labor time contained in commodities.

The total labor time expended by society yields a total social product that is divided between wages and profits. The larger the share of the total social product that falls to the capitalists, the less can fall to the workers, and vice versa. In reality neither total social production nor total labor power nor total capital is a directly observable magnitude whose interrelations could be ascertained. Capital is divided into many different capitals, which confront not the working class as a whole but smaller or larger groups of workers. As the capitals themselves differ, so do their abilities to yield surplus value. The "organic compositions"—the ratios of means of production (or constant capital) to labor power employed (or variable capital)—of individual capitals differ depending on the industries in which they are employed. According to the labor theory of value, only the living labor utilized produces surplus value. But as profit is surplus value measured against the total capital (i.e., against the sum of constant and variable capital), profits should be lower in industries with more constant than variable capital than in industries where these proportions are reversed. This, however, is not in general the case, exactly because the competition among capitalists and that of the buyers with them and with each other leads to a transformation of the true profits into socially average profits which, added to the costs of production, allow each capital to participate equally, in accordance with its size, in the total social surplus value.

If the formation of an average profit rate is explained by competition, the fact of competition does not explain the magnitude of this rate at any time. This magnitude depends on the unknown but nonetheless definitely given mass of profit yielded by the total social capital. And since the total value of the commodities conditions the total surplus value, while the latter governs the level of the average profit and thus the general rate of profit, the law of value regulates production prices.

Although the creation of surplus value by surplus labor takes place in production, the realization of profits is accomplished in the market. Though production is dominated by the accumulation of capital and realized on the market, it is its use-value side that determines the relation between supply and demand, with its influence on price relations and consequently on the division of the total surplus value among the various capitals. With the increase in demand for a particular commodity its production increases, as the decreasing demand for another diminishes its production. Thus capital moves from relatively stagnating into rapidly developing industries. The changes in the organic compositions of individual capitals resulting from this process do not affect their profitability. On the contrary, they lead to higher profits than those which fall to less productive capitals. The extra profit, in excess of the average profit, won at a given price level disappears again, however, with the influx of capital from profit-poor into profit-rich industries. The perpetual hunt for extra profit characterizes capitalist competition and leads by means of it to a higher organic composition of the social capital as a whole.

To understand changes in value relations and thus in prices, we must start from the process of accumulation. The modification of the general price level stems from capitalist accumulation as manifested in the rising productivity of labor. The general fall in commodity prices can be seen from the comparison of earlier with later production periods. Every individual commodity comes to contain less labor time than before. The decrease in value of the individual commodity is counterbalanced by the increase in the quantity of commodities, so that the profitability of capital is maintained despite falling prices. Thus the development of prices depends on the changing productivity of labor and so on the law of value. For the analysis of capitalist expansion, therefore, no particular price theory is needed, since the development of prices is already covered by the value analysis.

In the price relations effected by competition, the value designations of the individual commodities and individual firms' profits are lost from sight, as is also the division of the social product into wages and profits. But whatever the terms of this division, it operates at any given time on quantities of commodities requiring definite amounts of labor time, in turn divided first of all into time spent on value production and on surplus-value production. The actual distribution, expressed in price terms, presupposes this first division. Hidden by the market, this basis has just as much reality as the observable world of prices and commodities. In view of the latter the value relations appear to be simplifying abstractions from the complicated phenomena of the market; while if we focus on the fundamental relations of production, the world of commodities represents only a multifaceted modification of those relations. The relations of production can be understood without reference to the market, while the market cannot be understood without reference to them. It is therefore the production relations that must form the basis for any scientific analysis of capital and alone can make the possibilities and limits of market processes comprehensible.

The theory of value based on labor time is, then, abstract relative to the market and concrete relative to the relations of production. It is a mental construction only in the sense that value categories do not relate directly to market phenomena, so that the value relations hidden behind prices can be grasped only by way of thought. The pure market theory of bourgeois economics is naturally also an abstract affair, since it excludes the capitalist relations of production from consideration. In this way it shuts itself off from insight into the totality of the actual state of affairs and hence also from an understanding of market phenomena themselves. Value analysis, in contrast, makes possible the explanatory passage from abstract to concrete, since it can demonstrate the subordination of market relations to the production relations of modern society and so first bring to light the process of the capitalist economy as a whole.

The dual character of production as the production at once of commodities and of profits excludes the adaptation of production to real social needs or an equilibrium of supply and demand in the sense of an equilibrium of production and consumption. According to Marx, demand

> is essentially subject to the mutual relationship of the different classes and their respective economic positions, notably therefore to, first, the ratio of total surplus value to wages, and, second, to the relation of the various parts into which surplus value is split up (profit, interest, ground rent, taxes, etc.). And this thus again shows how absolutely nothing can be explained by the relation of supply and demand before ascertaining the basis on which this relation rests.[6]

However, due to the effort, growing out of capitalist competition, to heighten exploitation, this basis (the relations of production) is in a state of perpetual transformation, which manifests itself in changing relative prices of goods on the market. Therefore the market is continuously in disequilibrium, although with different degrees of severity, thus giving rise, by its occasional approach to an equilibrium state, to the illusion of a tendency toward equilibrium. The capitalist laws of motion exclude any sort of equilibrium, even when profit production and commodity production develop in tandem, since this very development stimulates the unfolding of a contradiction inherent in it that only further development can overcome.

Market and production, it goes without saying, form a unity and can be separated only in thought. However, market relations are governed by the production relations. The price of labor power can in general not fall below its value, i.e., the cost of reproduction of the labor force. It can never rise to the point at which it would abolish capitalist surplus value and so threaten the existence of the system. Whatever may happen in the market, its effects are determined by the relations of production, and the apparently autonomous operation of the market is restricted to the paths prescribed by these relations. However much the actual price relations may deviate from the value relations on which they are based, the total sum of commodity values can be no greater than the quantity of labor time expended in the production of the commodities. The sum of commodity prices can indeed lie below the total value, since total value and total price are equivalent only under the assumption that all the commodities produced are sold. There may, that is, be more value and surplus value created than finds expression in commodity prices, as happens when a part of production cannot be sold and therefore loses its value character. In any case the total prices realized are equal to the total value realized. In this way an analysis of capital's laws of motion based exclusively on value relations finds its justification.

While the phenomena investigated in Volume 1 of Marx's *Capital* are those "which constitute the *process of capitalist production* as such," in the third volume he attempts to "locate and describe the concrete forms that grow out of the *movements of capital considered as a whole.*" The configurations of capital, as

Marx describes them, "thus approach step by step the form which they assume on the surface of society, in the action of different capitals upon one another, in competition, and in the ordinary consciousness of the agents of production themselves."[7] But this step-by-step procedure does not negate the insights into the laws of capitalist development attained by analysis of the process of production as such. These insights remain valid for capital "considered as a whole," although they undergo various metamorphoses in the course of its investigation. The abstractions of Volume 1 represent not a mere methodology used to approach the inscrutable world of commodities but a representation of the actual foundation on which this world is based. Only if this foundation itself is exposed to view can the dynamic of the system, from which alone the multiple configurations of capital arise, be portrayed.

If the value of labor power is given by the cost of reproducing it, the labor time in excess of this amount has the form of surplus value. The increasing productivity of labor augments its use value relative to its exchange value and in this way enlarges the mass of capital derived from the surplus value. Capital formation can thus be shown to be the development of the productivity of labor. The increasing mass of capital determines the quantity of surplus value necessary for its further utilization or valorization (capital expansion by the investment of surplus value as additional capital). However, this process at the same time reduces the labor power employed relative to a given capital and accordingly diminishes the relative quantity of surplus value. With more rapid accumulation the employed labor power of course increases in absolute terms and declines only in comparison with the growing capital. But even this relative decline, in the context of the growing capital's increasing valorization needs, must in the course of time lead to a declining rate of accumulation. From this it follows that the accumulation of capital is constrained by definite value relations. If there is sufficient surplus value to valorize the capital already in existence, it secures its future development. If the surplus value is insufficient, then further rapid development of capital comes to an end.

The capitalist production of commodities is in reality the production of capital; the production of goods for use, that is, is only a means to the expansion of capital, and this has no subjective limits. A capital, as a sum of money invested in production, must emerge again from circulation as an enlarged capital if the conditions of capitalist production are to be met. Production is thus exclusively the production of surplus value and is governed by the latter. Since surplus value is unpaid labor time, the production of capital depends on the quantity of labor time appropriated. It is therefore of the essence of capital to increase the quantity of unpaid labor time. At a given stage of development and with a given number of workers, surplus value can be enlarged only by lengthening the time during which workers labor for the capitalists and shortening that during which they produce for themselves. Both methods face impassable objective barriers, since the working day cannot exceed twenty-four hours, and the worker's wage cannot be reduced to zero. The accumulation of capital possible under such conditions, as the accumulation of means of production, requires additional labor power and engenders a corresponding increase of the mass of surplus value. For accumulation to advance continuously, however, the productivity of labor must increase. This is accomplished by means of the development of technology and organization of the workplace. While these depend on accumulation, both of them promote an acceleration of accumulation, leading to an alteration of the value relations that constitute the organic composition of capital.

Under the assumption of a continuous accumulation of capital—an assumption in complete accord with reality—the increasing productivity of labor is reflected in a shift of the organic composition of capital toward its constant component. The variable capital grows, of course, but this growth lags behind that of the capital embodied in means of production. Despite the declining number of workers relative to the means of production confronting them as capital, the surplus value increases so long as the increasing productivity of labor adequately reduces the portion of the social labor time necessary to reproduce the workers. Thus despite the changing organic composition of capital, the valorization of capital and its further accumulation can take place.

While the rate of surplus value increases with the changing organic composition of capital, the latter exerts a contradictory effect on the rate of profit, since the first is the ratio of surplus value to the variable capital, while the rate of profit compares surplus value to both parts of capital, constant as well as variable. With the more rapid growth of the constant relative to the variable capital, a given rate of surplus value must mean a declining profit rate. The rate of profit can remain unchanged despite a higher organic composition of capital only if the rate of surplus value rises rapidly. With a quick enough increase of the rate of surplus value, the rate of profit can even rise. As the rate of surplus value can increase essentially only together with the rise in the organic composition of capital that accompanies accumulation, the accumulation process turns out to be governed by the general rate of profit, the movement of which determines all other movements of capital.

On the assumption of an irresistibly continuous accumulation of capital, the mutually compensating but contradictory movements of the rate of surplus value and the rate of profit must eventually create a situation excluding further accumulation. While the rate of surplus value must be increased enormously if the fall in the rate of profit is to be halted, the variable capital still continues to decline relative to the constant, and the number of producers of surplus value declines in comparison with the quantity of valorizing capital. Ever fewer workers must create an ever greater surplus value in order to produce the profits required by the capital already in existence if it is to continue to expand. Inevitably a point will be reached at which the greatest quantity of surplus value that can possibly be extorted from the diminished working class is no longer sufficient to augment the value of the accumulated capital.

This line of reasoning represents, to begin with, only the logical consequence of a hypothetical course of development. It refers to no more than the production and accumulation of capital in an imaginary system in which total capital confronts the working class as a whole—thus it refers to the pure operation of the mechanism of surplus-value production and the dynamic of the accumulation process. Marx's aim is to demonstrate the existence of a tendency, inherent in capitalist development and dominating it, by reference to which alone the real movement of capital can be explained. By this means he demonstrates that all the difficulties of capital arise from the nature of capital itself, from surplus-value production and the development, governed by it, of the social productivity of labor on the basis of the capitalist mode of production.

Just as the law of value cannot be observed directly in the actual events of the market but acts through market processes to accomplish the necessities of capitalist production, so the tendency of the rate of profit to fall (and thus the effect of the law of value on the accumulation process) is not a process observable directly in reality but a drive to accumulate manifested in market phenomena, whose results bring the capitalist mode of production into always greater conflict with real social needs. "The *real barrier* of capitalist production," wrote Marx,

> is *capital itself*. It is that capital and its self-expansion appear as the starting and the closing point, the motive and the purpose of production; that production is only production for *capital* and not vice versa, the means of production are not mere means for a constant expansion of the living process of the *society* of producers. The limits within which the preservation and self-expansion of value of capital resting on the expropriation and pauperization of the great mass of producers can alone move—these limits come continually into conflict with the methods of production employed by capital for its purposes, which drive toward unlimited extension of production, toward production as an end in itself, toward unconditional development of the social productivity of labor. The means—unconditional development of the productive forces of society—comes continually into conflict with the limited purpose, the self-expansion of the existing capital. The capitalist mode of production is, for this reason, a historical means of developing the material forces fo production and creating an appropriate world market and is, at the same time, a continual conflict between this its historical task and its own corresponding relations of social production.[8]

This analysis of capitalist accumulation exclusively in terms of the production process, which reveals the tendency of the rate of profit to fall, suggests the historical limits of this mode of production, without thereby being able to determine the exact time of its final denouement. But as this tendency characterizes the system from its beginning and is responsible for its dynamic, it must at all times appear in the actual events of the market, albeit in modified forms. It will be visible not as such but in the form of the measures taken to counter it, the processes Marx calls "counteracting influences ... which cross and annul the effect of the general law" of the falling rate of profit.[9] All of these countertendencies—the increasing intensity of the exploitation of labor, the depression of wages below the value of labor power, the cheapening of the elements of constant capital, relative overpopulation, foreign trade, and the increase in stock capital—are real phenomena whose function it is to improve the profitability of capital, i.e., to counteract the tendency of the rate of profit to fall. So long as they are successful and make possible the valorization of capital, the tendency of the rate of profit to fall is not observable as such and is *de facto* without force, although it is the cause of capital's activities to counteract it. Only in the actual crises which break out from time to time does the fall of the profit rate show itself in its own form, since the counteracting processes are then not sufficient to secure the further valorization of capital.

Marx's theory of accumulation is thus at the same time a theory of crisis, as it locates the origin of crisis in an insufficient valorization of capital, which in turn originates in the breakthrough of the tendency of the profit rate to fall. This kind of crisis arises directly from capital accumulation, governed by the law of value, and can be overcome only through renewed value expansion, i.e., through the reestablishment of a rate of profit adequate for further accumulation. Its basis is an insufficiency of the surplus value available in relation to the capital already accumulated; this transforms the latent fall of the profit rate into an actual profit shortage. The cessation of further accumulation constitutes the crisis situation, which Marx characterized as one of overaccumulation:

> Overproduction of capital is never anything more than overproduction of means of production—of means of labor and necessities of life—which may serve as capital, i.e., may serve to exploit labor at a given degree of exploitation; a fall in the intensity of exploitation below a certain point, however, calls forth disturbances and stoppages in the capitalist production process, crises, and destruction of capital. It is no contradiction that this overproduction of capital is accompanied by more or less considerable overpopulation. The circumstances which increased the productiveness of labor, augmented the mass of produced commodities, expanded markets, accelerated accumulation of capital

both in terms of its mass and its value, and lowered the rate of profit
—these same circumstances have also created, and continuously create,
a relative overpopulation, an overpopulation not employed by the surplus capital owing to the low degree of exploitation at which alone they
could be employed, or at least owing to the low rate of profit which
they would yield at the given degree of exploitation.[10]

In order to illustrate the concept of overaccumulation, Marx had
recourse to a further, not particularly well-chosen example:

> To appreciate what this overaccumulation is . . . one need only assume
> it to be absolute. . . . There would be absolute overproduction of capi-
> tal as soon as additional capital for purposes of capitalist production
> equals zero. . . . As soon as capital would, therefore, have grown in
> such a ratio to the laboring population that neither the absolute work-
> ing time supplied by this population, nor the relative surplus working
> time, could be extended any further (this last would not be feasable at
> any rate in the case where the demand for labor were so strong that
> there were a tendency for wages to rise); at a point, therefore, when the
> increased capital produced just as much, or even less, surplus value than
> it did before its increase, there would be absolute overproduction of
> capital. . . . [T] here would be a steep and sudden fall in the general
> rate of profit, but this time due to a change in the composition of cap-
> ital not caused by the development of the productive forces, but rather
> by a rise in the money value of the variable capital (because of increased
> wages) and the corresponding reduction in the proportion of surplus
> labor to necessary labor.[11]

As this example has given rise to many misunderstandings, it is
necessary to deal with it briefly. On its basis, for example, Martin
Trottmann[12] reproaches Henryk Grossmann, who explained overaccumulation in terms of insufficient value expansion of capital,[13]
for falsely identifying two different, completely contrary tendencies of capitalist accumulation as one and the same. Marx's concept of *absolute* overaccumulation, according to Trottmann, signifies overproduction not as a consequence of insufficient valorization but as the consequence of a shortage of labor power leading
to rising wages and declining surplus value. What Trottmann fails
to see is that the end result is the same in both cases, namely the
suspension of accumulation as a result of a lack of profits. It was

this state of affairs that Marx wanted to emphasize, although his example is doubly unfortunate, as it contradicts not only all experience but also his own theory of accumulation itself.

On the basis of the theory of surplus value, the limit of the capitalist mode of production is to be seen in the fact that "the development of the productivity of labor creates in the fall of the rate of profit a law which at a certain point comes into antagonistic conflict with this development and must be overcome constantly through crisis."[14] However, there is more to the regularity of crisis than this. On the one hand, the crisis appears as the breakdown of the continually evolving accumulation of capital that faces collapse due to the tendency of the rate of profit to fall inherent in it. On the other hand, it also appears in numerous additional contradictions, born in the market, which are of course accentuated by, as well as ultimately based on, the social contradiction of the relations of production. These partial crises cannot be understood apart from the general crisis originating in the capital-labor relation, just as market events in general cannot be understood except by reference to the relations of production.

In order to understand the crisis tendency, so closely bound up with the system, it is necessary always to bear in mind the dynamic character of the system, which rules out any sort of equilibrium. Against the equilibrium theorists of classical economics, who confused the process of circulation with direct barter and consequently imagined that every sale is a purchase and every purchase a sale, Marx maintained that "this gives poor comfort to the possessors of commodities who, unable to make a sale, cannot accordingly make a purchase either."[15] In barter one commodity is directly exchanged for another. But when exchange value is given a form independent of the object by being embodied in money, the sale of one commodity is an act distinct from the purchase of another. With this separation of purchase and sale the possibility of crisis already arises. "The *possibility* of crisis, which became apparent in the *simple metamorphosis* of the commodity, is once more demonstrated, and further developed, by the disjunction between the (direct) process of production and the process of circulation."[16] In this way demand and supply can fall asunder. Indeed, according to Marx, "in reality supply and demand never coincide, or, if they do, it is by mere accident, hence scientifically = 0 and to be regarded as not having occurred."[17] Thus an element of crisis is to be found in commodity production itself, in the contradiction, embodied in the commodity, between exchange value and use value. The contradictions—and thus the potentialities of crisis—already included in commodity and money circulation must however be explained on the basis of the specifically capitalist form of the circulation of commodities and money. Real crises "can only be deduced from the real movement of capitalist production, competition, and credit,"[18] namely, in terms of the aspects of this movement peculiar to capital, not those which would follow from the nature of commodities and money as they would exist in another social system.

In the direct process of production these elements of crisis do not appear, although they are contained in it implicitly, since the process of production is that of the creation and appropriation of surplus value. The possibility of crisis appears first in the process of realization, in circulation, which is implicitly and explicitly a process of reproduction, that is, of the reproduction of the surplus-value-producing relations of production.

> The circulation process as a whole or the reproduction process of capital as a whole is the unity of its production phase and its circulation phase, so that it comprises both these processes or phases. Therein lies a further developed possibility or abstract form of crisis. The economists who deny crises consequently assert only the unity of these two phases. If they were only separate, without being a unity, then their unity could not be established by force and there could be no crisis. If they were only a unity without being separate, then no violent separation would be possible implying a crisis. Crisis is the forcible extablishment of unity between elements that have become independent and the enforced separation from one another of elements which are essentially one.[19]

Although it first appears in the process of circulation, the real crisis cannot be understood as a problem of circulation or of realization, but only as a disruption of the process of reproduction as a whole, which is constituted by production and circulation together. And as the process of reproduction depends on the accumulation of capital, and therefore on the mass of surplus value that makes accumulation possible, it is within the sphere of production that the decisive factors (though not the only factors) of the passage from the possibility of crisis to an actual crisis are to be found. The crisis characteristic of capital thus originates neither in production nor in circulation taken separately but in the difficulties that arise from the tendency of the profit rate to fall inherent in accumulation and governed by the law of value.

Of course, according to Marx, "the conditions of direct exploitation, and those of realizing it, are not identical. They diverge not only in place and time but also logically. The first are only limited by the productive power of society, the latter by the proportional relation of the various branches of production and the consuming power of society."[20] These contradictions contain the possibility of crisis, which is the breaking up of the unity of production and circulation, and the necessity of a forceful reestablishment of this unity. Under the conditions of capital production, however, the reestablishment of this unitary reproduction process refers not simply to the overcoming of disproportionality and a strengthening of the capacity to consume as such but also to the adaptation of both production and circulation to the needs of capitalist reproduction, in other words, the need of capital for valorization. It is not that the crisis is a result of a lost proportionality of production and consumption; rather, the crisis, as a breakdown of the accumulation process due to other causes, expresses itself in disproportionality and a weakened capacity to consume.

This disproportionality and weakened consumer capacity are constant features of capitalism. It is here not a matter of more or less, not that in crisis the disproportionality is too big and consumption too small, because disproportionality and insufficient consumer power are both conditions and results of accumulation in general and are determined by it. Were this not the case, any crisis could be overcome by increasing consumption capacity and reducing the degree of disproportionality, even if this could only be done, within the framework of market relations, by the violent means of the crisis itself. Up to now, however, every real crisis has been overcome *without* abolishing the disproportionality of production and without increasing consumption capacity in relation to production. On the contrary, the disproportionalities are reproduced as part of the system of capitalist production, and the social capacity for consumption decreases relative to the accumulated capital.

Marx's critique of capitalism and of its economic theories is always a double one. On the one hand, he steps onto the terrain of these theories in order to demonstrate their untenability in the light of the theory of value. On the other, he takes his stance ultimately outside capitalist society and its value categories in order to demonstrate its historically limited character. From this viewpoint production cannot be identified with the production of producer and consumer *goods*, since this takes place only within the framework of the production of *capital* (self-expanding value), and its possibilities are determined and limited by this framework. The social capacity for consumption is not simply people's capacity to consume but this capacity as governed and necessarily limited by the requirements of surplus-value production. The capitalist economy is thus not only inadequate by its own standards and afflicted with crises, but, seen from a standpoint of opposition to this society, it is a social order antagonistic to the satisfaction of actual and potential social needs. While in the framework of capitalist production the overproduction of capital is a circumstance that generates crisis, from the standpoint of real social relations there exists no overproduction; indeed there is a lack of means of production capable of satisfying the needs and aspirations of mankind. The consuming power of society is not only limited by surplus-value production but can only find satisfaction under other social relations. In this way Marx condemns capitalism not only on the ground of its own deficiencies but also from the standpoint of another, not yet existing social order, which alone, by the abolition of value production, will make possible the adaptation of social production to social needs.

Marx stated his double critique of capital, so to speak, in one breath: a mode of exposition which has led to misunderstandings and to interpretations of his theory of accumulation as explaining crises either by the disproportionality (or anarchy) of capitalist production or in terms of underconsumption. On the basis of these interpretations, one would expect to find capitalism in continuous situation of crisis, since surplus-value production presupposes underconsumption, for "the working people can only expand their consumption within very narrow limits, whereas the demand for labor, although it grows *absolutely*, decreases *relatively* to the same extent as capitalism develops."[21] If it is said that the problem is not general overproduction but the existence of a disproportion between the different branches of production, this "is no more than to say that under capitalist production the proportionality of the individual branches of production springs as a continual process from disproportionality, because the cohesion of the aggregate production imposes itself as a blind law upon the agents of production, and not as a law which, being understood and hence controlled by their common mind, brings the productive process under their joint control."[22] The proportionality of which Marx speaks here, moreover, has nothing to do with the relationship between production and consumption but concerns the proportion between surplus value and accumulation required for the reproduction of capital and so with the increasing disproportionality of the capital relations, which become visible in crises.

Of course, Marx also wrote that "the more productiveness develops, the more it finds itself at variance with the narrow basis on which the conditions of consumption rest," so that the contradiction is intensified "between the conditions under which . . . surplus value is produced and those under which it is realized."[23] Thus "the ultimate reason for all real crises always remains the poverty and restricted consumption of the masses as opposed to the drive of capitalist production to develop the productive forces as though only the absolute consuming power of society constituted their limit."[24] However, these remarks provide no foundation for a theory of crisis based on underconsumption, nor can the realization of surplus value be made the principal problem of the capitalist mode of production. It goes without saying not only that the origin of crisis lies in an insufficiency of surplus-value production but also that crisis must manifest itself as a problem of the realization of surplus value and the insufficient buying power of the working population. For the very circumstances that lead to the fall of the rate of profit and with it to the restriction of the process of accumulation can be seen also on the level of the market in the form of insufficient demand and the growing difficulty of turning commodities back into money—in brief, in the interruption of the circuit of capital that underlies the entire process of reproduction.

In the early days of capitalist accumulation, when the organic composition of capital was low, the contradiction between production and consumption was less pronounced than it has become at a later stage of development, when the situation is the reverse. In the earlier period general poverty can be much greater than it would be at a later stage of accumulation, since with the lower rate of accumulation constant capital grows more slowly. Thus the realization of surplus value by way of capital accumulation still involves fewer difficulties than at a later stage of capital expansion. These difficulties multiply together with the difficulties of accumulation, which stem from the tendency of the rate of profit to fall and come to a head in a widening discrepancy between the production and the realization of surplus value, between social production and social consumption.

While it is this discrepancy alone that makes capitalist progress possible, at the same time it limits this progress, since it comes into conflict with the reproduction requirements set by the law of value for the total capital, that is, at the moment when the production of surplus value no longer suffices to continue a given tempo of accumulation. Only through the improvement of surplus-value production, through the restoration of the rate of profit necessary for further accumulation, can capital again overcome the breakdown of the reproduction process. It will not thereby have overcome the discrepancy between the production and realization of surplus value. On the contrary, the overcoming of the crisis, by way of the realization of surplus value thanks to further accumulation, also reproduces the divergence between the production and realization of surplus value and that between production and consumption in the sense of the satisfaction of real social needs.

Capital realizes surplus value by means of capitalistically unproductive consumption and by capitalist accumulation. So long as the latter meets with no obstacle, there exists no realization problem. There is none just because the tendency of the rate of profit to fall requires the perpetual increase of surplus value and thus the growth of the rate of accumulation. Capitalist production exclusively serves the accumulation of capital. But this mode of production, ruled by value production, cannot really free itself from the use-value character of social production, which of course, under capitalist conditions, means that it is not free from the limitations that the use value of labor power imposes on it.

Surplus value can never be anything but surplus labor, a portion of total labor; this in itself sets certain limits to accumulation. Thus despite capital's "accumulation for the sake of accumulation," there can be for it no unlimited "production for the sake of production." The rate of surplus value obtaining at any moment and the labor power profitably exploitable at that time set the limits of accumulation, which can be overstepped only through an enlarged production of surplus value. So every momentary overproduction of capital must appear as a crisis that has to put an end to this overproduction. This can be accomplished only by the restoration of a lost proportionality between surplus value and the production of capital, with respect to value relations which are at the same time use-value relations, even though the latter aspect is not consciously considered. More of the social labor must fall to capital, less to the workers.

The crisis serves to accomplish this in two different ways: first, by the destruction of capital, and second, by the increase of surplus value, until both processes have produced the needed relation between the rate of profit and the amount of surplus value required for further accumulation. A new cycle of accumulation begins. Like all the preceding cycles, it too must end in the overproduction of capital, when the uncontrollable passion for surplus value again drives accumulation beyond the point at which valorization is possible. Through the crisis "a large part of the nominal capital of the society, i.e., of the *exchange value* of the existing capital, is once and for all destroyed, although this very destruction, since it does not affect the use value, may very much expedite the new reproduction."[25] The lowered exchange value lowers the organic composition of capital, raising the rate of profit even with a constant rate of surplus value. But the intensified competition provoked by the crisis leads capitalists to cut their production costs and so to take measures in the sphere of production which in themselves raise the rate of surplus value. Thus the conditions for a resumption of the process of accumulation are re-created within the crisis, and with them the further potential for the realization of surplus value by way of capitalist expansion.

If this potential did not exist, the crisis could not be overcome at all, as neither the proportionality of the different branches of production nor the abolition of the divergence between production and consumption are (as we have seen) possibilities for capitalism. The proportionality of the various branches of production is determined by accumulation and achieved by the same processes that lead to the formation of the average rate of profit.

> [The] quantitative limit to the quota for social labor time available for the various particular spheres of production is but a more developed expression of the law of value in general, although the necessary labor time assumes a different meaning here. Only first so much of it is required for the satisfaction of social needs. The limitation occurring here is due to the use value. Society can use only so much of its total labor time for this particular kind of production under prevailing conditions of production.[26]

This adjustment, which is in practical terms an adjustment to market demand, is naturally accomplished, like the formation of the average rate of profit, "only in a very complicated and approximate manner, as a never ascertainable average of ceaseless fluctuations."[27] It is, however, accomplished in times of capitalist prosperity no less than in periods of depression and can therefore not be appealed to for an explanation of crisis. The divergence of production and consumption, which allegedly gives rise to crisis, not only persists during the crisis but acquires an even sharper form; nevertheless the crisis situation leads to a new upswing. So the crisis cycle cannot be explained by underconsumption.

A theory of the crisis cycle must explain prosperity as well as depression. But prosperity would be inexplicable if underconsumption and disproportionalities *per se* led to crisis, for then the first crisis would already have been the last. In fact capital has developed through numerous crises until the present day. This was made practically possible by the increase in the productivity of labor, which augmented surplus value by lowering the value of labor power—though without negating the improvement of the proletariat's living conditions, since a smaller exchange value can represent a greater quantity of consumer goods. Crisis must thus be understood not in terms of the observable phenomena of the market, superficial from the point of view of explanation, but in terms of the laws, directly unobservable yet fundamental to the capitalist economy, of surplus-value production. Here too Marx's dictum holds: "All science would be superfluous if the outward appearance and the essence of things directly coincided."[28]

While surplus value is created in production, "the conversion of surplus value into profit . . . is determined as much by the process of circulation as by the process of production."[29] It is this fact, which on the one hand leads to crisis, that on the other hand allows capital to escape from it. The destruction of capital that takes place in a crisis is a precondition for the powerful transformation of capital, concentrated in a short period of time, that is the prerequisite of further accumulation. The destruction of capital always accompanies capital formation, although in periods of economic prosperity, in a relatively moderate form. In the crisis the destruction of capital accelerates and accentuates this tendency, inherent as it is in the competitive concentration and centralization of capital with regard to both production and circulation. This process, together with the improvement of surplus-value production and the devaluation of capital, and despite a further increase in the organic composition of capital, leads to a restoration of the necessary rate of profit. The crisis manifests itself directly in overproduction of commodities and insufficient purchasing power. As "capital consists of commodities , . . . overproduction of capital implies overproduction of commodities."[30] From this it is not a big step to the idea that the ultimate cause of crisis is underconsumption. This idea is strengthened all the more by Marx's statement that "constant capital is never produced for its own sake but solely because more of it is needed in spheres of production whose products go into individual consumption."[31] If there is insufficient social purchasing power, however, the metamorphosis of money into commodities and the retransformation of commodities into money cannot take place, and this limits the production both of commodities and of constant capital.

Although this is what really happens, it does not explain how capital escapes from its dilemma, since in itself the crisis can only worsen this situation. If, as Marx here appears to maintain, this were really only a question of underconsumption, then the crisis could not be overcome by expanding the production of commodities and constant capital beyond that achieved at the point where prosperity gave way to crisis. But in fact every new prosperity arising out of crisis leaves the previous prosperity far behind with respect to the production of commodities and means of production. Had this not been the case, there would have been no capitalist development, no continuous accumulation of capital.

Marx's statement, then, represents either an error of judgment or unclear writing, especially since the disproportionality of the individual spheres of production and that between production and consumption are hardly contested by bourgeois economics. As the economists see it, however, the equilibrium tendencies of the market lead to the overcoming of these irregularities, i.e., the ensuing scarcity of commodities and capital restores the lost proportionality of production and consumption. If "constant capital is never produced for its own sake but solely because more of it is needed in spheres of production whose products go into individual consumption," then Marx's crisis theory would not be different from the bourgeois theories of the business cycle. Like them it would be a theory of the market in which the relations of supply and demand decide the extension or contraction of production.

In opposition to this, however, the Marxian theory speaks of accumulation as the factor exacerbating the contradictions of capitalism to the point of breakdown. The underconsumption theory as ascribed to Marx, which can indeed be read in some of his expressions, can be conclusively rejected on the basis of his double critique of capital. On the one hand, the overproduction of commodities and insufficient demand are characteristics of the overaccumulation of capital. On the other hand, from a position opposed to capitalism, the accumulation of capital is based on a perpetually widening divergence between production and consumption, so that the ultimate reason for all real crises remains indeed the poverty and restricted consumption of the masses—even if this is only to say that the crisis belongs to capitalism.

The capitalists experience the crisis as an insufficient demand for commodities, the workers as insufficient demand for their labor power. The solution for both lies in the growth of overall demand through the resumption of capital accumulation. But how can the expanded commodity production that goes with this find a market when current production has already outstripped demand? The answer is that capitalism produces precisely not to meet consumer demand but over and above it, until the limits of surplus-value creation are reached, limits that cannot be known when the goods are produced but can only be discovered in the market. Every crisis can be understood only in relation to the prosperity preceding it, just because prosperity derives not from the consuming power of society but from the accumulation requirements, imposed by capitalist competition, of the individual capitals, which at any time are growing to produce not for an *existing* but for an *expected* market. This is due to general social development and to the elimination of less competitive capitals, which yields the more competitive a larger market, along with accumulation.

Production always precedes consumption. In capitalism, however, it advances blindly, as each capital strives not only to win the greatest share of a given market but also to enlarge it ceaselessly and so to avoid losing it. The prerequisite of this is the rapid growth of productivity, which lowers costs, and with it the accumulation of capital in the form of means of production and the changing of the organic composition of capital that accompanies this. The general competition thus leads to a more rapid growth of the constant versus the variable capital, for the individual capitals as for the society as a whole. It is this very process that makes possible the realization of surplus value by way of accumulation, without respect for the restriction of consumption this presupposes. Surplus value becomes new capital, which in its turn produces capital. This process, senseless as it is, is actually the consequence of a mode of production oriented exclusively toward the production of surplus value. All good things come to an end, however, and this same process finds its nemesis in the tendency of the rate of profit to fall. At a certain point the realization of surplus value by accumulation is halted, when accumulation ceases to yield the surplus value necessary for the continuation of this process. Then it suddenly becomes apparent that without accumulation a part of the surplus value cannot be realized, since demand is insufficient to transform the surplus value lying hidden in the commodities into profit.

With respect to accumulation Marx asked why the rate of profit does not fall more quickly than it does, despite the enormous development of productivity. He answered his question by pointing to the countertendencies.[32] The point can also be put by asking not how crises begin but how capital has been able to accumulate despite all its crises. The crisis is easier to understand than prosperity, since the phenomena of overproduction, appearing on the surface of the market, are visible. One glance is enough to see that consumption cannot absorb everything that is produced. But it is not so easy to see how capital, given its inherent contradictions, can proceed for long periods of time from prosperity to boom, periods during which supply is often smaller than demand. This is comprehensible through the historically confirmed fact that the market formed by means of accumulation is nothing other than the development of capitalist society itself.

This development includes not only the accumulation of the existing capital but also the continuous creation of new capital: the spread of the capitalist relations of production over ever broader areas. The exploitation of greater masses of workers requires additional means of production, which must first be produced before they can be productively utilized. A part of the surplus value transformed into capital enters directly into accumulation through the continuous circulation among constant capitals. While one constant capital moves into commodity production, others withdraw commodities from circulation without at the same time producing commodities themselves. This uninterrupted process and its acceleration make it possible for the increasing quantity of commodities to find a market, as the latter is continually expanded by the process of accumulation.

Through the acceleration of accumulation, by perpetual reinvestment, the increasing production of final goods (which enter into consumption) can also find an outlet in the general circulation. Under these conditions—when one part of capital sets a series of other capitals in motion, the capitalists can consume more, and the fully employed workers also have more to spend—the accumulation of capital is more impeded than stimulated by the growing mass of commodities, so that the boom already bears within it the seed of crisis. Production shifts to the consumer-goods industries, which impairs the profitability of capital as a whole. The fall of the average rate of profit thereby accentuated then leads to the weakening of the prosperity and finally to crisis.

What this reveals is not simply a level of consumption too high in proportion to the requirements of accumulation but a shortage of surplus value resulting from the process of accumulation itself, which calls for the restriction of consumption if the going tempo of accumulation is to be maintained. If the amount of surplus value created in production was great enough to hasten accumulation even more, the increased consumption would be no hindrance to further accumulation but could grow together with it. The slowing of the rate of accumulation, however, reveals that the changing value relations, leading to a falling rate of profit, no longer allow the maintenance of the existing level of consumption; that is, that the organic composition of capital has reached a point at which the available surplus value is insufficient to secure both growing consumption and accumulation. On the terrain of the market, the declining rate of accumulation means the decline of new investments and its effects on production as a whole. The same process that opened the way to expansion now reverses direction, seizing on more or less all the branches of social production.

The relation between production and consumption is unaffected in an expanding capitalism, even if the production of consumer goods lags behind that of means of production. On the one hand, the growing productivity of labor makes possible the reduction of the costs of food production; on the other, rapid industrialization leads to a continuous improvement in the industrial products destined for consumption and thus an improvement in the general standard of living. Although accumulation requires the steady increase of means of production, the commodity market is at the same time continually broadened by the introduction of ever newer kinds of use values. Surplus-value production allows the construction of an infrastructure that involves ever greater numbers of people in the process of capital circulation as a whole. If the world market was a precondition of capitalist production, accumulation has led to an ever more rapid capitalization of world production, which does not conflict with the concentration of capital in a few capital-intensive countries as their production is integrated into that of the world. The accumulation of capital is thus not only the prosaic production of profit but also the conquest of the world by capital, an enterprise so demanding that no mass of profit, however great, will be enough.

Capital is always suffering from a lack of profit, in depression and in prosperity. Every capital must continually accumulate in order not to be driven out of business, and accumulation depends on the supply of capital, derived either from its own profits or from those of other capitals. The market grows together with the firms, and with the growth of the market the firms also must grow if they are not to be eliminated by their competition. There has never yet been a business smothered by its own profits, and capital "as a whole" has at no time bewailed an excess of surplus value. That a period of upswing turns into its opposite can only mean, from the standpoint of capital, that profits were too low to justify the expansion of production in terms of profitability. Of course, this situation appears to the capitalists only as a phenomenon of the market, since they do not understand that the level of their own profits is governed by that of the social surplus value, and since knowing this fact, if they did know it, could be of no use at all to them, since the only reaction open to them consists in further attempts to secure or restore their individual profits by the practically possible ways.

Capitalist prosperity depends on the continuous acceleration of accumulation, and this on the expansion of the mass of surplus value. Capital cannot stand still without calling forth crisis. Every equilibrium state—that is, every situation in which production does not exceed consumption—is a state of crisis or stagnation that must be overcome by an increase in surplus value if it is not to lead to the downfall of the system. Just as the tendency of the profit rate to fall exists in latent form even when the actual rate of profit is rising, crisis is already inherent, though invisible, in every prosperity. But like every other disproportionality of the system, that between surplus value and accumulation can also be altered only in accordance with the needs of accumulation, operating through anarchic market processes—only, indeed, through the violence of the crisis. This is a matter not of the restoration of a lost state of equilibrium between production and consumption but of the restoration of *the* disproportionality whose content is the "proportionality" of surplus value and accumulation.

If, according to Marx, the real crisis must be explained in terms of capitalist production, competition, and credit, it must be explained in terms of accumulation, for this is the meaning of production. It is hastened by competition and credit but also made increasingly prone to crisis, since the growing demand for surplus value can exceed by far that actually attained due to the tendency of the rate of profit to fall and despite the development of the productivity of labor. If at this point of overaccumulation the quantity of surplus value can no longer be increased, a situation arises that corresponds to that in Marx's abstract analysis, framed exclusively in terms of the production process, of an uninterrupted accumulation leading to the breakdown of the system. However, since this process is that of the reproduction of a total capital constituted by many capitals, the surplus value is accumulated from then on only in part; not only does the process of accumulation slow down, but the potential for structural changes of capital develops, making it possible to adjust the total surplus value to the needs of further accumulation at the cost of many individual capitals, as well as by higher rates of exploitation. In this sense the overproduction of capital is only temporary, although the tendency to overaccumulate is permanent.

Thus on the one hand capitalist prosperity depends on the acceleration of accumulation, while on the other hand this acceleration leads to the crisis of overaccumulation. For this reason capitalist development is a process shot through with, and inseparable from, crises in which the requirements of the reproduction of the capitalist mode of production assert themselves in a violent way. The reality of these crises naturally does not need to be proven, as they are directly experienced. The only question is whether they arise from the system itself and are thus inevitable, or whether they are caused by factors exogenous to the system and thus can be considered accidental, as imperfections of the system that can sooner or later be eliminated. For Marx accumulation without crisis was inconceivable. While from one viewpoint the crises sweep the difficulties to which accumulation gives birth out of the way, from another they are the surest sign of the ineluctable end of capitalist society.

The world trade crises must, according to Marx, "be regarded as the real concentration and forcible adjustment of all the contradictions of the bourgeois economy."[33] Even the aspects of the crisis that cannot be traced directly back to the capitalist relations of production derive from this source a particular character peculiar to capitalism. As crises of the world market affect all countries, although in different ways, and as the ultimate reason for crisis—the shortage of surplus value—appears on the market in inverted form as an unsalable excess of commodities, the conditions both of the crisis and its solution are so complex that they cannot be empirically determined. When the crisis will break out, its extent, and its duration cannot be predicted; only that there will be a crisis can be expected with certainty. Nonetheless Marx attempted to relate the periodicity of crisis to the reproduction of capital or, more exactly, to the replacement of fixed capital. As the accumulation of capital is largely a matter of the increase in the means of production, the replacement and enlargement of fixed capital should be at least a contributing factor of the periodicity of crisis.

The value invested in fixed capital is in the course of time transferred to the commodities produced and through their sale transformed into money. The retransformation of money into fixed capital (the replacement of the used-up means of production) is governed by the service life of the latter, which in turn is determined by the particular characteristics of the various branches of production. The replacement of fixed capital is, thanks to the development of technology, at the same time its improvement. This obliges capitalists, in order to remain competitive, to renew their fixed capital before it is worn out. This "moral depreciation" of fixed capital, as well as the general effort to partake in the changing technology, generates capitalist interest in the shortening of the turnover time of fixed capital. The shorter it is, the sooner the new investments can partake in the higher productivity achieved through the continuous revolutionization of the means of production, and the lower the costs of the "moral depreciation" that precedes the physical exhaustion of capital. As the average service life of fixed capital in his day was ten years, Marx wondered whether this might be related to the ten-year crisis cycle.

Of course, the service life of fixed capital can lengthen or shorten. However, according to Marx, the issue here is not a definite number of years. This much seemed evident to him:

> The cycle of interconnected turnovers embracing a number of years, in which capital is held fast by its fixed constituent part, furnishes a material basis for the periodic crises. During this cycle business undergoes successive periods of depression, medium activity, precipitancy, crisis. True, periods in which capital is invested differ greatly and far from coincide in time. But a crisis always forms the starting point of large new investments. Therefore, from the point of view of society as a whole, more or less a new material basis for the next turnover cycle.[34]

Marx did not follow up this vague hypothesis. Although crisis leads to a temporal concentration of investments and so to a sort of "material basis for the next turnover cycle," in the final analysis this is only to say that "a crisis always forms the starting point of large new investments," without thereby explaining the crisis or its periodicity. And although it is true that in the meantime the capital transformed into commodities piles up in the form of money, this does not mean that it must remain in this form until the replacement of the fixed capital. Since the service lives of different capitals are different, and since they renew themselves in accordance with their respective starting points, the turnover of fixed capital is being completed throughout the whole period of upswing, along with the new investments that constitute accumulation, which bring the cyclical upswing with them. This process is reversed in crisis, when capital is at first neither replaced nor newly invested. Only as the crisis proceeds are additional funds invested in order to raise the productivity of labor. These attempts give birth to the new prosperity, which is built not only on the replacement of fixed capital but on further accumulation.

Even if the turnover time of fixed capital plays a certain contributing role in governing the production process of capital as a whole, this does not suffice to explain the particular periodicity of crisis. Since crises are, according to Marx, "the real concentration and forcible adjustment of all the contradictions of the bourgeois economy"—contradictions whose particular contributions to the crisis cannot be estimated—the periodicity of crisis also cannot be treated as due to a particular aspect of the process as a whole. From the crisis cycle that Marx observed one can only conclude that the difficulties that characterized the process of development in his time made possible the maintenance of prosperity for no more than ten years at a time, and not that capital is therefore destined to a ten-year cycle.

Friedrich Engels wrote later that:

> The acute form of the periodic process, with its former ten-year cycle, appears to have given way to a more chronic, long drawn out alternation between a relatively short and slight business improvement and a relatively long, indecisive depression—taking place in the various industrial countries at different times. But perhaps it is only a matter of a prolongation of the duration of the cycle. In the early years of world commerce, 1815-47, it can be shown that crises occurred about every five years; from 1847 to 1867 the cycle is clearly ten years; is it possible that we are now in the preparatory stage of a new world crash of unparalleled vehemence? Many things seem to point in this direction. Since the last general crisis of 1867 many profound changes have taken place. The colossal expansion of the means of transportation and communication—ocean liners, railways, electrical telegraphy, the Suez Canal—has made a real world market a fact. The former monopoly of England in industry has been challenged by a number of competing industrial countries; infinitely greater and varied fields have been opened in all parts of the world for the investment of surplus European capital, so that it is far more widely distributed, and local overspeculation may be more easily overcome. By means of all this, most of the old breeding grounds of crises and opportunities for their development have been eliminated or strongly reduced. At the same time, competition in the domestic market recedes before the cartels and trusts, while in the foreign market it is restricted by protective tariffs, with which all major industrial countries, England excepted, surround themselves. But these protective tariffs are nothing but preparations for the ultimate general industrial war, which shall decide who has supremacy on the world

market. Thus every factor, which works against a repetition of the old crises, carries within itself the germ of a far more powerful future crisis.[35]

This is to say that the periodicity of crisis also has its history and is affected by historical circumstances. If the ultimate reason for every crisis is capitalism itself, each particular crisis differs from its predecessors just because of the continuous transformation of world market relations and of the structure of global capital. Under these conditions neither the crises themselves nor their duration and gravity can be determined in advance, and this all the less as the symptoms of crisis appear after the crisis itself and only bring the crisis to the attention of the population. Moreover, the crisis cannot be reduced to "purely economic" events, although it arises "purely economically," that is, from the social relations of production clothed in economic forms. The international competitive struggle, fought also by political and military means, influences economic development, just as this in turn gives rise to the various forms of competition. Thus every real crisis can only be understood in connection with social development as a whole.

Notes

1. *Capital*, vol. 1, Harmondsworth, 1976, pp. 96-97.
2. Ibid., p. 103.
3. Ibid., p. 102.
4. See V. I. Lenin, *Collected Works*, vol. 38, *Philosophical Notebooks*, Moscow, Foreign Language Publishing House, 1972, p. 180.
5. O. Morf, *Geschichte und Dialektik in der politischen Ökonomie*, 1970, p. 64.
6. *Capital*, vol. 3, Moscow, 1962, p. 178.
7. Ibid., p. 25.
8. Ibid., p. 245.
9. Ibid., p. 227; see chap. 14 *passim*.
10. Ibid., pp. 250-51.
11. Ibid., pp. 246-47.
12. *Zur Interpretation und Kritik der Zusammenbruchstheorie von Henryk Grossmann*, 1956.
13. See Henryk Grossmann, *Das Akkumulations-und Zusammenbruchsgesetz des kapitalistischen Systems*, 1929.
14. *Capital*, vol. 3, p. 253 [translation corrected].
15. Karl Marx, *A Contribution to the Critique of Political Economy*, Moscow, 1969, p. 97.

16. Marx, *Theories of Surplus-Value*, vol. 3, Moscow, 1968, p. 507.
17. *Capital*, vol. 3, p. 186.
18. *Theories of Surplus-Value*, vol. 2, p. 512.
19. Ibid., p. 513.
20. *Capital*, vol. 3, p. 239.
21. *Theories of Surplus-Value*, vol. 2, p. 492.
22. *Capital*, vol. 3, pp. 251-52.
23. Ibid., p. 240.
24. Ibid., pp. 472-73.
25. *Theories of Surplus-Value*, vol. 2, p. 496.
26. *Capital*, vol. 3, p. 621.
27. Ibid., p. 159.
28. Ibid., p. 797.
29. Ibid., p. 807.
30. Ibid., p. 251.
31. Ibid., pp. 299-300.
32. See ibid., p. 227.
33. *Theories of Surplus-Value*, vol. 2, p. 510 [translation corrected].
34. *Capital*, vol. 2, Moscow, 1961, p. 186.
35. Note in *Capital*, vol. 2, pp. 477-78.

3

The Epigones

The crises of the nineteenth century displayed characteristics which were connected equally with the level attained by capitalist development and with political events. Thus the crisis of 1816 was without a doubt closely connected with the many years of war preceding Napoleon's fall.[1] In particular English capital, despite the increasing mechanization of labor, had grown too quickly in relation to its valorization requirements to be able to avoid crisis by way of further expansion. The stagnation that set in manifested itself as overproduction, which, as a consequence of the impoverishment of continental Europe, could not be overcome by means of foreign trade. This resulted in a violent collapse of prices, which hit agriculture and the textile industry particularly hard and led to the introduction of protective tariffs in order to stabilize the still predominant agricultural production. There were many bankruptcies and bank failures. Wages were radically reduced, and growing unemployment engendered mass poverty, social unrest, the machine breaking of the Luddite movement, and also the theories, critical of capitalism, of Sismondi and Robert Owens. The general price collapse of the depression period, which was punctuated ten years later by a new crisis, only came to a stop in 1819.

The crisis of 1836 began in England and the United States. In both countries industrial development had led to widespread speculation and to a situation in which the production of profit no longer met the need for it. The crisis took the form notably of a money and stock-market crisis but affected the whole economy, ushering in a long period of depression that soon spread over all of Europe. The apparently permanent crisis led to the revolutionary events of 1848 and to the first beginnings of an anticapitalist labor movement. Even during the upswings within the depression, the living conditions of the workers improved only in unessential ways, only to sink all the deeper with the first economic downturn.

The low level of wages that prevailed was an expression of the still low productivity of labor. The relatively small amount of surplus value, along with the acuity of competition, stimulated accumulation, which of course soon reached the limits of exploitation set by the still narrow basis of the capitalist relations of production. The autonomous development of capital was not yet sufficient to enlarge the market decisively by itself. Crises appeared as commercial crises and found expression in a disastrous fall of commodity prices, which allowed for no further productive investment. Under these conditions only accidents like the discovery of the California gold fields led to a rise in prices and a new prosperity. Events like the American Civil War, which at first was a factor of crisis, later drove industrial and capitalist development forward at a more rapid tempo. With the geographical extension of capital production, crises acquired an even more international character, but at the same time enormously promoted every upswing of the economy. However, the actual development of capital allowed no other prognosis than the one Marx had made; his theory was directly confirmed by reality, which thus gave force to the revolutionary expectations connected with it. Although every crisis had a character of its own, to be explained only by reference to the total situation from which it had arisen, crises nevertheless were characterized in common by the interruption of accumulation and the overproduction accompanying it, which gave rise to mass misery. And although the crisis cycle was not a regularly periodic one, it nonetheless really existed as an irregular process. At the end of the nineteenth century, however, as Friedrich Engels said, crises appeared to become less severe and the periods of prosperity to lengthen; at the same time, the economic condition of the workers improved. The productivity of labor had been sufficiently increased to maintain the profitability of capital as it accumulated over longer periods of time. This situation gave rise to social democratic reformism and the abandonment of Marx's theory of accumulation as a theory of crisis and collapse.

While Engels saw in the increasing mildness of crisis the germ of more violent crisis in the future, Eduard Bernstein maintained in 1899 that

> Signs of an economic worldwide crash of unheard of violence have not been established, nor can one describe the improvement of trade in the intervals between the crises as particularly short-lived. Much more does a . . . question arise . . . (1) whether the enormous extension of the world market, in conjunction with the extraordinary shortening of time necessary for the transmission of news and for the transport of trade, has so increased the possibilities of adjustment of disturbances; and (2) whether the enormously increased wealth of the European states, in conjunction with the elasticity of the modern credit system and the rise of industrial cartels, has so limited the reacting force of local or individual disturbances that, at least for some time, general commercial crises similar to the earlier ones are to be regarded as improbable.[2]

Bernstein answered his own question with the statement that "the formula of the crisis in and for Marx was no picture of the future but a picture of the present day,"[3] so that today, "unless unforeseen external events bring about a general crisis . . . there is no urgent reason for concluding that such a crisis will come to pass for purely economic reasons."[4] For Bernstein and for reformism in general, a theory of class struggle based on a tendency toward crisis was outmoded, since a revolutionary situation created by the breakdown of capitalism was no longer to be expected.

In his reply to Bernstein's revisionism, Karl Kautsky explained that there is no theory of breakdown in Marx, but that this was a polemical invention of Bernstein's. "Crises," Kautsky argued,

> work in the direction of socialism by hastening the concentration of capital and increasing the insecurity of the proletarians' living conditions, thus sharpening the impetus that presses the workers into the arms of socialism. . . . Furthermore, the constant need to expand the market contains yet a further factor; it is clear that the capitalist mode of production becomes impossible from the historical moment when the market can no longer extend in the same tempo as production; that is, as soon as overproduction becomes chronic. Bernstein understands historical necessity to mean a situation of constraint. Here we have such a situation which, if and when it appears, will infallibly lead to socialism.[5]

Thus the upshot of Marx's theory, according to Kautsky, is the breakdown of capitalism, although there is no Marxian theory of breakdown. The attempt was made to overcome this contradiction with the hypothesis that chronic overproduction could be a long, dragged-out process, so that it was even doubtful whether the breakdown would actually occur. The class struggle could put an end to capitalism long before the system fell apart.

Heinrich Cunow brought this theory into closer connection with Marx's theory of accumulation. In his essays on the theme of "breakdown," Cunow argued that Marx and Engles had derived the system's collapse

> on the one hand from capitalist accumulation, and on the other hand from the split between the capitalist mode of production and its mode of exchange, which blocks the full utilization of the existing productive forces. . . . The capital wealth already generated finds no further adequate valorization, either in the process of production or in the process of commodity circulation; the developed expansive power of industry comes into ever sharper conflict with the mechanism of the capitalist form of economy, until the latter finally bursts.[6]

Of course, this process of breakdown was still put off into the distant future, since capital had learned to overcome its contradictions, growing out of commodity circulation, by means of the expansion of the capital and industrial markets on a global scale. Finally, however, the contradiction between social production and its mode of distribution remained decisive and was expected to put an end to capitalist production.

In this way attention remained fixed on the contradictory development of production and distribution, on the increasing difficulty with which surplus value is realized as a result of capitalistically limited consumption. In order to demonstrate the viability of capital, it was necessary to deny the ability of this disproportionality to menace capital. This Tugan-Baranovsky attempted to do. In his book on commercial crises he described the crisis cycle as did all the others who explain crisis in terms of a disturbance of the proportionality of supply and demand.[7] This disproportionality, which also can be understood as a disproportionality between the different branches of production, Tugan-Baranovsky held to be the sole cause of crisis. A distribution of capital in accordance with the real demand for commodities would be enough to eliminate crises. Arising from the planlessness of capitalist competition, they can be made less severe by increasing control over the economy and can in principle be overcome.

If according to Tugan-Baranovsky the origin of crisis is to be found in the disproportionate distribution of capital, it is not to be found in the distribution of the social product between labor and capital. The restriction of consumption does not for him impose a limit on accumulation or on the realization of surplus value, since restriction of the demand for consumer goods is in no way identical with restriction of the demand for commodities *per se*. "The accumulation of social capital leads to a restriction of the social demand for consumer goods and at the same time to an enlargement of the total social demand for commodities."[8] Thus the "accumulation of capital can be accompanied by an absolute decline of social consumption. A relative decline of social consumption—relative to the sum total of the social product—is in any case inevitable."[9]

Tugan-Baranovsky appealed to Marx with regard to two points. Like Marx he saw the fundamental contradiction "between production as a means to satisfy human needs and production as a technical aspect of the creation of capital, that is, as an *end in itself*."[10] He admitted that "the poverty of the masses of people, poverty not in an absolute but in a relative sense, in the sense of the insignificance of labor's share of the total social product, is one of the preconditions of commercial crises"; but it would be false to suppose "that the distress of the workers . . . makes the realization of ever expanding capitalist production impossible because of insufficient demand, . . . since capitalist production creates its own market for itself." On the contrary, "the smaller the share of the workers, the greater is the share of the capitalists—and the more quickly capital accumulates—necessarily accompanied by slowdowns and crises."[11]

To demonstrate the possibility of unlimited accumulation Tugan-Baranovsky made use of the Marxian reproduction schemas in Volume 2 of *Capital*. As he saw it, these schemas granted the possibility of a continued and crisis-free total reproduction of capital so long as the requisite proportions between the individual spheres and branches of production are maintained. Since these proportions are difficult to maintain because of the anarchy of the economy, crises occur, but not the objective impossibility of further accumulation. Thus every theory of breakdown must be rejected, and the abolition of capitalist society must be considered a matter of the development of socialist consciousness.

In dealing with Marx, Tugan-Baranovsky of course forgot the theory of value on which the Marxian theory of accumulation is based. Or rather he referred to Marx without taking account of his theory, as he, like Bernstein and other reformists, had already taken up the subjective value theory of bourgeois economics. Thus, as he himself said, he did not utilize "the usual Marxian terminology (constant capital, variable capital, surplus value)," since, according to him, "in the creation of the surplus product—thus of rent—no distinction between human labor power and the dead means of labor is to be made. One ought to call the machine variable capital for the same reason as human labor power, since both yield surplus value."[12] Consistently, he accepted (with some reservations) the equilibrium theory descended from Say, namely the idea that with a proportional distribution of social production, the supply of commodities must be equal to the demand, and he interpreted Marx's reproduction schemas in this sense. In this way the contradiction of accumulation stemming from the fall in the rate of profit vanished from his conception, and with it all the limits of capitalist production.

Oddly enough, this fact went unnoticed in the polemic directed against Tugan-Baranovsky within Social Democracy. Kautsky, though granting that "a lack of proportionality in production can also provoke a crisis," nevertheless continued to insist that "the ultimate reason for periodic crises is to be found in underconsumption." He directed his energies against the equation of human labor power with the dead means of production, in order, however, only to point out that "in the last instance human labor alone is the value-creating factor, so that in the last instance the extension of human consumption determines the extension of production."[13] On this account the accumulation of capital depends on the workers' consumption—as there is no insufficiency of capitalist consumption—and the expansion of capital is tied to human needs, since "the consumption of the means of production is nothing other than the production of consumer goods."[14]

For Conrad Schmidt as well the volume of consumption determined the volume of production, and overproduction arose from the restricted consumption of the working population.

> Capitalist competition, with the increasing difficulty of finding markets, must, given its tendency, be manifested in an increasing downward pressure on prices and thus in a fall in the rate of return or in the *average rate of profit*—a fall making the capitalist type of economy ever more unprofitable and risky even for the majority of private entrepreneurs, while at the same time the labor market becomes progressively unfavorable to the workers, and the ranks of the *industrial reserve army* swell terribly.[15]

Schmidt too did not appeal to Marx's theory of accumulation, and he rejected the labor theory of value. Like Adam Smith before him, he explained the fall in the rate of profit by the intensification of competition. Although for him the crisis arose from insufficient consumption, he nevertheless agreed with Tugan-Baranovsky that crisis did not imply an eventual breakdown of capitalism, since the improvement in the workers' living conditions achieved through social struggles would weaken, if not completely eliminate, the roots of crisis, the restriction of consumption.

The vast debate about the crisis and collapse of capitalism (which we will not discuss further here) reflected the ambiguities in Marx's depiction of crisis. As already pointed out, for Marx the crisis was due, on the one hand, to the fall in the rate of profit inherent in accumulation and independently of all the phenomena of crisis visible on the surface of society; but on the other hand, it also originated in the underconsumption of the workers. Thus Kautsky could appeal to Marx with as much right as Schmidt or Tugan-Baranovsky. The confusion became all the greater since the underconsumption theory could support the conclusion that capitalism must break down. The debates on crisis and breakdown have continued to the present day, in part thanks to the ambiguity of Marx's statements, although the latter indeed signify no more than Marx's own unsureness, as they were written many years before the publication of Volume 1 of *Capital* and at a later moment would most probably have been reformulated in a less contradictory way.

However this may be, both the actual development of capitalism and the analysis of accumulation in terms of value and surplus value unambiguously show that the continuing accumulation of capital is linked to the disproportionality between production and consumption corresponding to the valorization of capital, and that only the maintenance of this situation makes it possible to overcome the crises that occur. Of course, if the crisis can no longer be overcome in a capitalist way, permanent depression must set in, with an absolute pauperization of the workers and unemployed. This state of affairs would exhibit the contradiction of capital as a conflict between the capitalist mode of production and the consumption needs of society.

With Tugan-Baranovsky's reference to the Marxian reproduction schemas in Volume 2 of *Capital*, the debate on crisis took on a new dimension. The problem of crisis was seen no longer as a question of the overaccumulation of capital or of underconsumption but as one of social equilibrium or of the proportionality of the reproduction process. It will be necessary here to go briefly into the Marxian reproduction schemas. The process of production is at the same time a process of reproduction, which is completed through circulation. For theoretical ends and for the illustration of this process it is sufficient to divide total social production into two departments in order to represent the conditions of an imaginary, frictionless exchange. Although capitalist production is the creation of exchange value, it nevertheless remains tied to use value. While every capitalist seeks only to enlarge his capital as capital, he can accomplish this only in the framework of social production, which is at the same time a social metabolism concerned with use values. In the social framework a theoretically conceivable equilibrium of capitalist exchange presupposes the production in the correct proportions of the use values necessary for reproduction.

Just as competition cannot be explained by competition, the circulation process cannot be explained in terms of circulation. It presupposes definite labor-time relations as value and use-value relations and a definite division of them to make reproduction possible. It goes without saying that the Marxian reproduction schemas do not refer to the real production process but to the requirements of capitalist reproduction that underlie the real process, which are indeed not consciously taken into account in capitalism but must nevertheless be satisfied in one way or another if the accumulation of capital is to go on. The function of the reproduction schemas is simply to indicate that accumulation as well as production requires definite proportions of kinds of product, which must be established via the market. The schemas are formulated in such a way that with both simple and enlarged reproduction there is an equilibrium of exchange between the two departments of production. This, however, does not mean that the actual capitalist reproduction process proceeds or can proceed following the pattern of the schemas of simple or enlarged reproduction.

The illustrative and explanatory function of the reproduction schemas was then confused with that of representing a process actually occuring in reality, and the relations of exchange defined by them were treated as examples either proving or disproving the tendency of the system to equilibrium. For Tugan-Baranovsky the reproduction schemas provided proof of the possibility of unlimited capital accumulation, so long as the necessary proportions were maintained. This idea was taken up by Rudolf Hilferding. He agreed with Tugan-Baranovsky, and with Marx, that capitalist production depends not on consumption but on the need of capital for valorization. But he also wanted to do justice, in some fashion, to the idea of underconsumption and so maintained that "the conditions of valorization rebel against the extension of consumption, and as they are decisive, the contradiction grows to the point of crisis."[16] To be sure, he immediately took this back, pointing out that "the periodic character of crisis . . . cannot be explained in general from a *permanent* phenomenon (namely, underconsumption)."[17] For Hilferding the crisis is, "in general, a disturbance of circulation" that violates the necessary equilibrium conditions of the social reproduction process. For him the Marxian schemas also show that

In capitalist production reproduction both on the simple and on the enlarged scale can proceed undisturbed so long as the [necessary] proportions are maintained. Conversely, the crisis can arise even with simple reproduction if, for example, the necessary proportion between used-up and newly invested capital is violated. It does not in the least follow from this that the cause of crisis must be the underconsumption of the masses inherent in capitalist production. A too rapid expansion of consumption would in itself give rise to crisis as much as would a stabilization or contraction of the production of means of production. Just as little can the possibility of general overproduction of commodities be deduced from Marx's schemas; rather they allow for any expansion of production on the basis of the existing forces of production.[18]

For Hilferding capital's propensity to crisis due to disproportionality changed with the restriction of competition by the trustification and cartelization of capital. Although the overproduction of commodities can in part be overcome through a better adaptation to demand, a crisis involves an overproduction not of commodities but of capital. This means only "that capital has been invested in production to such a degree that its conditions of valorization have come into conflict with its realization conditions, so that the marketing of commodities no longer yields the profit on which a further expansion, a further accumulation, depends. Sales stagnate because the expansion of production comes to a halt."[19] Since for Hilferding the crisis is a "disturbance of circulation," his explanation is based not on the fall in the rate of profit resulting from a growing organic composition of capital but on a lack of sales relative to too quickly growing production or on a contradiction between the "valorization conditions and the realization conditions" of capital—thus, after all, on a divergence between supply and demand, even if independent of the restricted consumption of the workers. Such "disturbances of circulation" are made not less but more acute by the advance of cartelization, without thereby leading to a breakdown, since an economic breakdown is for Hilferding "in general not rationally conceivable."[20]

The abolition of capitalist society can therefore be achieved only by a political process, which in any case is prepared for to an ever greater extent by the cartelization of capital and the absorption of industrial capital by bank capital, a process described by Hilferding as the formation of finance capital. "Finance capital signifies the tendency to establish social control over production. But it is socialization in an antagonistic form; control over social production remains in the hands of an oligarchy. The struggle for the dispossession of this oligarchy is the final phase of the class struggle between the bourgeoisie and the proletariat."[21] For this it is sufficient "for society to take control of finance capital through the conscious organ of the people, the state captured by the proletariat, in order immediately to extend control over the most important branches of production."[22]

While in Hilferding's view there were no economic limits to capitalist accumulation, it was nevertheless a process marked by crises that only the socialization of production by socialism could overcome. Under capitalist management accumulation compelled, along with the perpetual expansion of production, the export of capital and a struggle for markets and for sources of raw materials in order to increase the surplus value of the nationally organized capital. Imperialism, a direct consequence of the capitalization of the world economy, was as much a factor of crisis as the overcoming of crisis. Inseparable from capitalism, imperialism took on particularly ominous forms around the turn of the century, as the imperialist powers prepared for new confrontations. Imperialistic policy and colonialism found opponents and supporters even in the Social Democratic camp, a situation reflected in Rosa Luxemburg's work on the accumulation of capital.[23]

Taking Heinrich Cunow's crisis theory as a point of departure, but completely ignoring Hilferding's, Luxemburg saw imperialism as an immediate consequence of capitalist production. This she wished to prove scientifically. The attempt to give a "strictly economic demonstration" of the necessity of imperialism led her, in her own words, "to Marx's diagrams at the end of the second volume of *Capital*, which have seemed weird to me for a long time, and which I now find full of hot air."[24] By "hot air" she meant the equilibrium conception of capitalist reproduction she took Marx to have. Luxemburg's analysis of Marx's schemas of enlarged reproduction led her to the reverse of Marx's apparent results, namely to the impossibility of equilibrium. "If we take the schema literally," she wrote, ". . . it appears that capitalist production would itself realize its entire surplus value, and that it would use the capitalized surplus value exclusively for its own needs."[25] But, according to Luxemburg, this would mean that "these capitalists are thus fanatical supporters of an expansion of production for the sake of the expansion of production. They see to it that ever more machines are built for the sake of building—with their help—ever more new machines"; that is, they accumulate their surplus value not as capital but in the form of a pointless production of means of production.[26] In this conception surplus value would be created "from the very beginning . . . in a natural form exclusively designed for the requirements of accumulation."[27] This, however, is not the case in reality, as capital must first sell in order to be able to accumulate. But where are the capitalists to find the buyers who will allow them to realize their surplus value? Capitalist accumulation, for Luxemburg, is "the heaping up of money capital," which presupposes the realization of the surplus value produced. How can this be accomplished,

> if the capitalists as a class are themselves always the only buyers of their total product—apart from the portion which they must at the moment pay the working class for its maintenance—if they must always buy their commodities from themselves and must "cash in" the surplus value contained in them with their own money—then the heaping up of profits which is accumulation must be impossible for the class of capitalists as a whole.[28]

She found the answer to her questions "in the dialectical contradiction that capitalist accumulation needs noncapitalist social formations as the setting for its development, that it proceeds by assimilating the very conditions which alone can ensure its own existence."[29] Internal capitalist trade can, as she saw it, "at best realize only certain quantities of value contained in the social product: the constant capital that has been used up, the variable capital, and the consumed part of the surplus value. That part of the surplus value which is earmarked for capitalization, however, must be realized "externally.""[30] Thus capitalism,

> thanks to its interactions with noncapitalist social strata and countries, expands itself more and more, in that it accumulates at their expense but at the same time erodes and displaces them step by step in order to take their place. But the more capitalist countries participate in this hunt after territories for accumulation, and the scarcer the noncapitalist

areas still open to the global expansion of capital become, the more bitter will be the competitive struggle of capital over each such territory and the more its campaigns in the world theater will turn into a series of economic and political catastrophes: world crises, wars, revolutions.[31]

Imperialism can be explained apart from Luxemburg's "strictly economic reasoning." It can be treated in connection with accumulation, without reference to the need for noncapitalist markets for the realization of surplus value, as for example in Hilferding's theory. The importance of Luxemburg's work, however, lay not so much in the explanation of imperialism as in the demonstration that capitalism has absolute, impassable limits, and that the more closely the system approaches them, the greater the social shocks will be. It was the idea of Tugan-Baranovsky and Hilferding, based on the reproduction schemas, that nothing stands objectively in the way of accumulation, which impelled Luxemburg to investigate the equilibrium conditions of the schemas and thereby to conclude that the impossibility of realizing surplus value within the capital-labor relationship gives rise to a perpetual element of disequilibrium, in the form of an unsalable quantity of commodities that cannot be turned into money and the value of which can only be realized as capital outside the system. Thus it was not the problem of the production of surplus value and the difficulties it encounters as accumulation proceeds but that of the realization of surplus value which Luxemburg saw as decisive for the future of capitalism. The periodic crises were accordingly for her crises of overproduction, characterized by quantities of unsold goods, and could not be overcome within the system. This idea had a certain plausibility, as capitalism had in fact spread geographically and incorporated one new country after another into the world economy; but it had nothing to do with Marx's theory of accumulation. As a result Luxemburg's theory came in for extensive criticism both from the right and from the left wing of the social democratic movement.

The discussion around Marx's theory of accumulation and crisis led to the development of two antithetical views, each giving rise to several variants. One insisted that the accumulation of capital has absolute limits and that an economic breakdown of the system is inevitable. The other held this to be absurd, maintaining that the system would not disappear from economic causes. It goes without saying that the reformists, if only to justify themselves, adopted the latter position. But even ultraleftists—Anton Pannekoek, for example—saw the idea that the breakdown of capitalism would be a "purely economic" process as a falsification of historical materialist theory. Pannekoek thought the problematic itself was false, whether it led to Tugan-Baranovsky's conclusion that accumulation has no limits or to Luxemburg's breakdown theory. He thought the shortcomings of the capitalist system as Marx described them and the concrete phenomenon of crisis, produced by the anarchy of the economy, were sufficient to provoke the development of revolutionary consciousness among the proletariat and thus to lead to proletarian revolution.

Although Pannekoek attacked Tugan-Baranovsky's harmonizing interpretation of Marx's reproduction schemas[32] on the grounds that the circuit of capital is in reality a process shot through with crises and that the function of Marx's formulas in his theoretical analysis was only that of a preliminary and simplified description, he also held Luxemburg's critique to be a misunderstanding,[33] since in his opinion capital is able to realize its surplus value without the help of a noncapitalist market. By the same token, imperialism, while an incontestable fact, was not a necessary presupposition of capitalist production. The whole hypothesis of a final and automatic breakdown of capital, he thought, contradicts Marx's approach, in which the objective and subjective conditions of revolution cannot be separated. The revolution depends on the will of the working class, even if this will develops in response to economic circumstances. Thus the proletariat is not going to meet a final crisis but will experience many crises, until the decisive element, revolutionary consciousness, is sufficiently constituted to put an end to the capitalist system.

Luxemburg's *Accumulation of Capital* met with almost universal rejection among the theoreticians of Social Democracy, not so much because she dared to criticize Marx or to explain the reality of imperialism by the realization difficulties encountered by accumulation, but because by evoking the inevitable end of capitalism she supported a politics of proletarian class struggle diametrically opposed to the dominant reformist attitude. On the other hand, it was just her insistence on the inescapable end of capital that assured her a following among the workers of the left opposition, whether or not they accepted her specific argument for it, as they did not care very much whether and how capital would break down from these or from any other causes, as long as it was doomed to break down from some cause.

Among the many theoreticians who argued against Luxemburg, Otto Bauer and Nikolai Bukharin merit particular attention. Bukharin's delayed critique[34] reflected not only theoretical interest but also the struggle the Bolsheviks were waging at that time against "Luxemburgism" in order to clean the tradition linked to her out of the communist parties. Bukharin found nothing to object to in Marx's reproduction schemas and rejected Luxemburg's critique on this subject. Of course, the circuit of capital, represented at a very high level of abstraction, required later completion on a lower, more concrete level of abstraction. In any case, the reproduction schemas admitted of neither Tugan-Baranovsky's nor Luxemburg's interpretations. According to Marx and Lenin, even in a "pure" capitalist system nothing stands in the way of accumulation and the realization of surplus value. Bukharin saw the basis of Luxemburg's false theory in her identification of the accumulation of capital with that of money capital. She imagined that the share of the surplus value that must be accumulated as additional capital must first be transformed into money already at hand within the system. Only then would the surplus value be realized, and the expanded reproduction would be the reproduction of capitalist accumulation. Without this metamorphosis of surplus value from the commodity form into the money form, accumulation could not take place. Bukharin, however, pointed out that, like capital itself, surplus value appears in various forms: as commodities, as money, as means of production, and as labor power. For each of these the money form is not to be identified with the total surplus value in its various forms. Surplus value must go through its money phase, only not as a whole, at one time, but rather bit by bit, through innumerable commercial transactions, in the course of which a given sum of money can repeatedly accomplish the transformation of commodities into money and money into commodity. The total surplus value does not have to encounter a sum of money equivalent to it, although every commodity, in order to be realized, must be turned into money. The fact that the growing capital is accompanied by an increasing mass of money does not mean that capital and money capital have to accumulate at the same rate. Capital is objectified in many forms, of which that of money is one, but not the exclusive, functional form of realized surplus value.

This critique of Luxemburg's theory was related to Bukharin's own crisis theory, which relied on Lenin. It did not differ essentially from the disproportionality theories of Tugan-Baranovsky and Hilferding, although Bukharin attempted to take a position opposed to Tugan-Baranovsky. This putative opposition consisted in the inclusion of underconsumption within the disproportionality between the production of producer's goods and that of consumers' goods. One might consider this a tautology, but for Bukharin it was the decisive factor that distinguished Marx's theory from Tugan-Baranovsky's. Here we find ourselves facing the question raised earlier, whether Marx had two crisis theories, one deriving crisis from the theory of value as the falling rate of profit, and the other deriving it from the insufficient consumption of the workers. Neither Lenin nor Bukharin saw a contradiction here. On the one hand, they maintained that the production of means of production took place in complete independence of that of consumer goods; on the other hand, it was for them the insufficient consumption of the workers that set limits to the accumulation process, because Marx had declared that in the final analysis the production of means of production always only serves consumption. Accordingly they held Tugan-Baranovsky's hypothesis of the limitless expansion of capital to be false, even though they did not deny the possibility of a balanced proportionality of the different departments of production.

It was thus not the falling rate of profit resulting from accumulation which Lenin and Bukharin opposed to Tugan-Baranovsky's imaginary unlimited capital expansion but the underconsumption of the workers, which, in the context of all the other disproportionalities, limited accumulation in a particular way. It followed that the increasing consumption of the workers would help make possible the realization of the surplus value destined for accumulation. Thus Bukharin suggested that variable capital grew together with constant capital, with the result that an increasing part of the surplus value could be realized. Of course, in practice this could only mean that the capitalists would give back to the workers a part of the surplus value just extracted from them; they could have saved themselves the trouble if they had only taken that much less surplus value from the workers in the first place! Although it is sometimes (but not always) true that additional means of production require additional labor power, this in no way alters the fact that the ratio of constant to variable capital shifts in the course of accumulation in favor of constant capital. Despite the absolute increase of the number of workers, they become fewer relative to the more rapidly growing constant capital, so that the surplus value extracted from them increases, and the problem of its realization—if there is such a problem—not only remains but becomes more severe.

Now Marx's theory of accumulation as a whole is based on the assumption that the workers are always paid according to their value, measured by their production and reproduction costs. The surplus value can therefore only go to the capitalists and must be realized by them through their own consumption and their accumulation. Assuming for the moment that nothing stands in the way of this realization, Marx pointed out that even under these benign circumstances, accumulation depresses the profit rate until accumulation finally founders on the lack of profit. This does not mean that the process of realization proceeds as smoothly as the general theory of accumulation makes it appear; but it does mean that, quite independently of all its difficulties with realization, capital meets a limit in surplus-value production itself. If the accumulation process can be depicted in abstraction from the circulation process, the process of reproduction can also be traced without considering the realization problems it encounters in reality in order to explain the meaning of the circuit of capital. One can find this mode of procedure reasonable or not; at any rate Marx believed that although his abstract model of the capitalist process of circulation did not correspond to reality in some ways, it could nevertheless contribute to a better understanding of reality. But just as

Tugan-Baranovsky's conclusions cannot be justified by appealing to the reproduction schemas, they also cannot be contested by the meaningless assertion that the workers realize a part of the capitalists' surplus value and that a crisis must set in if this no longer happens to a sufficient degree.

For Bukharin the crisis results from a conflict between production and consumption or (what is the same) from overproduction. The anarchy of capitalist production includes in its various disproportionalities that between production and consumption. From this it would follow that without these disproportionalities the capitalist reproduction process could proceed frictionlessly. And as the crisis only appears periodically, prosperity appears when the elements of the system are adequately proportional. Moreover, it follows from this that with the correct proportionality the process of reproduction would proceed as portrayed in Marx's schemas. If we bear this in mind, it becomes comprehensible why Lenin took the side of Otto Bauer in the debate between Luxemburg and Bauer, with which we shall now deal.[35] That it occurred to neither Lenin nor Bukharin to investigate the problem of crisis from the standpoint of the theory of value is already evident in the fact that Bukharin agreed with Luxemburg that if the fall in the rate of profit were to be responsible for the end of capitalism, this "would take as long as the cooling of the sun."[36] At the same time, however, he turned this remark against Luxemburg herself, since her theory also depends on the continuous fall in the rate of profit, though due to the disappearance of noncapitalist markets.

Since the whole debate about the Marxian reproduction schemas can be followed in the original writings of the participants, and since the particular, arbitrarily chosen magnitudes of these diagrams are of no consequence for us, it is enough here to repeat: Marx wanted to show that with certain exchange ratios between the department of production producing means of production and that producing consumer goods, both can not only renew their constant and variable capital but also grow through capitalizing their surplus value. Marx represented this process first as a closed circuit, i.e., as the "simple reproduction" of a given state of the economy, and then as a process of expansion, or "expanded reproduction," in which simple reproduction is included as a part of the total process. The static case appeared to all the participants in the debate as equally clear; only when it came to expanded reproduction were minds divided. For with the inclusion of circulation the static circuit become "a spiral, winding higher and higher, as if under the compulsion of a mathematically measurable natural law."[37]

According to Marx, Luxemburg explained,

> reproduction expands in strict conformity with the laws of circulation: the mutual supply of the two departments of production with additional means of production and consumer goods proceeds as an exchange of equivalents. It is an exchange of commodities in the course of which the very accumulation in one department is the condition of accumulation in the other and makes this possible. The complicated problem of accumulation is thus converted into a diagrammatic progression of surprising simplicity.[38]

Just because of this it is necessary

> to take care lest we should only have achieved these surprisingly smooth results through simply working out certain foolproof mathematical exercises in addition and subtraction, and we must further inquire whether it is not merely because mathematical equations are easily put on paper that accumulation will continue *ad infinitum* without any friction.[39]

Nevertheless Luxemburg began by busying herself very intensively with these equations in order to establish that Marx's calculations did not work out right and that the surplus value cannot be realized within the terms of his model, which rules out the reproduction process on an expanded scale as he presented it. Otto Bauer then took on the task of repulsing this attack on Marx. He maintained, to begin with, that every society with an increasing population has to enlarge its productive apparatus, so that accumulation is unavoidable.

> One part of the surplus value is transformed into capital; this means that one part of the surplus value accumulated goes to variable, another to constant capital. The capitalists carry out this accumulation in order to increase their profits, but its social effect is the provision of the consumer and producer goods necessary for population growth.[40]

While in this way, according to Bauer, the capitalists increase their capital, despite their self-interestedness, in a way that conforms to social needs, as a result of the anarchic character of production the danger always exists that accumulation will lag behind population growth or get ahead of it. Thus the first thing to investigate is "how the accumulation of capital should be carried out if it is to remain in equilibrium with population growth."[41] Taking various hypothetical starting points (such as that of a 5 percent yearly growth of population and so of variable capital and a constant rate of surplus value), Bauer calculated a series of transformations of the economic system. His tables indicated that with an increasing organic composition of capital, the rate of accumulation must rise yearly if the equilibrium between accumulation and population is to be maintained.

Bauer dealt first with the total capital, subsequently differentiating between the two departments of production. A higher organic composition of capital implies the transfer of a part of the surplus value accumulated in consumer goods production into the department producing means of production. In Bauer's opinion there is nothing to prevent this, since it results directly from the requirements of production and the relations of exchange. Bauer did not deny the arbitrary elements Rosa Luxemburg criticized in Marx's schemas; but believing that Marx's reasoning was nevertheless correct, he sought to answer her criticisms with a better schema. In Bauer's schema the only remaining arbitrary elements were the hypotheses defining the starting point of accumulation; given these the magnitudes represented in his schemas followed with mathematical necessity. The only result of interest to us here is that all the commodities of both departments could be sold and realized.

Bauer then asked how Luxemburg could have come to the opposite view and thought he could explain this as the result of a misunderstanding. She assumed that, following the schema, the surplus value to be accumulated must be realized year by year. However, this was only a simplifying assumption, made for heuristic reasons; in reality the surplus value created in one year may be realized over a period of many years. The unrealizability of a part of the surplus value is "only a transitory phase in the whole circuit, which extends over many years."[42] Once this is understood, and the time scale covered by the schema prolonged, a harmonious process of accumulation results.

> The workers' consuming power grows as quickly as their numbers. The capitalists' consuming power grows first as rapidly, since with the number of workers the mass of surplus value also increases. The consuming power of the whole society thus grows as rapidly as the value product. Accumulation alters nothing in this; it means only that fewer consumer goods and more production goods are required than with simple reproduction. The extension of the domain of production, which is a presupposition of accumulation, is here made possible by the growth of the population.[43]

How can such harmonious circumstances lead to a crisis? The equilibrium of accumulation and population growth can only be maintained, according to Bauer, "when the rate of accumulation grows so rapidly that despite the rising organic composition of capital, the variable capital grows as quickly as the population."[44] Otherwise a situation of *underaccumulation* arises. This leads to unemployment and downward pressure on wages, but also to a rise in the rate of surplus value. Assuming a constant rate of accumulation, if the rate of surplus value rises, the portion of surplus value accumulated will also grow. "Thus the mass of surplus value invested in the enlargement of the variable capital also grows. It will continue thus to increase until the *equilibrium* between the growth of the variable population and the growth of the population is reestablished."[45] In this way the underaccumulation is always counteracted again, so that the periodic crisis represents only a transitory phase of the industrial cycle. Underaccumulation is the obverse of the overaccumulation described by Marx.

> Prosperity is overaccumulation. It provides its own counteraction in the crisis. The depression that follows is a period of underaccumulation. It resolves itself by creating out of itself the conditions of a return to prosperity. The periodic return of prosperity, crisis, and depression is the empirical expression of the fact that the mechanism of the capitalist mode of production by itself overcomes overaccumulation and underaccumulation, perpetually adapting the accumulation of capital to the growth of the population.[46]

Rosa Luxemburg had the opportunity to answer her critics. Against the theoreticians of harmonious development, she held that under the assumption of limitless capitalist accumulation, "socialism loses the granite bedrock of objective historical necessity. We are lost in the fog of the pre-Marxist systems and schools that want to derive socialism from the pure injustice and wickedness of the modern world or from the pure revolutionary will of the working class."[47] That objective necessity could also have another foundation did not enter her mind. Therefore she found nothing to revise in her theory. Despite her insight "that mathematical schemas in general prove nothing with respect to the question of accumulation,"[48] she nevertheless stuck too doggedly to her interpretation of Marx's reproduction schemas to be able to give her theory of imperialism another basis.

Giving special attention to Bauer's criticism, but without going into his calculations, Luxemburg attacked his theory of population, rejecting it as senseless. In this she stood completely on the terrain of Marx's theory, for which it is the mechanism of production and accumulation that adapts the number of employed workers to the valorization requirements of capital, and not accumulation that is adapted to population growth. She also rejected Bauer's speculation that she had interpreted Marx's schemas as referring to calendar years, although without going deeper into the implications of this. She drew attention to the necessary distinction between the realization of the surplus values produced by the individual capitals and those produced by the total capital, without noticing that the total surplus value can only be realized via the realization of the individual capitals' surplus values, for the total capital exists only as the sum of all the individual capitals. While the magnitudes postulated by Marx's reproduction schemas were for her a "scientific fiction," operating with theoretical assumptions about total capital and total surplus value can itself be only a heuristic procedure: a means to the understanding of reality, not reality itself.

In general Luxemburg was never clear about the function of the reproduction schemas, as can be seen from her hypothesis that they "anticipate the actual tendency of capitalist development."[49] Marx assumed, she wrote, "that the complete and absolute domination of the whole earth by capitalism, the furthest extension of the world market and the world economy, toward which capital and the whole of present-day economic and political development *in fact* are heading, had already been achieved."[50] If this was Marx's procedure, then it would speak not for Luxemburg but against her, for without a doubt the reproduction schemas show that even under the conditions they assume, the circuit of capital is conceivable on an expanded scale. Since according to Luxemburg capitalism can simply not exist under these conditions, Marx on her interpretation would have imagined an absolute impossibility. In fact, however, Marx's intention was

> to view the process of reproduction in its basic form—in which obscuring minor circumstances have been eliminated—in order to get rid of the false subterfuges that furnish the semblance of "scientific" analysis when the process of social reproduction is immediately made the subject of the analysis in its complicated concrete form.[51]

Thus Marx was dealing not with a future state of capitalism but with the investigation of the fundamental structure of capitalist reproduction, its inner relations, unobservable at the surface level.

While Rosa Luxemburg did not go into Otto Bauer's calculations, Henryk Grossmann accorded them all the greater attention. Grossmann completely rejected her theory, but he also rejected Bauer's critique of it. His own interpretation of Marx's theory of accumulation started from Marx's theory of value and treated the problem of accumulation as one of valorization that arises out of capitalist production, although it manifests itself in the process of circulation. But he could not resist entering into the whole discussion about accumulation, and particularly into Bauer's contribution to it. Grossmann emphasized that Bauer had succeeded "in constructing a reproduction schema that indeed meets . . . the formal requirements that can in general be set for this type of construction and presents none of the defects for which Rosa Luxemburg criticized Marx's reproduction schema."[52] Certainly Bauer's population theory is "a pure and simple abandonment of the Marxian theory of population," but "in and of itself Bauer's reproduction schema has nothing to do with his population theory and can be considered independently of it."[53] On the basis of Bauer's assumptions, Grossmann showed that extending Bauer's calculations from the period of four years worked out by Bauer to one of thirty-five years led to results fully at odds with Bauer's conclusions.

Bauer knew, of course, that the rising organic composition of capital implies a falling rate of profit, a phenomenon that can of course be accompanied by a more rapid growth of the rate of surplus value. But in his schema the rate of surplus value remains constant instead of increasing with the growing organic composition, a contradiction that Luxemburg had already pointed out in her *Anti-Kritik*.[54] According to Bauer this contradiction could be eliminated by supplementing his schema by introducing a rising rate of surplus value, although he himself did not undertake this task. Were this done, the rate of profit would fall in his schema, in which the constant capital grows at twice the rate of the variable capital. But this fall of the rate of profit does not prevent the growth of capital and increasing capitalist consumption during the period considered by Bauer. By extending Bauer's schema beyond this period, Grossmann showed that on Bauer's own assumptions there necessarily comes a point after which the surplus value no longer suffices to continue accumulation. Thus, in Grossmann's eyes, Bauer's schema itself provided proof that the system faces an objective limit set by the tendency, inherent in it, of the profit rate to fall.

The law of the falling rate of profit, however, has nothing to do with the reproduction schemas, either Marx's or Otto Bauer's. It follows from the rising organic composition of the total capital, independently of the exchange relations between the two chief departments of production. According to Marx crises can arise also from disproportionalities within the production and circulation processes. But as these disproportionalities—maldistributions of capital among branches of production—can also in turn be overcome by way of these same crises, the process of reproduction can be represented as crisis free, just as an equilibrium of supply and demand, which in real life does not exist, can be imagined. Crises of this kind, arising exclusively from the disproportionalities of the system, are only an expression of the anarchy of capitalism and not of the exploitative character of the relations of production that underlie this anarchy; they are resolved, therefore, by the redistribution of surplus value, without the production of additional surplus value. The crises that arise from the nature of capitalist production, in contrast, do not solve themselves but can be counteracted only by the adjustment of surplus value production to the valorization needs of the altered capital structure—only, that is, by an increase in exploitation.

Otto Bauer did not concern himself with crisis resulting from the relations of production and the production of capital. He explained crisis as a result of disproportionality, not as Tugan-Baranovsky and Hilferding understood it but as the disproportionality between accumulation and population growth. On this basis he showed that Marx's reproduction schemas can be used to prove the potential for accumulation of a "pure" capitalism. With this Grossmann agreed, but at the same time he showed that this did not eliminate the crisis problem, since it ignored the valorization problem involved with accumulation. Since the whole discussion of crisis turned around Marx's reproduction schemas, it was necessary for Grossmann to deal with them. This was all the more important as the preoccupation with the schemas gave rise to the impression that this was Marx's real crisis theory, while the theory, advanced in the first volume of *Capital*, of a breakdown engendered by accumulation was taken to be an idea later abandoned by Marx. In this interpretation crisis remained a matter solely of the disproportionality of the system, which awakened the conviction that any crisis could be overcome through the restoration of the lost proportionality and that crises could perhaps be completely eliminated by a better organization of the system. Indeed it was just these views that led Rosa Luxemburg to attack the harmonizing interpretations of the reproduction schemas, with the upshot that in the end she denied that they had any heuristic value.

For Grossmann no conclusions about reality can be drawn directly from the reproduction schemas. In the form Marx gave them, they indicated neither an equilibrium nor a disequilibrium state of the economy. Since they dealt only with the value side of reproduction, they were unable to "represent the real process of accumulation with respect to *both values and use values.*"[55] They must be understood, Grossmann thought, in the light of Marx's method of approximations, which require subsequent modification and completion to give a full picture of reality. With the reproduction schemas "Marx wanted to bring out that the exchange of commodities is a necessary presupposition of the capitalist mode of production; he therefore necessarily had to describe not one capitalist but at least two independent commodity producers or production groups";[56] hence the two departments of the reproduction schemas. But the reproduction schema "does not claim to be in itself a replica of concrete capitalist reality; it is only a link in Marx's chain of approximations, which, together with the simplifying assumptions that lie at the base of the schema and the subsequent modifications in the direction of a progressive concretization, form a coherent whole."[57]

This particular step in a series of approximations leading to an understanding of capital as a total process was of particular importance for Grossmann, as in his view it was the central element in the structural plan of *Capital*. Pointing out that Marx had altered the plan of his work in 1863, Grossmann held it to be very likely that this was connected with Marx's discovery, made at the same time, of the reproduction schema. This interpretation is supported by the "methodological viewpoint actually adopted in the final version of *Capital*—the arrangement of the empirical material by reference to the functions that capital carries out in its circuit."[58]

In 1857, when he wrote the *Grundrisse*, however, Marx had already developed a reproduction schema, though a simpler one, illustrating the circulation between different departments of production.[59] Grossmann could not have known this at the time of his own work, since Marx's earlier text had not yet been published, but the idea of the reproduction schemas did not, therefore, have to await Marx's discovery of 1863. Although the latter may well have influenced the final form of the schemas, it did not determine the structural plan of *Capital*. In any case, what is important is that already in the *Grundrisse*, Marx subordinated the problem of exchange to that of the valorization of capital. In the process he called simple reproduction,

At a given point in the development of the productive forces—for this will determine the relation of necessary labor to surplus labor—a fixed relation becomes established, in which the product is divided into one part—corresponding to raw material, machinery, necessary labor, surplus labor—and finally surplus labor divides into one part which goes to consumption and another which becomes capital again. This inner division, inherent in the concept of capital, appears in exchange in such a way that the exchange of the capitals among one another takes place in specific and restricted proportions—even if these are constantly changing in the course of production. . . . *Exchange* in and for itself gives these conceptually opposite moments an indifferent being; they exist independently of one another; their inner necessity becomes manifest in the crisis, which puts a forcible end to their seeming indifference toward each other.[60]

The valorization of capital is for Marx "production of new and larger values,"[61] so that the reproduction of capital can be understood only as accumulation. Every revolution in the productive forces alters the relations of exchanges, "whose foundation—from the standpoint of capital and hence also of that of realization through exchange—always remains *the relation of necessary to surplus labor* or . . . of the different moments of objectified to living labor."[62] However this may affect exchange, "the relation of surplus labor to necessary labor" must remain "the same—for this is equal to the constancy of the valorization of capital."[63] The crisis makes its appearance "in order to restore the correct relation between necessary and surplus labor, on which, in the last analysis, everything rests."[64] Exchange, Marx continues,

> does not change the inner characteristics of valorization; but it projects them to the outside, gives them a reciprocally independent form, and thereby lets their unity exist merely as an inner necessity, which must therefore come forcibly to the surface in crises. Both are therefore posited as the essence of capital: the devaluation of capital in the production process, as well as the suspension of devaluation and the creation of the conditions for the valorization of capital."[65]

The crisis appears here not as the result of the disappearance of a proportionality in the relation between production and consumption, but as a means to restore the "proportionality" between necessary labor and surplus labor that has been lost through the uncoordinated movement, rendered independent, of exchange and production. In other words: the process of production and of circulation, although a necessary unity, is actually unified and is coordinated temporarily only through the crisis. Regulation here means essentially nothing but the reestablishment of valorization, which of course must manifest itself also in shifts of the relation between the spheres of production and in those of circulation. The changes in the process of capital as a whole are thus determined by the changes of profit and of accumulation. The *concrete forms* these phenomena take could, according to Marx, be developed only with a treatment of competition and an analysis of real capital.

The titles of the three volumes of *Capital*—"The Process of Production," "The Process of Circulation," and "The Process of Capitalist Production as a Whole"—illustrate the structure of the work. The process as a whole, as a unity of the production and circulation processes, represents the real process of capitalist reproduction. It is presupposed by the separate analyses of production and circulation, which is as much as to say that the volumes on the process of production and circulation, based on the theory of value, deal with matters that appear in a different form in reality. This does not mean that the analysis of production in terms of value, or of circulation in terms of the exchange of values, is not an analysis of the real world. It is, but its categories represent the world as experienced in a modified form. Just as "capital in general, as distinct from the particular real capitals, is itself a real existence,"[66] the exchange of values, like the labor-time value of commodities, also really exists, although these too can only be seen in the capitalist economy's submission to the laws of value intrinsic to it. The transformation of values into prices of production makes neither value nor reproduction schemas framed in terms of value fictional, since the basis of the prices of production encountered in reality is nothing other than the labor-time values.

Thus a study of circulation in isolation from the system as a whole does not require investigation of the actual exchange relations of reproduction. Even on the abstract basis of the reproduction schemas, the process of reproduction requires a definite proportionality of exchange relations. It was to represent them that

Marx devised the schemas, which make no further claim to description of reality save that they represent a process that must be carried out in actual reproduction, although in forms different from those of the abstract model. As accumulation can only proceed when there is a proportional or adequate relation of surplus labor to labor as such, this relation must also appear in the proportions obtaining between the two departments of production and the exchanges between them. Where this proportionality is not present, crisis will ensue in order to produce the proportionality required for further accumulation. If one wanted to call the presence of the necessary proportionality between profit and accumulation an "equilibrium" state (which it certainly is not), one could describe the absence of this proportionality as a state of "disequilibrium." But both terms would signify no more than a rate of profit either sufficient or insufficient for accumulation.

To Grossmann's observation that the reproduction schemas are not designed "to represent the real process of accumulation in terms of value and use value," it must be added that Marx did not intend the schemas as pictures of the "real process of accumulation"; the schemas nevertheless deal with values as much as with use values. Their function was precisely to indicate that while in reference to the individual capitals,

> the bodily form of the commodities produced was wholly immaterial for the analysis, . . . [t]his merely formal manner of presentation is no longer adequate in the study of the total social capital and of the value of its products. The reconversion of one portion of the value of the product into capital and the passing of another portion into the individual consumption of the capitalist as well as the working class form a movement within the value of the product itself in which the result of the aggregate capital finds expression; and this movement is not only a replacement of value but also a replacement in material and is therefore as much bound up with the relative proportions of the value components of the total social product as with their use value, their material shape.[67]

The analysis of production in terms of value was for Marx the unavoidable precondition for understanding capital and its laws of motion, even though not value but prices of production govern the market, and the prices coincide with values only in the theoretical analysis of the total capital. In the same way, the analysis of the circulation process in terms of value was a necessary first step in the scientific understanding of capitalist production, although here too exchange is governed by prices of production, which in the first place reflect the use values of commodities. What Marx sought to make clear was that independently of the modifications of the value relations due to market relations, the value relations themselves already carry the germ of crisis. As a result, just by being based on value-regulated exchange, which is at the same time an exchange of use values, the reproduction of capital is a process shot through with crises.

> The fact that the production of commodities is the general form of capitalist production implies the role which money is playing in it not only as a medium of circulation but also as money capital, and it engenders certain conditions of normal exchange peculiar to this mode of production and therefore of the normal course of reproduction, whether it be on a simple or on an extended scale—conditions which change into so many conditions of abnormal movement, into so many possibilities of crises, since a balance is itself an accident owing to the spontaneous nature of this production.[68]

Marx then showed how the double character of the commodity, as value and use value, transforms even the apparent equilibrium of simple reproduction into disequilibrium. Thus, for example, the wear and tear and replacement of fixed capital can produce dislocations in the value-defined conditions of exchange, destroying any possibility of equilibrated reproduction.[69] Without going into Marx's examples of the appearance of disproportionality within simple reproduction, it here needs to be stressed only that they apply exclusively to *capitalist* reproduction.

> Once the capitalist form of reproduction is abolished, it is only a matter of the volume of the expiring portion—expiring and therefore to be reproduced in kind—of fixed capital . . . varying in various successive years. If it is very large in a certain year . . . , then it is certainly so much smaller in the next year. The quantity of raw materials, semi-finished products, and auxiliary materials . . . does not decrease in consequence. Hence the aggregate production of means of production

would have to increase in the one case and decrease in the other. This can be remedied only by a continuous relative overproduction. There must be on the one hand a certain quantity of fixed capital produced in excess of that which is directly required; on the other hand, and particularly, there must be a supply of raw materials, etc., in excess of the direct annual requirements. . . . This sort of overproduction is tantamount to control by society over the material means of its own reproduction. But within capitalist society it is an element of anarchy.[70]

Thus the point of the schemas of simple and enlarged reproduction is not the demonstration of the possibility of a frictionless exchange bringing the two departments of production into equilibrium but the demonstration that such a hypothetical situation could arise neither in capitalism nor in a socialist society. Moreover, while in socialism overproduction would be indispensable to assure the satisfaction of social needs and would therefore be considered normal, the same situation in capitalism, where it must appear as an excess or deficiency of reproduction, represents a problem bound to manifest itself in disorganization and crisis. It did not occur to Marx that the idea of a harmonious course of capitalist accumulation could be derived from his reproduction schemas, if only because the first volume of *Capital*, which unambiguously predicted the breakdown of capitalism, preceded them.

Perhaps, however, to forestall all harmonizing interpretations, it would have been better not to treat the circulation process on the basis of value exchange, since calculation with values only makes sense in reference to the total capital. Grossmann's explanation, that the reproduction schemas were necessary because the exchange of commodities requires at least two exchanging social groups, is not convincing, for this obvious fact needs no demonstration, and since actual exchange takes place in price, not value, terms, so that the division of the system into two parts can be represented using prices of production, without any preliminary description using values.

Rosa Luxemburg's objections were directed at Marx's construction of his reproduction schemas in value terms, on which basis she showed that the equilibrium assumed by Marx cannot be maintained (something Marx himself had demonstrated, although with different arguments). Grossmann corrected Luxemburg by showing that the disequilibrium in the value-based reproduction schema could lead to equilibrium in a schema based on prices of production. Thus he showed that the portion of the surplus product she had thought to be unsalable within the system could be completely absorbed by it thanks to the formation of an average rate of profit due to competition and the ensuing distribution of the total surplus value.

Nevertheless, according to Grossmann Marx's reproduction schema represented

> the median line of accumulation, thus the ideal normal path on which accumulation takes place equally in both departments of production. In reality there are departures from this median line, but these deviations are only understandable on the basis of that ideal average line. Rosa Luxemburg's error consists exactly in the fact that she treats as an exact description of the real process what is supposed to represent an ideal normal course among many possible cases.[71]

This explanation, however, brings us back to the theories of Tugan-Baranovsky, Hilferding, and Otto Bauer, which indeed also deal only with an "ideal normal course," which in reality would be disrupted by all manner of disproportionalities or "deviations" from the "median line." With these authors too it is a matter only of a theoretically conceivable "normal course" of accumulation in which the "deviations" from the "median" always lead back to it, so that equilibrium asserts itself as a tendency, thus justifying the assumption that the system has no objective limits. In this way Grossmann's attempt to counterpose a Marxian equilibrium to Luxemburg's disequilibrium (once as the "midline" of the fictive reproduction in value terms and then as the solution of the disequilibrium by means of the transformation of values into prices by competition) leads to the completely unnecessary concession that the reproduction schemas, in one version or another, demonstrate the possibility of a frictionless exchange between the departments of production.

For Marx, as stated above, the difficulties basic to capitalism arise not from the exchange relations between the different capitals, although these also exist, but from the production relations which *appear* as exchange relations. The realization of surplus value is a problem that capital must solve for itself and is a consequence of the production relation of exploitation that underlies it. If capital could not realize the surplus value, it could not exist, for it is nothing but surplus value. The very existence of capital proves that it is able to transform surplus value into capital. The increasing accumulation furnishes the proof that it is in a position to realize an increasing mass of surplus value. The realization of surplus value has, in general, nothing to do with the workers, since they produce both their own value and the surplus value and realize their own value in their consumption. The surplus value is realized in accumulation and capitalist consumption (which includes the unproductive costs of the society).

What mattered to Rosa Luxemburg was not so much the realization of the surplus value itself, which could not be doubted, but the *mechanism* through which it took place. This mechanism was not visible in the reproduction schemas, as it was already implicit in the assumption that the surplus value is realized in the circulation of capital. Now, Marx could also have elaborated a reproduction schema in which this was not the case; but this would have been pointless, as the accumulation of capital, theoretically and practically, presupposes the realization of surplus value. Luxemburg thought this presupposition would not hold for a closed system, even entirely apart from the reproduction schemas, since she could not see how the transformation of the accumulated surplus value into money could be accomplished.

It was clear to her that foreign trade between capitalist nations provided no solution here but only repeated the problem on a wider plane. There must be buyers who do not themselves sell but exchange money for the surplus value created in the capitalist lands in the form of commodities. She did not explain where these buyers would obtain the necessary money, but it must derive from noncapitalist exploitation relations, which accordingly must be fruitful enough to absorb all the surplus value produced in the capitalist countries and destined for their accumulation. Thus the production of surplus value indeed depends on the exploitation of the workers in the capitalist countries, but without ensuring its accumulation, so that the accumulation of capital has as its ultimate condition the exploitation of noncapitalist countries.

It follows from this fantastic idea that the total accumulated capital of the capitalist world is only made possible by the exploitation of the noncapitalist world and that the latter must absorb a quantity of commodities with a value great enough to be adequate, when realized in money, for accumulation to continue. If this were possible, which it is not, it would only mean—as is true for foreign trade in general—that "the involvement of foreign commerce in analyzing the annually reproduced value of products can . . . only confuse without contributing any new element of the problem or of its solution."[72] Money is also a commodity; and the exchange of commodities for money, whether within capitalist areas alone or on the world market, remains the exchange of commodities, in which the money form of the commodity is only one phase of the process of circulation.

Marx also recognized a problem of realization. But for him it was a problem specific to the capitalist world, which could not be solved through the existence of noncapitalist countries. The anarchy within capitalist production and accumulation *permanently* excludes the realization of a part of the produced surplus value, so that the realized surplus value is always different from that produced. Whether commodities are over- or underproduced relative to the market can only be discovered after their production. The value and surplus value contained in unsalable commodities is lost and cannot be capitalized. When the production oriented toward expansion reaches a point that puts its valorization in jeopardy, it ceases to expand and thereby produces an unsalable mass of commodities whose value cannot be realized by accumulation and so cannot be realized at all. In this way the suspension of accumulation appears as a problem of realization, since in fact produced commodities cannot be sold. Overproduction, as the appearance in the market of the overaccumulation of capital, is only perceived in the form of the increasing difficulties of realization and is therefore explained in terms of them, although its real origin is the (unobservable) increasing divergence between production and valorization. Thus for Marx there are two sorts of realization problem: first, the ever present expression of capitalist anarchy; and second, the crisis problem, as the appearance on the market of the divergence between the profit produced and the surplus value requirements of an enlarged reproduction.

It is therefore not the accumulation of capital that depends on the realization of surplus value, but the realization of surplus value that depends on accumulation. To say this, however, is not to explain the mechanism of the realization process. For every individual capital the sum of money resulting from the sale of its commodities must be greater than the sum of the capital advanced. In the same way, in comparison to the total capital expressed in money, the total surplus value must amount to a greater value in money terms. What is the source of this additional money? Marx saw no problem here but located this source provisionally, but completely adequately for the purposes of his abstract analysis of the circulation problem, in gold production and credit. Only a discussion of the concrete market relations would, in his opinion, make it necessary to go more deeply into the broader development of the money function within the circulation process of surplus value.[73]

In the earlier discussion of the answers given by Bukharin and Otto Bauer to Rosa Luxemburg's question as to the source of the money for the transformation of commodity values into additional capital, we already encountered Marx's answers to this question. In addition, this problem was for Marx not so much a question whether gold production could furnish a sufficient and so perpetually increasing supply of money, but just the reverse: he saw it as important for capital to restrict the production of gold for monetary use as much as possible in the interest of accumulation.

> The entire amount of labor power and social means of production expended in the annual production of gold and silver intended as instruments of circulation constitutes a bulky item of the *faux frais* of the capitalist mode of production, of the production of commodities in general. It is an equivalent abstraction from social utilization of as many additional means of production and consumption as possible, i.e., of real wealth. To the extent that the costs of this expensive machinery of circulation are decreased, the given scale of production or the given degree of its extension remaining constant, the productive power of social labor is *eo ipso* increased. Hence, so far as the expediences developing with the credit system have this effect, they increase capitalist wealth directly, either by performing a large portion of the social production

and labor process without any intervention of real money, or by raising the functional capacity of the quantity of money really functioning.[74]

As a means of circulation, commodity money in gold and silver represents a great and unnecessary expense. For this reason capital has always striven to replace commodity money by symbolic monetary instruments. Commodity money lost its earlier importance with the development of banking and credit. As the social category of money is already included in that of the commodity, the gold standard was a historical but not a necessary phenomenon of commodity circulation. Since all commodities potentially represent money, and money has all commodities at its command, on the national level and recently increasingly on the international level also, any instrument of payment can serve as a means of exchange. Money is created within the banking system. The volume of credit offered by the banks is determined by the governmental creation of money—through note issues and treasury certificates —and by varying reserve requirements set by the government as a function of deposits. If credit is only partially covered by bank reserves, it is nevertheless generally guaranteed by capital owned by the borrowers. Where there is no capital equivalent at hand, there is also no credit, which thus relates not to the *money* on hand but to the existing *capital*.

In the process of circulation the accumulated capital takes on the commodity form at one moment and the money form at another. Means of production and commodities can be transformed into money and *vice versa*, so that the ownership of capital can be expressed as ownership of money. Although "capital" means money, it also includes all commodities, so that any commodity has the capacity to take the place of money. Although the quantities put on the market must be transformed into money, they embody only a part of the existing capital, so that only a part of capitalist property needs to take on the money form. In general the necessary volume of money is determined by the prices of the commodities entering into circulation and by the turnover velocity of money, modified by the mutual cancellation or the postponement of payments.

Aside from the fact that money has been accumulated for

centuries in the form of commodity money (which has continually increased also through the production of precious metals) and can therefore be directly exchanged against other commodities, capitalist accumulation has freed itself from these limitations by the mechanism of credit, based on capital already accumulated. The transformation of surplus value into additional capital can be accomplished without additional commodity money, and capital can be accumulated in its commodity form. No actual commodity money corresponds to the credit money necessary for this; it is the "symbolic form" of an additional sum of money that does not exist in reality; but it suffices to carry out the transformation of the commodity values into additional capital: additional capital that in turn determines the future expansion of credit. Thus it is the accumulation of capital itself which solves the problem of the additional money necessary and eliminates the difficulties of realization by means of the techniques of finance.

For money to function as capital, it must first of all cease to be money—i.e., it must be invested in means of production and labor power. The transformation of surplus value into money is only a stage, carried through in the market, in its transformation into additional capital. It is of no consequence at all whether this transformation is accomplished with commodity money or symbolic money. The latter, however, can be increased at will and so adapted to the needs of accumulation. Its growth accompanies that of the accumulating capital but is also limited by the latter. In this way we return to the point which appeared so unlikely to Rosa Luxemburg, namely the production for the sake of production, which she believed impossible in a closed system, having failed to find an explanation for the additional money required.

If capital can realize its surplus value through accumulation, then the enlarged capitals are represented as increased sums of money capital. But accumulation depends not on money or credit but on profitability. If profits fall, and with them the rate of accumulation, then the demand for credit declines along with the total demand. The insufficient demand appears as a lack of money and the crisis of production also as a financial crisis. It therefore seemed important to Marx "first and foremost to assume here, as everywhere, metallic circulation in its simplest, most primitive form, because then in the flux and reflux, the squaring of balances, in short all elements appearing under the credit system as consciously regulated processes present themselves as existing independently of the credit system, and the matter appears in primitive form instead of the later, reflected form."[75]

In addition, at the time Marx was writing *Capital*, the expansion of production and the creation of new money capital were favored by a credit system of which "metallic circulation remain[ed the] basis,"[76] a situation that has changed with modern modes of credit creation. But the perpetual development of new methods for realizing surplus value in additional capital is only of historical interest and only shows the effect of the increasing weight of the accumulating capital. The system of credit based on metallic money served no other function than the creation of credit without this basis. In both cases credit is governed by the movement of capital. It cannot become autonomous, as it has meaning only in relation to the actual processes of social production on which it rests. Like money, credit can create nothing; it can only provide the means by which the surplus value created in production finds its way into accumulation. If the actual surplus value is insufficient to be capitalized and at the same time valorized, credit cannot alter this and will fail as an instrument facilitating capital accumulation.

Accumulation for the sake of accumulation—that is, without regard for actual social needs or even for the valorization requirements of capital—is exactly what is characteristic of surplus value production and nothing to be wondered at. Competition on the basis of value production impels every capital, in the interests of self-preservation, to accumulate. It must grow or go under, and the total result of all these strivings is the growth of the total capital and the resulting changes of the value relations, which bring with them the fall in the profit rate as soon as the blind drive to accumulate overshoots the actual productivity of labor.

If the surplus value is not sufficient to pursue the process of accumulation profitably, it can also not be realized through accumulation; it becomes the unrealized surplus value of overproduction. Where there is no surplus value to be transformed into additional capital, there also no additional money and no credit can transform surplus value into capital. In order to avoid this crisis state, capital must accumulate without cease, but this is only possible with a simultaneous, continuous increase in labor productivity, which keeps the tendency of the rate of profit to fall latent. That such a coordination of material production with the value requirements of capital accumulation is denied to capital is apparent in the crises, which must restore from outside the lost inner coherence of capitalist production if a further expansion of capital is to be possible.

Surplus value is the decisive element of capitalist production. It can become too small as a result of the tendency of the rate of profit to fall, but it can never be too big. This holds not only for the society as a whole but also for each individual capital. Capitalist production therefore always aims at the enlargement of surplus value in order to secure its own existence. For capital the increasing surplus value always seems insufficient, no matter what its magnitude. If the market limits capital in one branch of production, capital emigrates into another or opens up new branches, until these too reach the limits imposed by the market. In the course of accumulation the material side of market relations thereby changes, bringing with it the elaboration of new needs as an expression of the expanding productive forces of society and their application on a greater scale and in broader areas. Material wealth grows along with the development of accumulation in value terms. The capitalists' consumption can increase enormously, the mass of the unproductive strata of society can grow, and even the workers can improve their situation thanks to the fall in the value of consumer goods. With all this the pressure on surplus value also grows, compelling always new attempts to increase it in order to keep the process going. Under these conditions there can be no excess of surplus value but only a lack of it, which must finally appear on the market as overproduction and insufficient demand. Every equilibrium state is therefore a state of crisis, which in this dynamic economy can lead only to a breakdown or to a new takeoff. Any concept of equilibrium thus contradicts capitalist reality and can at most serve as a methodological means for the investigation of particular properties of the dynamic course of the economy. Nevertheless, Marxists, in unison with bourgeois economists, have spoken of supposed equilibrium tendencies of the capitalist economy and its development. To take only one example, according to Bukharin

> The whole construction of *Capital* . . . begins with the analysis of a
> completely stable equilibrium system. Complicating factors are gradual-
> ly introduced. The system fluctuates, becomes dynamic. Its fluctua-
> tions, however, remain regulated by laws, and despite the sudden break-
> downs of equilibrium (crises), the system as a whole continues. The dis-
> ruption of equilibrium leads to a new equilibrium, so to speak, of a
> higher order. Only after we understand the laws of equilibrium can we
> go on to investigate the system's fluctuations. The crises themselves are
> treated not as the destruction but merely as disturbances of equilibrium;
> and yet Marx thought it necessary to discover the law of this movement
> and to understand not only how the equilibrium is disturbed but also
> how it is reestablished.[77]

Bukharin summarizes his equilibrium conception in the following
way:

> The law of value is the law of equilibrium governing the system of sim-
> ple commodity production. The law of production price is the law of
> equilibrium governing the modified commodity system, the capitalist
> system. The law of market price similarly governs the fluctuations of
> this sytem. The law of competition governs the continual reestablish-
> ment of disrupted equilibrium. The law of crises governs the necessary
> periodic disturbance of the system's equilibrium and its restoration.[78]

This postulate of equilibrium is the starting point of all disproportionality and underconsumption theories, which accordingly view crises as disturbances of equilibrium and their overcoming
as its restoration. Marx, in contrast, uses the idea of equilibrium
only as a provisory methodological hypothesis with a role to play
in the elaboration of his abstract theory but with no claim to represent processes in reality. Often it is a matter of pure tautology, as
with the assumption of an equilibrium of supply and demand,
which plays no role either in the analysis of the total capital or in
that of the process of production in isolation from the total system; and often the concept is a *starting point* for the description
of the development of capital, and which in the framework of that
development itself no longer has any significance. For Marx it is

not equilibrium tendencies that govern the economy but the law of value, which asserts itself in the same way as "the law of gravity . . . when a person's house collapses on top of him." [79]

Crisis therefore represents not an insurmountable disturbance of equilibrium but a temporary breakdown of the valorization of capital, which neither before nor after its collapse is characterized by any equilibrium. The fact that the crisis is overcome likewise indicates not the restoration of a lost equilibrium but shows that despite the continuing dynamic of the system, it was possible to increase the surplus value enough for a further round of expansion. "With respect to the volume of production there is no equilibrium state to which the system returns after some deviations. . . . [T]he industrial cycle is no oscillation around some mean given by some necessity." [80] Even though Marx writes in one place that "permanent crises do not exist," [81] this does not mean, as Bukharin maintained, that "the disturbance of the equilibrium leads to a new equilibrium of a higher order" but only that the accumulation interrupted at a certain level of capitalist production can be continued at another level. That this cannot always be the case follows from the abstract analysis of value-determined accumulation. But so long as capital is actually able to adapt the surplus value to the needs of accumulation by way of crisis, every crisis is temporary.

But even a crisis theory disregarding all considerations of equilibrium must deal with the problem of how capitalism can collapse when it can overcome all of its crises. Thus, for example, Otto Benedikt demanded of Henryk Grossmann, for whom the breakdown of the system would be an insurmountable crisis, "why its 'economic end point' is different from the surmountable crisis? Why is the last crisis no longer surmountable?" [82] Following Lenin's disproportionality theory, Benedikt came to the conclusion that aside from its validity or lack of it, Grossmann's crisis theory is just a theory of crisis and not a theory of breakdown. According to Benedikt the question of crisis concerns neither the possibility nor the impossibility of continuous accumulation, "but a growing, inevitable dialectical process of disturbances, contradictions, and crises—not an absolute, purely economic impossibility of accumulation, but a constant alternation between the overcoming of crisis and its reproduction at a higher level until the destruction of this schema by the proletariat."[83]

Grossmann could have given the same answer as Benedikt himself gave, along with all the discussants of the crisis problem, with either different reformist or revolutionary variations. In the final analysis there cannot be a "purely economic" or "automatic" breakdown. For Tugan-Baranovsky, Hilferding, and Otto Bauer it is ethical and politically conscious social movements that will transform the evil into a better social order; for Rosa Luxemburg and Anton Pannekoek it is the class-conscious workers who, long before any theoretically determinable final stage of capitalist expansion, will put an end to capitalism; so also for Grossmann "no economic system, no matter how weakened, collapses by itself in an automatic fashion. It must be 'overthrown.' . . . [T]he so-called 'historical necessity' does not operate automatically but requires the active participation of the working class in the historical process."[84] But this is a matter for the class struggle, not for economic theory, which can only bring to light the objective conditions under which the class struggle unfolds and which determine its direction.

Oddly enough, the most diverse analyses of crisis were all offered to explain the inevitability of capitalism's decline and the abolition of the system to be effected by political movements evoked by this decline. We have already seen this in the example of Rosa Luxemburg and Henryk Grossmann. But disproportionality theorists like Bukharin as well maintained "that the process of capitalist decadence necessarily sets in once the enlarged negative reproduction has swallowed up the social surplus value. Theoretical investigation cannot determine with absolute certainty exactly when the period of decadence begins and by what specific figures this process is characterized. This is already a *questio facti*. The concrete situation in the European economy in the years 1918-20 shows clearly that the period of decadence has already begun and that there are no signs of a resurrection of the *old system* of production relations"[85] A consistent application of the underconsumption theory could also lead to the conclusion that capitalism must collapse. For instance, Natalie Moszkowska wrote that

> if the gap between production and consumption reaches a certain size, and if the deficiency of consumption reaches a certain amplitude, relative pauperization becomes absolute. Production is reduced, and the workers are thrown into the streets. If classic capitalism was characterized by relative pauperization, late capitalism is characterized by absolute pauperization. And this absolute pauperization, not supportable for long, leads to the end of capitalism.[86]

That the economic conditions during and after the First World War gave support to the idea of capitalist decline is not surprising. Even in the bourgeois camp this period not only awakened a deep pessimism but also undermined the earlier conviction that society can master its crises. Indeed, Adolf Löwe remarked that "the crises intrinsic to the economic system have lost their virulence; but if we consider an international destruction of value like the world war as the modern form of crisis in the age of imperialism, and there is much to be said for this view, there is little room for extravagant hopes for spontaneous 'stabilization.'"[87] In such a situation there was not much sense in maintaining that for capital there is "no situation absolutely without a way out" or in assuming the opposite. Under the circumstances both were conceivable. Since for Marxism it is not the economy that conditions the given class relations but the capitalist relations of production—*qua* class relations—that under the conditions of the market economy take on the fetishistic form of economic relationships, every "purely economic" conception of capital and its laws of motion is from the start inappropriate. Nevertheless, although for Marx "the whole economic shit ends in the class struggle," he took pains during decades of work to demonstrate the transitory nature of capitalism even when viewed in terms of its own economic categories.

The trend of capitalist accumulation toward its abolition can only be demonstrated with a model respecting the essential bases of the system. In Marx's theoretical construction capital must perish as a result of its contradictions; and since history itself does nothing but is made by people, it follows directly that the historical limit of capital lies in proletarian revolution. Conversely, however, such an upheaval presupposes a disintegration of capitalism. Through its accumulation capital produces its own gravediggers, so that the process of accumulation already contains its final end, and one can rightly speak of the theory of accumulation as a theory of breakdown, without thereby adopting a "purely economic" or "automatic" breakdown theory.

The interpretation of the great crisis between the two world wars as a possible final crisis of capital made the wish the father to the thought. But this could only be known afterwards. In principle in developed capitalism any great crisis can become the final crisis. If it does not, it remains a presupposition of further accumulation. This is not to say that there cannot arise a situation of "permanent" crisis, since this concept must also be construed not as referring to eternity but only in contrast to temporary, quickly surmounted crises. In this sense the "permanent" crisis is just as conceivable within the Marxian system as surmountable crises. When Marx denied that there are permanent crises, he was referring only to the business cycle of the previous century and to Adam Smith's theory of accumulation, in which the profit rate must always fall. That under the present-day conditions of world capital a state of persistent economic and political crisis can arise is just as possible as that the crisis will give capital a chance to begin a new expansion.

Notes

1. A short but adequate empirical presentation of the crises since 1816 is to be found in Maurice Flamant and Jeanne Singer-Kérel, *Modern Economic Crises and Recessions*, New York, Harper-Row, 1970.

2. E. Bernstein, *Die Voraussetzungen des Sozialismus und die Aufgaben der Sozialdemokratie*, English trans. as *Evolutionary Socialism*, New York, Schocken, 1961, pp. 79-80.

3. Ibid., p. 85.

4. Ibid., p. 93.

5. Protocol of the Hannover Party Congress, cited after L. Woltmann, "Die Wirtschaftlichen und politischen Grundlagen des Klassenkampfes," *Sozialistische Monatshefte*, February 1901, p. 128.

6. In *Die Neue Zeit*, 17(1), p. 358, 1898-99.

7. Tugan-Baranowsky, *Studien zur Theorie und Geschichte der Handelskrisen*, Jena, 1901.

8. Tugan-Baranowsky, op. cit., p. 25.

9. Ibid., p. 27.

10. Ibid.

11. Ibid., p. 33.

12. Ibid., p. 18, n. 1.

13. K. Kautsky, "Krisentheorien," *Die Neue Zeit*, 29(2), pp. 112 and 117, 1901-2.

14. Ibid., 118.

15. C. Schmidt, "Zur Theorie der Handelskrisen und der Überproduktion," in *Sozialistische Monatshefte*, September 1901, p. 675.

16. R. Hilferding, *Das Finanzkapital*, 1909. Cited from the edition of 1968, Frankfurt on Main, p. 330.

17. Ibid.

18. Ibid., p. 347.

19. Ibid., p. 411.

20. Ibid., p. 501.

21. Ibid., p. 503.

22. Ibid.

23. *Die Akkumulation des Kapitals*, 1912. Quotations will be from the translation, *The Accumulation of Capital*, London, Routledge, 1951.

24. Letter to Constantin Zetkin, November 16, 1911, in Rosa Luxemburg, *Briefe an Leon Jogisches*, Frankfurt, 1967, p. 332.

25. R. Luxemburg, *The Accumulation of Capital*, p. 329 [translation corrected].

26. Ibid., pp. 334-35.

27. Ibid., p. 345.

28. R. Luxemburg, *Was die Epigonen aus der Marxschen Theorie gemacht haben*, 1921, p. 17.

29. *The Accumulation of Capital*, p. 366 [translation corrected].

30. Ibid., pp. 366-67 [corrected].

31. *Was die Epigonen*, p. 20.

32. "Herrn Tugan-Baranowskys Marx-Kritik," *Die Neue Zeit*, 26(1), 1909.

33. Article in *Bremer Bürger-Zeitung*, January 29-30, 1913.

34. N. Bukharin, *Der Imperialismus und die Akkumulation des Kapitals*, Vienna-Berlin, 1924.

35. In his 1914 article on Marx for the Russian *Granat Encyclopedia*, Lenin wrote: "The Marxian theory of capital accumulation is dealt with in a new book by Rosa Luxemburg. Analyses of her erroneous interpretation of Marx's theory are to be found in O. Bauer's article in *Die Neue Zeit* (1913), in Eckstein's review in *Vorwärts*, and in Pannekoek's review in the *Bremer Bürger-Zeitung*."

36. R. Luxemberg, *Was die Epigonen*, p. 38.

37. R. Luxemburg, *The Accumulation of Capital*, p. 117 [translation corrected].

38. Ibid., p. 118.

39. Ibid., p. 119.

40. O. Bauer, "Die Akkumulation des Kapitals," *Die Neue Zeit*, 31(1), p. 834, 1912-13.

41. Ibid., p. 835.

42. Ibid., p. 867.

43. Ibid., p. 869.

44. Ibid.

45. Ibid.

46. Ibid., p. 872.

47. *Was die Epigonen.* p. 37.

48. Ibid., p. 26.

49. Ibid., p. 107.

50. Ibid.

51. K. Marx, *Capital*, vol. 2, Moscow, 1961, p. 457.

52. H. Grossmann, *Das Akkumulations- und Zusammenbruchsgesetz des kapitalistischen Systems*, Leipzig, 1929, p. 101.

53. Ibid., p. 104.

54. *Was die Epigonen*, p. 62.

55. Grossmann, op. cit., p. 105.

56. Ibid., p. 48.

57. H. Grossmann, "Die Änderung des ursprünglichen Aufbauplans des Marxschen *Kapital* und ihre Ursachen" (1929), in H. Grossmann, *Aufsätze über die Krisentheorie*, Frankfurt, 1971, p. 32.

58. Ibid., p. 17.

59. K. Marx, *Grundrisse*, English translation, Harmondsworth, 1973, p. 441.

60. Ibid., pp. 443-44.

61. Ibid., p. 442.

62. Ibid., p. 444.

63. Ibid. [translation corrected].

64. Ibid., p. 446.

65. Ibid., p. 447.

66. Ibid., p. 449.

67. K. Marx, *Capital*, vol. 2, p. 394.

68. Ibid., p. 495.

69. See ibid., pp. 466 ff.

70. Ibid., pp. 468-69.

71. H. Grossmann, *Das Akkumulations- und Zusammenbruchsgesetz*, p. 246.

72. K. Marx, *Capital*, vol. 2, p. 470.

73. Ibid., p. 346.

74. Ibid.

75. Ibid., pp. 500-501.

76. Ibid.

77. N. Bukharin, *Ökonomie der Transformationsperiode*, Hamburg, 1922, pp. 158. ff.

78. Ibid.

79. K. Marx, *Capital*, vol. 1, Harmondsworth, 1976, p. 168.

80. A. Pannekoek, "Theoretisches zur Ursache der Krise," *Die Neue Zeit*, 31(1), pp. 783 and 792, 1913.

81. K. Marx, *Theories of Surplus-Value*, vol. 2, p. 497 n.

82. O. Benedikt, "Die Akkumulation des Kapitals bei wachsender organischer Zusammensetzung," *Unter dem Banner des Marxismus*, 6, p. 887, December 1929.

83. Ibid., p. 911.

84. H. Grossmann, "The Evolutionist Revolt against Political Economics," *Journal of Political Economy*, 1943, p. 520.

85. N. Bukharin, op. cit., p. 53.

86. N. Moszkowska, *Zur Kritik der modernen Krisentheorien*, Prague, 1935, p. 106.

87. A. Löwe, *Die Wirtschaftswissenschaft nach dem Kriege*, vol. 2, p. 371.

4

Splendor and Misery of the Mixed Economy

The second global economic crisis of this century was transformed, due to the provocation of imperialist competition, into the First World War. To the usual devaluation of capital by crisis, combined with its concentration and centralization, was now added the physical destruction of means of production and labor power. Connected to this was a shift in the balance of economic power from the European nations to the United States. America became the greatest exporting and creditor nation in the world. The territorial changes brought about by the war, the removal of Russia from the world economy, the capitalist reparations policy, the breakdown of currencies and the world market—all this made the reconstruction much more difficult than it would have been in the case of a "purely economic" crisis. The revival of the European economies proceeded so slowly that with the exception of America, the crisis that had turned into the First World War extended through it into the Second World War. America's special situation was thus a limited privilege, which came to an end in 1929. The American economic collapse drove the world economy into a general decline. Capital had indeed made an effort, in the form of American loans, large-scale cartellization, rationalization of production, and inflation, to escape the crisis, but without success. To look only at the poorest and the richest capitalist countries of that time, we note that between 1929 and 1932 industrial production in Germany fell by around 50 percent, while the unemployed numbered seven million, and the national income fell from 73.4 to 42.5 billion marks. In America around 1932 the national income had also fallen by about half, from $87.5 to $41.7 billion, and the sixteen million unemployed reflected the 50 percent contraction of industrial production. A world economic crisis of this extent went beyond all previous experience and could not, like the first postwar crisis, be ascribed to the circumstance of the war.

The partisans of Marx's crisis theory, of all shades, saw in the persistent crisis the confirmation of their critique of capital, and they looked for an overcoming of the crisis either in reform of the system or in its overthrow. The static theory of general equilibrium was unable to explain the crisis, as the postulated equilibrating tendencies refused to work. And because the various governments of the capitalist nations relied, at first, on the deflationary crisis mechanism to solve the problem and did not interfere in the economic process, the deepening of the depression could not be blamed on erroneous government policies. There was nothing left to blame for the crisis but the workers' unwillingness to accept lower wages. The persistence of the crisis and the constantly increasing unemployment, however, finally impelled the bourgeois economists to a revision of their theory, which has taken its place in history as the "Keynesian Revolution."[1]

Without opposing neoclassical theory in general, Keynes recognized the evident fact that the traditional theory was not in accord with the actual situation. The full employment assumed by the theory appeared to him now as a possible but not necessary presupposition of economic equilibrium. Say's thesis, that supply and demand must always coincide, was now—a hundred years late—recognized as erroneous, since "savings" do not necessarily lead to new investments. In Keynes's view, while production must serve consumption, the latter decreases with the increasing satisfaction of needs, so that the extension of production must decrease and with it the labor market. Thus in mature capitalist society new investments would be always less and less profitable, even in the case of a radical reduction of wages. And while it is true that low wages yield high profits, so inducing new investments, it is nevertheless not only wrong but dangerous to leave the economy at the mercy of the economic course of events, in view of the difficulties that stand in the way of such wage decreases and of the inevitable long-run decline of the rate of accumulation. The depression therefore must, according to Keynes, be combated with a policy of state stimulation of expansion, based at once on an inflationary monetary policy and on public works paid for by the public debt.

Although Keynes tried to explain the cyclical movement of capital as due to the changing profitability of capital, he really developed no theory of crisis. According to him it was the declining propensity to consume that reduced the rate of accumulation and induced the capitalists to stop transforming their money into capital. Were they to continue to invest, it would be only to earn a declining rate of profit, which would find its lower limit in the given rate of interest. In order to escape the depression, it would be necessary to add new anticrisis measures to the familiar ones. Wages would have to be cut by means of inflation, the profit rate supported by lowering the interest rate, and the remaining unemployment absorbed by public works, until these measures produced the beginning of a new prosperity, at which point the economy could be left once again to the automatic mechanism of the market. Since Keynes was essentially concerned with the overcoming of the crisis of his day, the long-term developmental tendency described by his theory remained only a philosophical ornament, which drew no great interest at the time. His theory remained on the terrain of static equilibrium and was therefore unable to come to terms with the dynamic of the system.

The Keynesian theory was necessarily restricted to the national economy rather than to the capitalist world economy, as the state interventions it called for could be applied only in a national framework. Of course, it included the hope that the increase in production in individual countries would favorably influence world trade, so that international competition would become less fierce. The measures required to counter unemployment compelled a return to classical macroeconomics, which investigated society as a whole in its economic aggregates, in contrast to microeconomics—then almost the only kind of economics cultivated—which concerned itself only with the fragmentary analysis of isolated economic processes. Whatever practical proposals were made, of course, hardly represented new discoveries but rather the reemployment of expedients that had been relegated to the background during the flowering of laissez faire. Despite an enormous flow of technical economic neologisms, the pretensions of the "new economics" clothed only the ordinary capitalistic principle of increasing profits by means of governmental interventions in market relations.

The need for state intervention dictated by the crisis soon became, in the hands of the economic theorists, a virtual principle of economic management. The traditionally dominant view that all public expenditures have an unproductive character was now seen as an error, and it was asserted that public spending has the same beneficial effect on production and income as private investments. According to Alvin Hansen,

> The development of a public park, swimming pool, playground, or concert hall makes possible a flow of real income no less than the erection of a radio factory. . . . [P]ublic expenditures may also be . . . income-creating in the sense that they tend currently to expand income and employment. . . . [W]ars not only promote employment during the emergency, but may stimulate postwar private investment by creating accumulated shortages in housing and other investment areas. . . . Indeed, when private business outlays decline, the government alone is in a position to go forward and sustain the income through increased expenditures.[2]

Since the economists do not distinguish between economy in general and the capitalist economy, it is impossible for them to see that "productive" and "capitalistically productive" mean two different things, and that public like private investments are capitalistically productive only if they create surplus value, not because they supply material goods or amenities.

Contemporary economists imagine that both private capital and the government contribute to the national income, as both draw from the great "stream" of income. Although the government's contribution depends on taxes and borrowing, the debt service that goes with this is supposed to be paid out of the increased national income achieved through public works. Inflationary consequences were held to pose no danger so long as the increasing money supply could be balanced by an equal increase of production and real income. In order to demonstrate this, economists appealed to a so-called "acceleration principle" and to a "multiplier effect," or to a combination of the two, whose operation could be established mathematically on the basis of certain imagined assumptions. Whether these "principles" yield the same or similar results in reality can of course not be proven due to the empirical complexity of economic processes. But even theoretically nothing follows from them but the obvious insight that like all other spending, state expenditure also can lead to further private expenditure, so that the total new purchasing power is higher than that contributed by the original state expenditure.

Alvin Hansen denied that his theory could be included under the ordinary rubric of underconsumption theories. In his view crisis resulted not from insufficient demand for consumer goods but from spontaneously originating overinvestment. As the dynamic of the system drives the production of means of production forward faster than social consumption, the rise in consumption must be raised to a dominant principle of the system if overproduction is to be avoided. In modern capitalist society investments are no longer determined by consumption, according to Hansen, so that the cycle theories of the classical and neoclassical economists, with their supply-demand equilibrium, are in conflict with the actual facts. Consumption is now a function of accumulation, as a result of which the crisis cycle is an inevitable result of capitalist expansion. In order to eliminate unemployment and overproduction, *public consumption* must be increased by means of public spending to produce a kind of mixed economy in which the price relations are so integrated with monetary and fiscal measures that the economy can continue to develop.

This "revolution" in theoretical economics had already been preceded by a matching practice born of necessity. It took different forms in different countries. While, for example, in the United States unemployment relief, paid out of public funds, counteracted a noticeable radicalization of the working population, the make-work program in Germany had the form of rearmament in order to undo the results of the First World War and overcome the crisis imperialistically at the expense of other nations. Thus the integration of the market economy with state economic management served, on the one hand, the defense of the political status quo and, on the other, the attempt to disrupt it. The general crisis situation and the conflicting capitalist interests mixed the fight against the crisis with a series of imperialist adventures and social conflicts, which more or less affected all countries and finally resulted in the Second World War, which powerfully advanced the integration of state and economy. The fully developed mixed economy began in the form of a war economy that put an end to the apparently permanent state of crisis through the destruction of unbelievable quantities of capital value and the mutual extermination of the producers.

Only after the war did the "new economics" become the ideology of the ruling classes, when state involvement in the economy could not be eliminated in the chaos of the postwar period. With the exception of America, the world, in the eyes of the bourgeoisie, had been utterly shattered and required political and military intervention if total anarchy was to be avoided. The economic functions of the state, evolved in the course of war and crisis, could be altered but not eliminated. The confrontation that immediately broke out between the victorious powers over the division of the spoils of war and the creation of new spheres of influence gave the governmental institutions yet greater influence on economic affairs. The newly established borders had to be secured and the capitalist world economy put on the road to reconstruction with the help of the state. An increasing part of social production was devoted to these ends, and the state budgets continued to swell thanks to taxation and borrowing.

The idea that "mature" capitalism is inevitably doomed to stagnation and increasing unemployment, which can be overcome only by public expenditure, remained a leitmotif of the "new economics." The fact of full employment during the war was held to be sufficient proof that state interventions could have the same results under all conditions and that the state-integrated economy could end the crisis cycle and make possible an unbroken expansion of the economy. The incorporation of economic growth into economic analysis necessitated the construction of a dynamic theory that could be adjoined to the static equilibrium theory. Among others, R. F. Harrod[3] and E. D. Domar[4] attempted to provide theoretical proof of the possibility of an equilibrium economic growth rate by a dynamization of the Keynesian model of income determination, together with the accelerator and multiplier principles.

This equilibrium growth rate was supposed to be determined, on the one hand, by the propensity to save and, on the other, by the capital required and the returns from it. Growth, however, would mean the departure from an equilibrium state; once embarked upon, growth would tend to continue autonomously in the same direction and thus to become always more unstable. Since new investments have two sides, increasing incomes and productive capacity—the first representing demand and the second supply—a growth rate guaranteeing economic stability must harmonize the increasing productive capacity with the increasing demand. For this to be possible, it is not sufficient to achieve an equilibrium of savings and investment, but investments must exceed savings if unemployment is to be avoided. As a result, economic growth, while a means of fighting unemployment, becomes a source of new unemployment as soon as growth leaves the path of equilibrated development.

If the static equilibrium is already recognized to be an illusion, a balanced rate of development is even less credible. But what an autonomous process of growth cannot achieve may be accomplished by its conscious direction. The economy and its development can, according to Paul Samuelson, be compared to "an unmanned bicycle, which is unstable if disturbed from the vertical" but "can be converted into a stable system by a steadying and compensating human hand." In the same way "a Harrod-Domar growth path that would be unstable under laissez-faire [can] be made stable by compensating monetary and fiscal policies in a mixed economy."[5] And "although nothing is impossible in an inexact science like economics," at the present day "the probability of a great depression—a prolonged, cumulative, and chronic slump like that of the 1930s, the 1890s, or the 1870s—has been reduced to a negligible figure."[6]

This confidence appeared to be justified by the facts of economic development and had in addition the "merit of having proved that among other possibilities of development, that of growth without disturbances of equilibrium also exists, something which was earlier contested by various investigators (including Marx, with his breakdown theory)."[7] In this way the question of the dynamic of capitalism was expounded in a manner satisfactory to bourgeois economics, without abandoning the equilibrium approach, and was developed in the neo-neoclassical theory, in which static and dynamic analysis were united.

The various growth theories, however, were less concerned with the economic processes of the developed countries than with the question, raised by the outcome of the Second World War, of the capitalist development of the underdeveloped nations. Of course, this question could be answered quickly and easily, though the realization of the proposal contained in these answers—namely, to repeat the process already completed in the developed countries—ran into insurmountable difficulties. Nevertheless, concern with underdevelopment opened up a new branch of theoretical economics that sought to explain the success of the mixed economy to the whole world and recommend it for imitation. As this evolutionary theory of development, however, has nothing to do with the problem of crisis, we can neglect it here.

From the standpoint of Marx's crisis theory, the prosperity which began, with some delay, after the war is not surprising, since it is the function of crisis to lay the groundwork for a new upswing. This is not to say that every crisis can introduce a new period of accumulation; it may lead also only to a situation of relative stagnation, as was the case in many countries after the First World War, and thence to a new crisis. With the growing destructive powers of capital, war as crisis becomes an obstacle to rapid recovery and can only slowly give way to a new expansion. Under these circumstances it is necessary to continue state intervention in the economy, and this in fact appears to be an essential instrument of the new upswing.

If the stagnation of the capitalist economy leads to state intervention in order to restart the economy and conquer unemployment, it does not follow that these interventions are to be thanked for the new prosperity that finally arises. It may be due instead to the restoration of the profitability of capital, achieved at the same time as, but relatively independently of, these interventions, as in earlier crises, in which the state's deflationary policy aggravated rather than attenuated the crisis. The reduction of the state budget failed as a means to improve the profitability of capital, and likewise an increase in public works does not guarantee a solution to the crisis. In both cases the continuation of accumulation depends in the final analysis on transformation of the capital structure and a rate of surplus value that can valorize the expanding capital. Without a doubt the expansion of capitalist production after the Second World War can be explained only by the still unbroken, or restored, expansive power of capital, and not by the effect of state-induced production. But if this is true, a new overaccumulation crisis is certain, and with it the necessity of further state intervention.

From the standpoint of the "new economics," however, a sufficient autonomous expansion of capital could no longer be counted on, so that continuing capitalist development was thinkable only in the form of the mixed economy. A skeptical minority of economists remained true to the principle of laissez faire and saw the mixed economy as the pure and simple destruction of the market economy, which must lead in the end to the collapse of private capitalism. The sustained prosperity in the Western countries, which could not be simply explained as the result of state interventions, pushed the Keynesian conceptions into the background, and in the academic world microeconomics again took the dominant place. Governmental involvement in the economy was considered not only superfluous but as obstructing the free movement of capital, and it was thus seen as a hindrance to development. Of course, this new capitalist self-confidence was rooted in the prevailing prosperity; and just as the "new economics" could not completely vanquish the laissez-faire doctrine, the latter was not able to compel the "new economics" to retreat purely because of the fact of prosperity. The mixed economy had already become the unalterable form of modern capitalism, although the mix itself could be altered. State interventions could be increased or decreased to meet the changing needs of the yet uncontrolled development of the economy.

The expansion of Western capital was unexpectedly rapid and durable. Economic downturns were of such brief duration as to inspire the replacement of the concept of "depression" by that of "recession," and the share of state-induced production increased more slowly than production as a whole. This affected not only the tenor of Keynesian theory but also Marxist views, leading in the end to various new revisions of Marx's theory of capital and crisis. Drawing nearly universally on the Keynesian theory of insufficient demand as the cause of stagnation, a series of authors[8] represented the position that capitalism's difficulties arise not from a shortage of surplus value but from an excess of it. Structural transformations favorable to capital production—such as the cheapening of constant capital due to modern technology and the arbitrary manipulation of prices that accompanies monopolization —were held to result in the production of more surplus value than could possibly be accumulated, and which could be spent only by way of public expenditures. As the capitalist mode of production rules out an improvement in the working population's standard of living proportional to the rising capacity to produce, the economy fluctuates between stagnation and overcoming it through a policy of waste in the form of space exploration, armaments, and imperialistic adventures. Thus crises were not eliminated by the excess of profit, while they did not arise from the tendency of the rate of profit to fall. In other words, these authors, taking their own routes, had returned to the conviction of Tugan-Baranovsky and Hilferding that capital has no objective limits, since it can increase production indefinitely despite its antagonistic conditions of distribution, even if a portion of it must be "irrationally" wasted.

Without going into the internal contradictions intrinsic to these theories here,[9] it should be noted that they reflect the visible upswing of capitalism in the West, which not only made possible further accumulation with a simultaneous improvement in the workers' standard of living but also remained undamaged by the growth of public spending. Contrary to what had been assumed during the depression, it was not the additional public spending that kept the economy going but the high profits that permitted the luxury of waste production and, beyond that, the alleged transformation of capitalism into an "affluent" or "consumer society."

Of course, this period of prosperity does call for an explanation, which can only be found in the actual course of economic events. For Marxism the general explanation of prosperity is simply the existence of profits sufficient to continue accumulation, just as crisis and depression arise in the absence of this state of affairs. Every cyclical wave can be explained more specifically, if only in retrospect, in terms of the phenomena it displays.

If the long depression of the prewar years was characterized by a general lack of profit, disinvestments, and an extremely low rate of accumulation, this was not because the productivity of labor had suddenly decisively decreased but because the existing productivity was not great enough to assure the existing capital a further profitable expansion. The average rate of profit determined by the existing capital structure was too low to inspire the individual capitals to increase their production by enlarging the productive apparatus, although they experienced the fall in the average rate of profit not directly but as the growing difficulty of selling their commodities. The need for profit on the part of capital—swelled by fictitious and speculative capital values—cannot be satisfied by the mass of profit at hand, and the resulting decline of profit for each individual capital leads through the interruption of further expansion to a general situation of crisis.

The way out of this situation lies in its reversal, in the creation of a capital structure and a mass of surplus value that make further accumulation possible. The combination of the destruction of capital throughout the long period of depression with the enormous acceleration of this process by the destruction of capital values during the war created a new world for the surviving capital in which the given mass of profit was at the disposal of a much diminished capital, which accordingly increased its profitability. At the same time, the technological development forced by the war led to a significant rise in labor productivity, which, in connection with the altered capital structure, raised the productivity of capital sufficiently to increase production and enlarge the productive apparatus.

American capital was unable to accumulate during the war, since about half the national product was used for military ends. The postwar period was a period of making up for lost accumulation and the replacement of the means of production that accompanies this. The result was prosperity in which unemployment was for a time reduced to its indispensable minimum. The years between 1949 and 1968 saw "a 50% increase in the amount of capital for each unit of labor employed." This was largely responsible for "the marked acceleration in output per man-hour from 2.3% to 3.5%." As this increase in the productivity of labor was "in excess of the increase in real wages," the rate of profit on capital, while relatively low, was nevertheless stable.[10] The reconstruction of the European and Japanese economy was in part initiated and financed by American grants and loans, which stimulated American exports and secured markets for the growing output far greater than those due to domestic accumulation alone. The private export of capital followed the lead of the government at the first signs of profitability, above all in the form of direct investments, which internationalized the accumulation of American capital and facilitated its valorization. Access to advanced technology, together with restriction of wages, gave the capital newly forming in the reconstructing countries a competitive position in the world market in a number of areas of production.

The productivity of labor rose in Germany, for example, by around 6 percent yearly, and a quarter of total production was invested as additional capital. With the exception of England, things were not much different in the other European countries, while in America the rate of accumulation remained below its historic average. The higher profit rates in the more rapidly accumulating European countries caused an accelerated export of American capital, and this in turn hastened the general economic development of the capital-importing countries. Conditions due to the outcome of the war led to an extraordinary increase in multinational corporations, largely American in origin, which further hastened the general process of capital concentration through actual fusions and liquidations. Without going further into this well-known story, which was widely celebrated as an "economic miracle" and has been excessively documented, it should be said that it represents no more than an accelerated rate of accumulation which, just because of this acceleration, raised the profit rate to a point permitting an increase in the product share intended for consumption along with production as a whole.

The "new economics," however, had been developed to meet the challenge of a crisis apparently without end. Keynesianism had taken two directions. One tendency aimed at overcoming the crisis by state interventions ("pump priming") in order to give the economy free rein again once expansion was achieved. The other was convinced that capitalism had already reached a stationary state and would therefore always require state intervention. As we know, the actual development of the economy confirmed neither of these views but led to a combination of prosperity and continuing state management of the economy. In Western Europe this took the form of a state-forced acceleration of accumulation, so that the "social market economy" did not differ from the "mixed economy." In America, however, it remained necessary to keep the level of production stable by means of public spending, which led to slow but sure growth of the national debt.

The growth of the public debt can also be traced to America's imperialistic policy and, later, to the war in Vietnam in particular. But since unemployment did not fall below 4 percent of the total labor force and production capacity was not fully utilized, it is more than plausible that without the "public consumption" of armaments and human slaughter, the number of unemployed would have been much higher than it actually was. And since about half of world production was American, despite the upswing in Western Europe and Japan, one cannot really speak of a complete overcoming of the world crisis, particularly not when the underdeveloped countries are taken into consideration. However brilliant the prosperity was, it was nevertheless confined to no more than a part of world capital and did not result in a general upswing encompassing the world economy.

However this may be, what the "new economics" maintained was that capitalist crisis had lost its inevitability, as every downturn could be counteracted by governmental measures. The crisis cycle was supposedly a thing of the past, for every setback to private production could be compensated by an equivalent increase of state-induced production. A whole arsenal of methods of economic management was now available to secure economic equilibrium and equilibrated development. An expansive monetary policy to stimulate private investments, fiscal flexibility, built-in stabilizers like unemployment insurance—such means, together with the deficit financing of public expenditure, guaranteed a regulated economy with full employment and price stability, which needed only the government's decision to be made a reality.

To demonstrate the illusory character of the idea of a state regulation of the economy by way of compensatory measures, the Marxian critique of economics only has to point out the profit-oriented nature of capitalist production. This is not to deny all efficacy to Keynesian methods. Just as the expansion of private credit can stimulate economic activity beyond the level to which it would otherwise be limited, the expansion of public spending realized through credit can also at first have a stimulating effect on the economy as a whole. But both methods find their limits in the actual production of profit. Because of these limits it is possible to abstract from credit in the theory of capitalist development without thereby denying the actual role of credit. Where there is no profit to be had, credit will not be sought; and when the economy is in a downturn, credit is seldom granted. Of course, capitalist production has been based on credit for a long time without this affecting its susceptibility to crisis. While the extension of the credit system can be a factor deferring crisis, the actual outbreak of crisis makes it into an aggravating factor because of the larger amount of capital that must be devalued, although in the end this devaluation in turn is a means to overcome the crisis.

The fact that state-induced production has been expanded by means of credit already indicates that the private expansion of credit has not been able to sustain prosperity. Since state-induced production in competition with private capital would increasingly aggravate the economic difficulties of the latter without changing the low profitability, the state produces not goods for the market, where their value could be realized and accumulated, but goods for "public consumption." This "public consumption" is at all times paid for by taxation of the workers and the surplus-value-producing capital in order to satisfy the general needs of capitalist society. The extension of "public consumption" through deficit financing also implies a deduction from surplus value and a decrease in private consumption, although with a delay, since this financing is accomplished not through additional taxation but through the mobilization of private money capital for a long period—i.e., through the public debt.

The whole matter finally comes down to the simple fact that what is consumed cannot be accumulated, so that the growth of "public consumption" cannot be a means to transform a stagnating or declining rate of accumulation into a rising one. If the rate of accumulation is improved, it is due not to public expenditures but to a restored profitability of capital, accomplished by the crisis, sufficiently vigorous to launch a new expansion despite the increase in public expenditures. This also is not altered by the fact that the economic stimulation due to state expenditures can be an impetus to further expansion, since the *expansion itself* can only be achieved through the actual increase of private surplus value. Without this, state-induced production can lead only to a further collapse of the rate of accumulation.

"Mixed economy" means that a part of the national production remains production for the profit of private capital, while a smaller part consists of state-induced production yielding no surplus value. Thus the total production has a smaller mass of profit at its disposal. Since in general the state does not own means of production and raw materials, it must make use of unutilized capital to get state-induced production going; that is, it must place orders with various enterprises that sell the product requested to the state. These enterprises must valorize their capital and extract surplus value from the workers they employ. This surplus value, however, is not realized on the market by exchange against other commodities but is realized by the money borrowed by the government. The products themselves are either used or wasted.

For the capitalists filling the state's orders, life has been made easier, as they do not have to worry about production and realization. The part of capital blessed with government orders realizes its profit exactly like the part that produces profitably for the market. But its income has an equivalent in taxation and public debt. It seems as if the state-induced production has increased the total profit. But in reality only the surplus value realized on the market is newly produced surplus value, while the surplus value "realized" through state purchases is surplus value previously produced and objectified in money capital.

If the crisis would completely and generally destroy the profitability of capital, capitalist production would stop. In reality, even in the depth of crisis a portion of capital remains sufficiently profitable to continue producing, although on a reduced scale. Another part falls victim to the crisis and thus helps preserve the profitability of the remaining capitals. If this process develops freely, as was generally the case with the crises of the nineteenth century, a shorter or longer period of suffering gives way to a situation in which capital, with an altered structure and a higher rate of exploitation, can recommence accumulation, pushing it beyond the level reached before the crisis. Under the circumstances of the present day, this "healing process" is socially too risky, requiring state interventions to avoid social upheavals.

Due to the high level of capital concentration already achieved, the devaluation of capital by way of competition and the improvement of profitability by way of concentration have lost much of their effectiveness unless these processes are extended beyond national boundaries to the world economy, which must lead to armed confrontations. Since the concentrated capitals totally disregard social needs, even as capitalistically defined, these needs must be supplied by political means, for example, by state subsidization of profit-poor but necessary branches of production. In short, the viability of society requires state intervention in the distribution of the total social profit.

This redistribution of the social profit in the form of state-induced production in no way changes the quantity of this profit. Since the additional production yields no profit of its own, it is of no service to the accumulation of capital. Since the crisis results from insufficient accumulation, it is not eliminated by state-induced production. On the assumption of a capitalism incapable of further accumulation, thus of a situation of permanent crisis, which is a real possibility, the attempt to combat the crisis through deficit-financed, unprofitable public spending would take the following form: the state borrows money to buy products that otherwise would not have been produced. This additional production has an immediate positive effect on the economy as a whole (although this cannot be ascribed to the fashionable but purely speculative "multiplier," based on the untenable bourgeois economic theory). It is obvious that every new investment, whatever its origin, must stimulate economic activity unless it also leads to disinvestment counteracting this stimulative effect. Products are manufactured and workers hired, and the general level of demand must rise along with the new investments. But since the additional production yields no profit, the accumulation difficulty of capital is not solved. *At first*, however, this difficulty merely persists, without being aggravated by the state-induced production.

Since under our assumption private capital is not accumulating and state-induced production, as production for "public consumption," can contribute nothing to accumulation, the maintenance of the existing level of production continually requires additional state expenditures and therefore the perpetual growth of the national debt. Its interest obligations require the state to impose correspondingly higher taxes on productive capital. Of course, these interest payments are a source of income for the state's creditors and as such reenter consumption or are again invested either in the private economy or in state paper. But we are dealing here in any case with one and the same sum which is given up as profit in order to appear elsewhere as interest. Since a nonaccumulating capitalism is not simply a stationary state but implies a regressive situation, the decline in the economy must lead to more and more governmental interventions, which increasingly weaken any new possibility of an upswing for private capital. The compensatory state-induced production thus changes from the means of easing the crisis it originally was to a factor deepening the crisis, as it divests an increasing part of social production of its character as capital, namely its ability to produce additional capital.

The purpose of this picture of a state of permanent crisis is only to demonstrate that unprofitable state-induced production, far from being a means of overcoming crisis, must in the course of time call the capitalist mode of production itself into question. However, since the crisis develops within itself the conditions required to surmount it, the need for continually increasing state-induced production disappears, apart from the fact that the governments concerned, since they are capitalist governments, themselves feel the need to dismantle state intervention at the point at which it becomes dangerous for the system. To preserve the capitalist economy not just production but the production of profit is required. If profit could be increased simply by additional production, capital would see to it itself, and state intervention would not be needed.

Bourgeois economics does not think in terms of the categories of value and surplus value. From its point of view profit is not seen as the determining factor of the economy and its development; indeed, it disputes even the existence of profit. "Much of what is ordinarily called profit," writes Paul Samuelson, for example, "is really nothing but interest, rents, and wages under a different name."[11] When no distinction is made between wages and profits, the relationship between production and profit production is also obscure, and every sort of activity is represented equally in the national income, from which every individual draws his share in proportion to his contribution. In the total production expressed in money terms, the difference between profitable and unprofitable production disappears, and state-induced production and private production are confused in a night in which all price relations, like all cats, are gray. As a result bourgeois economics is unable to foresee the consequences of its own prescriptions.

Nevertheless, the "new economics" claimed the honor of having found the key to the solution of the problem of crisis. Only later was it apparent that it had strutted in borrowed plumes, and that the actual overcoming of the crisis owed nothing to the *Keynesian* anticrisis mechanism. As already pointed out, this is no reason to deny that it has had any economic effect, since it can serve to initiate a new prosperity when the potential for such a prosperity already exists. In itself, however, additional state-induced production cannot increase the social surplus value and must decrease it if it continues to expand. Nevertheless, the extension of production that accompanies it, like any extension of credit, can mitigate the conditions of crisis, since its negative effect on the total profit will only be visible at a later point. *In the short run* the state-induced production offers private capital a wider range for action and an improved basis for its own efforts to escape from the shortage of profits for accumulation. If in the meantime private capital succeeds in extricating itself from the crisis, this may appear to be a result of the state's interventions, although the latter would have had no success without the improvement, independent of them, of capital's ability to expand itself.

There is therefore no contradiction in seeing both a crisis-mitigating and a crisis-sharpening factor in governmental fiscal policy. The additional production made possible by deficit financing does appear as additional demand, but as demand unaccompanied by a corresponding increase in total profits. The additional demand consists of money injected into the economy by the state in the form of governmental credit. It nonetheless functions immediately as an increase in demand that stimulates the economy as a whole and can become the point of departure for a new prosperity if insuperable barriers do not stand in the way of such a prosperity. But only under such circumstances can the unprofitable expansion of production smooth the way for a profitable expansion without even then losing its capitalistically unproductive character. It is the capitalistically unproductive nature of state-induced production that sets definite limits to its utilization in capitalist society, limits that are reached more quickly the longer capital remains in crisis.

In all circumstances the production it induces is due not to the state itself but to its creditworthiness. It is private capital that must foot the bill and spend the money to increase demand. Thus it is private capital itself that finances the deficit, and it is ready to do so precisely because it is unable to operate or even think in terms of society as a whole. The money placed at the government's disposal yields interest, and it is this interest that gives some number of capitalists sufficient reason to lend their money to the state. Once this process is set in motion, it leads to the imposition of a growing tax burden on the capital still producing at a profit, which is thereby drawn into the financing of the deficit. In this way the total capital, both money capital and productive capital, becomes bound up with unprofitable production. The part of capital that (as we saw above) makes a profit even during the crisis, without transforming it into additional capital, sees its profitability cut even further as a result of the growth of state production, until in the course of time the unwillingness to invest becomes the objective impossibility to do so. In this sense, in the absence of a spontaneous reprise of profitable accumulation, state-induced production will change from a result of a crisis into a cause of its further aggravation.

The positive effect of state intervention on the economy is thus only temporary and turns into its opposite if the expected stimulation of profitable production does not occur or takes too long. The representatives of the "new economics" had, so to speak, a stroke of luck, in that the new prosperity, which they *did not* expect, developed along with the state interventions. If it had not developed, the stimulating effect of the state-induced increase in production would have progressively declined, until the government's action itself became an obstacle to the surmounting of the crisis. If Keynesianism does not deserve the credit for the actual prosperity, it does not provide weapons for fighting crisis either; hence the capitalist law of crisis continues to dominate the system, just as before the discovery of the "new economics."

The lengthy period of upswing, however, was impressive enough to stimulate the expectation—just as at the turn of the century—that the business cycle was tending to flatten out, so that the periods of depression, now grown milder, could be counteracted by less stringent state measures. Those breaks in expansion that still occured were seen as no more than "growth recessions," which did not threaten the existing level of production, or simple "pauses" within a continual increase of production. At the onset of such pauses the governmental money and fiscal policy would be enough to overcome the gap between demand and supply and so clear the way to further growth.

The relative reduction of the deficit financing of public expenditures made possible by the rapid development of profitable production strengthened the conviction that the interplay of the market economy and state economic regulation had once and for all eliminated the crisis problem. While taxation absorbed a great part of the national income—in America, e.g., 32 percent and in West Germany 35 percent—state expenditures nevertheless did not grow faster than total production. And while the national debt continued to grow, it was at a slower pace. In America, for example, the national debt amounted to $278.7 billion in 1945 and $493 billion in 1973. The interest obligations increased during the same period from $3.66 billion to $21.2 billion. The share of interest costs in the national product nonetheless remained the same, namely 1.7 percent. Similar proportions held in other countries. What is important here is to see that with a more rapidly growing total production, the interest burden can be kept stable despite a growing national debt.

144

The increased share of the state in the national product represents a drain on the total surplus value, absorbing a portion of the surplus value that can therefore not enter into the accumulation of private capital. But the fact that private capital accumulation did continue kept the size of the state's share of surplus value *relatively* stable; it grew slowly though *absolutely*. The resulting relationship between state-induced production and total production, between national debt and national income, can manifest itself as a steady growth of production with a constant rate of accumulation along with a relatively lower rate of profit. But this relationship is extremely delicate just because of the low profit rate, which in addition is influenced adversely by the continuation of accumulation. On the one hand, as we know, accumulation increases the productivity of labor; on the other, by raising the organic composition of capital it depresses the rate of profit. Every new divergence between profitability and accumulation will turn a hitherto supportable state deduction from the total social profit into a factor impeding the accumulation process. Thus private capital's first reaction to the fall in the already low rate of profit is to demand the cutting of public expenditure or the reestablishment of a relationship between state-induced production and total production that does not threaten accumulation.

The more capital accumulates, the greater is its sensitivity to the quantity of profit. To escape the pressure of the declining average rate of profit and to safeguard the valorization of the existing capital, monopolizing capital seeks to set its supply price to meet its own profit requirements so as to make its own accumulation independent of the market. Of course, this is possible only within certain limits. Since neither the total social product nor the total surplus value can be enlarged by price manipulations, monopoly profits can only arise from the further fall of the profits of the competitive capitals, still ruled by the average rate of profit. To the extent that monopoly profit exceeds the average profit, it reduces the latter and thus continually destroys its own basis. In this way monopoly profit tends toward the average profit, a process that is of course retarded by the international extension of monopolization. But this unequal appropriation of the total social surplus value cannot change the magnitude of this surplus value unless monopolization affects not only price determination but also the production process, as when the destruction of competitive capital leads to an increase in the productivity of labor and so the growth of surplus value.

The development of capital in the mixed economy and under the pressure of monopoly is far more dependent on the rapid increase in the mass of surplus value than it was under laissez-faire conditions. Since the growth of production excludes an equivalent growth of profits and must therefore grow more rapidly than profit if the latter is to remain adequate to the requirements of accumulation, a slowing rate of accumulation must lead to crisis. Inversely, accumulation in turn depends on sufficient profits. But just as monopoly profits can be achieved for a long time at the expense of the general profit, so also the general profit can be maintained for a considerable time at the expense of the society as a whole. The means to this end are to be found in the state's money and fiscal policy.

The accumulation of capital in itself represents no problem so long as the necessary profits are available, and capital was accumulated for a long time in general independence of state expenditures. The utilization of state monetary and fiscal policy to influence the economy indicates a situation in which accumulation has become a problem, and one that can no longer be handled without conscious management of the economic process. The problem is summed up in the single word "profit." Each capital must worry about its own profit, but it is just this that leads to the crisis of overaccumulation whose periodic appearance becomes ever less bearable. The consequences of the crisis—overproduction and unemployment—can be mitigated by increasing public works, but the cause of the crisis—the lack of profit that hinders further accumulation—cannot be dealt with in this way. With public works as without them, it is up to capital to get itself out of the crisis. In order not to place further difficulties in capital's path, the increased public expenditures are financed by way of deficits. The taxation of capital can therefore be fairly restrained at first in order not to diminish further the needed surplus value. This, however, engenders an inflationary process which, once under way, conditions the further development of capitalist production.

Inflation is a weapon in the Keynesian arsenal. Through the more rapid increase in prices relative to wages, the profit necessary for expansion grows, while the accelerated creation of money reduces the interest on debt, which makes investment easier. Inflation is here seen as a method for enlarging surplus value. The surplus value gained in this way, equal to the reduction in the value of labor power plus the surplus value transferred from money capital to productive capital, permits a corresponding increase in accumulation.

The money borrowed by the government is injected into the economy through the conduit of profitless production. Although its *final products* fall in the sphere of "public consumption" and so do not appear on the commodity market, this production directly enlarges the total demand. The increased sum of money entering into circulation allows the prices of commodities intended for private consumption also to rise. This process is clearly observable in war time, and governments attempt to avoid the inflation then resulting from the interaction of a decreased or constant commodity supply with the increased money income due to war production by such means as forced savings and the rationing of use values. If in a weaker form, the increase in the money supply due to deficit financing leads to an endless process of inflation, since nothing opposes the increase in prices the expansion of the money supply makes possible.

The increased sum of money entering into circulation confronts, at first, an unchanged total surplus value in the form of a certain quantity of commodities. The increase in prices made possible by monetary growth improves the profitability of capital. To the surplus value created in production is added the value derived from price increases or the loss in the buying power of money. This increase in profit represents a new division of the total social income to the advantage of capital; it cannot alter the size of the total product or its value as such. The value of labor power is lowered by the detour of circulation, as is the income share of those groups within the population who live on surplus value, with a corresponding increase in the share going to capital. Only if the additional surplus value extracted via the circulation process is accumulated, so as to increase the productivity of labor and thereby the social product, has the increased mass of profit changed from the money form into the capital form. Otherwise the increased profitability leads only to a further fall in private demand and to more unused capital.

The real gains that inflation yields to capital are thus only another form of the devaluation of labor power, which happens in every crisis. What used to be accomplished by deflationary means is now effected by inflationary means, not by lowering wages but by raising prices—or by a combination of both. The increase in profits by means of inflation encounters definite barriers, however, as the reduction of the value of labor power has absolute limits, and even these cannot be reached because of the resistance of the workers. Moreover, the increase in total demand brings with it an increase in the demand for labor power, which in itself restricts the lowering of wages by price inflation.

The crisis can only be said to have been overcome when capital value can be expanded without reducing the value of labor power, so that the new prosperity brings increasing wages with it. This cannot be achieved through the "public spending" of the government, as this, in the final analysis, accomplishes only the draining of a growing portion of the surplus value existing in the form of money into "public consumption." If the policy of public spending is nonetheless adopted, it is because there is no other alternative for capital to the risk of increased unemployment and an extensive destruction of capital. "Public consumption" also represents destruction of capital, accepted and regulated in the hope that the system on its own will create the conditions for a continuance of capital accumulation; it represents, in other words, management not of the economy but of the crisis.

If the growing public expenditures are not to become a factor deepening the crisis, capital must succeed, first, in keeping the growing national debt within the limits set for it by the actual creation of surplus value, and second, in reestablishing the conditions of further accumulation—that is, in increasing profit more quickly than it is spent in unprofitable production. A certain amount of surplus value is absorbed by the state in any case, apart from the amount used for the reduction of unemployment by state-induced production. This share has steadily grown. Here, however, we are concerned only with the increase in the additional amount deducted from surplus value for state-induced production. This presents a further obstacle to capital accumulation, although it is an obstacle that can be pushed aside if capital succeeds in abolishing unemployment by continuing to accumulate. This, however, requires a rate of accumulation high enough for the absolute number of surplus-value-producing workers to increase fast enough to offset its relative decline (the rising organic composition of capital). Such a rate of accumulation was approached in the postwar decades by several Western European countries; the ensuing prosperity even led to the import of labor power, although this of course indicated the persistence of unemployment in other countries. In the United States the unemployment level stabilized at about 4 percent of the total active population—an officially recognized percentage that came to be accepted as "normal" and as compatible with the concept of "full employment."

The fact that state-induced production, insofar as it was represented by the national debt, has so far amounted only to a rather small fraction of total production, together with the fact that its costs were at first limited to the interest payments on the national debt and so claimed only a fraction of the capital disappearing into "public consumption," postponed the reckoning imposed on private capital and had no immediate negative effect. Of course, the money loaned to the government has turned into the national debt, backed by nothing but the government's promise to meet its obligations someday and meanwhile to pay the creditors the interest due them. The money capital utilized by the government is not invested as capital and so preserved but disappears into "public consumption." If the state debt is ever paid off—which may well not happen—it can only be paid out of new surplus value freshly created in production. And this would in no way alter the fact that the surplus value represented in the national debt has vanished without a trace instead of adding its volume to the accumulation of capital.

It follows that the state's use of increased public spending to fight crisis ends by consuming capital. This consumption of capital appears as a growth of production and employment, but due to its unprofitable character, it is no longer *capitalist* production and really amounts to a hidden form of the expropriation of capital by the state. The state uses the money of one group of capitalists to buy the production of another group, with the intention of satisfying both groups by assuring for one the interest on and for the other the profitability of its capital. But the incomes that appear here as interest and profit can only be paid out of the total social surplus value actually produced, even if the reckoning can be deferred. As a result, from the standpoint of the system as a whole the proceeds of state-induced production must count as a deduction from the total profit and therefore as a diminution of the surplus value needed for accumulation. Since the crisis results from a shortage of surplus value, it can hardly be overcome by increasing this shortage.

It is true, of course, that the profit shortage manifested in the form of crisis is neither aggravated nor diminished directly by state-induced production, and that production, employment, and income increase just because means of production and labor power, which would not have been utilized without the state's intervention, are set in motion. But the means of production and the consumer goods consumed by workers employed in this part of production do not form part of capital, if viewed from the standpoint of the system as a whole. For the individual capitals involved, their outlays on means of production and labor power function as capital and yield them profits. But their profit means a loss of profits for all other capitalists and so stimulates their attempts to shift this loss to the shoulders of the population as a whole by means of price increases. Since the loss of profits due to state-induced production is spread over the society as a whole, it remains tolerable for a long time, without thereby ceasing to diminish the total profit.

This is not the place to go into the wider implications of state-induced production. What is important for us is only to see clearly that capitalism's susceptibility to crisis cannot be overcome by this means. Whatever effects state-induced production may have in a crisis situation, it cannot increase profits and is therefore no instrument for overcoming crisis. Its continuing use can only enlarge the unprofitable portion of society's production and in this way progressively destroy its capitalist character. True prosperity, in contrast, depends on the increase in surplus vaue for the further expansion of capital. It must be admitted that capital has succeeded in creating, out of its own resources, the prosperity of the recent past; but with it it has also created the conditions for a new crisis.

However, this statement must be qualified. Just as the last great crisis differed from its predecessors, and in its length, extent, and violence shook the world uniquely, so the prosperity that began after the Second World War had a particular character differentiating it from earlier prosperities. It was accompanied from the start by an extraordinary growth of credit and so of money, which left the increase in production far behind and stimulated and sustained the prosperity by means of inflation. The growth of credit is a characteristic of every prosperity, and its acceleration, according to Marx, is a symptom of approaching crisis. In bourgeois economic theory also the rapid expansion of credit and the accompanying price inflation have been viewed as signs of a prosperity nearing its end and the approach of a period of economic downturn, since the reserve requirements of the banks set definite limits to the extension of credit. As these limits are approached, the price of credit soars, and the demand for it falls, bringing the inflationary effects of the boom to an end. If the prosperity does not rest on resources sufficient to continue it, i.e., on a rate of profit sufficient for accumulation, it can, however, be sustained by a looser state monetary and credit policy, though at the cost of increasing inflation.

A "cheap money" policy cuts down on the general debt burden and lightens the interest service on the national debt, on the one hand, and adds to the state's demand for credit the demands of industry and consumers, on the other. It makes possible a rapid advance of production at the cost of increasing indebtedness and rising inflation. In the United States, for instance, the total product grew between 1946 and 1970 by around 130 percent in real terms, but by around 368 percent in money terms. Total debt—excluding government debt—rose during the same period by 798 percent. Just like the government's demand for credit for the deficit financing of public expenditure, the expansion of private credit also increases economic activity beyond the level it would otherwise have reached, but without thereby being able really to change the productivity of labor and the quantity of surplus value, which develop independently of the growth of credit. Like governmental deficit financing, private indebtedness also depends on the expectation that production will grow without limit and can be extended in proportion to the expansion of credit.

What this proportion is, however, cannot be established. In the expectation of continuous and increasing production, with the higher incomes this will allow, and driven by capital's need to expand if it is to maintain itself, capitals compete by means of the credit system, which thus runs the danger of development far beyond the basis afforded by the actual level of social production. Of course, the danger is not so great for the creditors, who to a great extent are free to raise the price of credit and can include their apparent losses in setting interest rates, which in itself leads to higher prices. In part the risk is shifted to the population as a whole by allowing capitalist debtors to deduct debt and interest payments from their taxes. Nevertheless, inflationary credit escapes the control of governmental monetary and credit policy, since inflation itself counteracts the state's raising of the cost of credit by manipulating the interest rate, and since the demand for credit can increase even with higher interest rates. Naturally, the government can halt the expansion of credit by increasing reserve requirements, but this would threaten the prosperity on which the government itself depends. Whenever this way of halting inflation has been tried, the resulting recession has forced a return to the inflationary credit policy.

If the extraordinary growth of private debt was a means of maintaining the prosperity thanks to which the growth of the state debt could be slowed down, the money and credit inflation was both a cause and a consequence of a prosperity that to an increasing extent was based on future profits, and that was therefore bound to collapse when they did not appear. As the inflation-caused differential between price and wage formation allowed profits to rise, the pressure of accumulation on the rate of profit was less noticeable. However, the sole result of this—at least for America, as noted above—was a profit rate stabilized at a relatively low level, which without the government's inflationary policy would not have sufficed to enlarge production to the degree attained. Of course, the inflation contains its own contradictions;

from a stimulus to the economy it can turn into a factor undermining it, since the real contradictions of capitalist production cannot be eliminated by techniques of finance. If the expansion of private credit reaches the limits set by the actual profitability of capital, then the prosperity it has engendered comes to an end, requiring additional state-induced production if the economic decline is to be halted, without thus being able to prevent it.

From the standpoint of the "new economics," the inflationary money and credit policy was a method of surmounting crisis and restoring full employment. The illusion that this policy could lead to the restoration of an equilibrium based on price stability soon disappeared, however, in response to empirical facts if not to theoretical insight. The economist A. W. Phillips, in a historical investigation of the relation between wages and employment levels in England, made the not very surprising observation that rising wages and prices are correlated with decreasing unemployment, and falling wages and prices with increasing unemployment. Following the custom of economists, this observation was graphed, by the so-called Phillips curve, which represents changes of wages and prices as a function of employment. This was supposed to show clearly that growing employment implied wage and price inflation, so that the only choice is between inflation and unemployment.

For example, it was calculated on the basis of the Phillips curve that in postwar America, without inflation unemployment would rise to between 6 and 8 percent of the working population, while with a 3 or 4 percent rate of inflation it could be reduced to 4 or 4.5 percent. Thus there was not only the choice between unemployment and inflation but also the possibility of using state intervention to restore the balance between unemployment and inflation necessary for prosperity. Any excessive increase in unemployment could be overcome through a corresponding increase in inflation, which, in the eyes of the economists, was really not too high a price to pay for permanent prosperity. This is because, in the words of a theoretician of "functional finance,"

> Inflation does not constitute a reduction in the goods available for people to buy. The idea that the buyer's loss from inflation can be treated as a social loss contravenes the first principle of elementary econom-

ics: the principle of remembering that if anybody pays any money somebody else must be getting it. Every 1% increase in prices, although it means that the buyers have to pay 1% more, also means that the sellers receive 1% more. Since both the sellers and the buyers are members of the society, society in the aggregate neither loses nor gains. Indeed, most people are both buyers and sellers, at different times of the week or even of the day; so that the greater part of the losses when buying and the gains when selling cancel out, and perhaps only one quarter of the 1% of the national income involved is an actual transfer from some people to other people. This net transfer of 1/4 of 1% from the buyers to the sellers changes the distribution of income and wealth, but there is no more reason for supposing that the new distribution is worse than the old distribution than for supposing that it is better.[12]

This cold-blooded falsification of the real function of inflation enabled the representatives of the "new economics" to see their theory empirically confirmed by an inflationary prosperity with a stable level of unemployment—until, one day, the increasing rate of inflation was accompanied by growing unemployment, and the theory was revealed to be false. With this bourgeois economic theory fell into a second crisis, if we see its first crisis in the general confusion that preceded Keynesianism and was seemingly resolved by it. It was realized that the regulative measures suggested by Keynesian theory are not only limited and double-edged but also subject to contradictions inherent in the capitalist system. Economics, which according to Paul Samuelson had been transformed, thanks to Keynesianism, from a dismal into "a cheerful science,"[13] relapsed into its original gloom. "In the post-Keynes era," Samuelson explained,

> we have at our disposal the instruments of a monetary and fiscal policy that can create the purchasing power necessary for the avoidance of great crises. No well-informed person still worries himself about the size of the public debt; so long as the Gross National Product and the nation's fiscal capacity keep pace with the growth of the interest on the national debt, this problem is only a worry of the seventeenth rank, and no-one is losing sleep over growing automation or business cycles. However, along with all our triumphant self-satisfaction there is still a spectre that haunts us: galloping inflation. It is the new scourge, which the pre-1914 theoreticians did not foresee. . . . With what we know today, we

154

are indeed able to avoid a chronic recession, or to initiate a needed spending policy. But we don't yet know how to stop a cost-push inflation, without the cure being nearly worse for the economy than the disease.[14]

It completely escapes Samuelson that the dread "scourge" of inflation and the "triumphant" monetary and fiscal policy are one and the same and that inflation cannot be fought with inflation. Of course, he distinguishes between two types of inflation: first, one stemming from an excess demand pushing up prices, which can be easily controlled by cutting incomes; and second, the supply inflation of recent times, which arises "from the pressure of wage costs along with the attempts made by giant firms to maintain undiminished profit margins."[15] For this second type no solution has yet been found, for experience teaches that government-imposed wage and price controls have only short-term effects.

Since the capitalist crisis was supposedly caused by insufficient demand, which was mastered exactly by means of the "triumphant" monetary and fiscal policy, it is difficult to understand how this triumph over crisis has itself turned into an inflationary state of crisis that is manifesting itself once again in growing unemployment. To surmount this new crisis situation, according to Samuelson, profits and wages must be decreased, which would inevitably result in an insufficient demand, which in turn would have to be mastered anew with the "triumphant monetary and fiscal policy."

Samuelson considers it "a truism, that the price level must rise when all the factors of cost rise more quickly than the volume of production."[16] But why doesn't the volume of production rise? Because "wages rise more quickly than the average productivity of labor," answers Samuelson. But why doesn't labor productivity rise faster than wages? Since the rise in productivity depends on technological development, and this depends on capital accumulation, it must be because capital is not accumulating fast enough. But why not, when "the giant firms maintain undiminished profit margins"? Well, we just don't know. "A good scientist," says Samuelson, "must be able to admit his ignorance"[17] —the ignorance that for this good scientist led to the Nobel Prize.

Another Nobel Prize winner, Kenneth Arrow, observed with resignation that

> the resolution of any problem always creates a new problem. From the beginning of the Keynesian era, the fear has been expressed that vigorous full-employment policies will lead to inflation. Standard economic theory has been built in large measure about the idea of equilibrium, that an exact balancing of supply and demand on all markets, including the labor market, will lead to steady prices, while an excess of supply leads to a downward pressure. Thus, unemployment ought to lead to wage declines; they manifestly have not done so in recent years. The coexistence of inflation and unemployment is thus an intellectual riddle and an uncomfortable fact.

Until this riddle is solved, together with the elimination of this uncomfortable fact, we should nevertheless bear in mind that

> the rates of inflation with which we have had to contend impose no insuperable problem or even major difficulty to the operation of the economic system, nothing comparable to the major depressions of the past. Individuals will learn and have learned to deal with inflation, making their plans to take expected inflation into account.[18]

The ignorance that Samuelson admits and Arrow's unanswered riddle cannot be dealt with on the basis of bourgeois economic theory. But this theory cannot be renounced without giving up an important component of the ideology necessary to capitalist society. However, it is not only that the "riddle" of inflation with growing unemployment spells the bankruptcy of the Keynesian theory of full employment in its neoclassical version; in view of present-day conditions, the whole conceptual scheme of bourgeois economics has lost even that semblance of relevance to reality required by its ideological function. Even many economic ideologists have come to find the encumbrance of the neoclassical equilibrium price theory unsupportable and have attempted to free themselves from it and to develop theories that fly less in the face of real economic relations.[19] Of course, the so-called crisis of academic economics is not a general phenomenon. The majority of economic theorists still remain undisturbed by the divergence between theory and reality. This is not to be wondered at, since this phenomenon can be noted in other ideological areas also: there is no God but there are many hundreds of thousands of theologians.

For another group of theorists the "second crisis" of economics stems not from the riddle of the failure of monetary and fiscal policy to sustain full employment but from the problem of distribution, left unexamined by the neoclassical economists. Along with neo-Marxists like Baran and Sweezy, "left" Keynesians[20] accepted the proposition that Keynesian methods could achieve full employment. In contrast to the neo-Marxists, the "left" Keynesians do not believe in the necessity of waste production. Full employment, they believe, can also be maintained by increasing the consumption of the population. Theoretically the concept of marginal productivity is seen as untenable as a basis for explaining the distribution of income and as no more than an apologia for the prevailing unfair mode of distribution. Practically the Keynesian methods of increasing production by state intervention should be matched by a politically determined distribution coordinated with it. By concerning itself with problems of the distribution of the social product, as in Ricardo's original formulation of its goals, economics should return to its origin in political economy.

Thus, while the current state of affairs presents the representatives of the "new economics" with an unanswered riddle, "left" Keynesianism is still occupied with the hypothesis of a crisis-free economy in which the only problem is how the benefits of steadily increasing production are to be shared among the whole society. This would require not only a different principle of distribution than the existing one but also a different division of social labor, transferring resources from waste production to production for private consumption. Since this would require the direct competition of state-induced production with production for private account, which would only lead to the further subordination of the private sector of the economy to the state sector, this program could be carried out only through a struggle against private capitalism. And in fact "left" Keynesianism inclines toward state-capitalism and in this sense converges with neo-Marxism, without thereby losing its lack of relation to reality.

The still unsolved "riddle" of economic stagnation with growing unemployment and an increasing rate of inflation, given a name with the concept of "stagflation," is in fact no riddle but a phenomenon known for a long time and put to use in the drive for higher profits under conditions unfavorable for the production of surplus value. Mass unemployment accompanied the "classic" German inflation after the First World War. Today it accompanies the forced accumulation in the capital-poor countries. The creeping inflation that is a constant feature in the capitalistically developed countries also indicates a level of profitability too low for the accumulation requirements of capital, which is certainly masked, but not overcome, by the increase in production. Inflation is not a natural phenomenon but the result of monetary and fiscal policies that could also be discontinued. If a government is unwilling to abandon the inflationary course, it is because of anxiety about the resulting economic stagnation, for this would be as injurious to it as to capital itself, since every deflationary measure, every economic downturn also decreases the share of surplus value going to the government.

It is impossible to establish empirically either the accumulation requirements of capital or, therefore, the mass of surplus value that would satisfy them. That the relation between the two is not "in order" is only indicated indirectly through events in the market. Whether the state's interventions through money and fiscal policy are able to restore the necessary relationship between profit and accumulation can likewise be discovered only in further market events. Thus the state can only react blindly to uncomprehended economic fluctuations in its attempt both to stimulate the economy and to secure the profitability of capital and its accumulation. But the first of these contradicts the second, although of course this, too, becomes apparent only later, in the market, through the combination of inflation with growing unemployment.

If the inflationary monetary and credit policy is a means to increase production, then the newly arising unemployment should in turn disappear with the acceleration of inflation. But the theoreticians of inflation themselves shrink before this consistent application of their theory, which would lead from creeping to galloping inflation. The deficit financing of public expenditures and the inflationary monetary and credit policy ought, they say, not be pushed too far, for this would call the future existence of the system itself into question. This confession is of course also an admission that creeping inflation can be useful to capital only insofar as it fosters an increase in profit at the expense of society as a whole. But this does not mean that the increase in profit makes possible a rate of accumulation that could be described as capitalist prosperity. The appearance of growing unemployment with creeping inflation reveals that profits cannot be sufficiently increased by means of inflation to head off the incipient stagnation.

Inflation is a worldwide phenomenon. This indicates not only the mutual interdependencies and the complexity that characterize the global economy but also the sharpening general competition, which is also waged with the weapons of currency policy. The hunger for profit is universal, and the longing for additional capital can find no satisfaction in a world in which ever greater capital masses oppose each other competitively and must always continue to grow, not only to be able to hold their own but also to escape the economic stagnation that would otherwise set in. It is without a doubt true that monopoly profit can be maintained and indeed increased even under the conditions of stagnation, but only at the cost of aggravated stagnation and an irresistible decline in the economy. From this arises the need for further state interventions, which of themselves contribute to the disintegration of the system. Thus the future of capital still depends upon accumulation, even if accumulation promises it no future.

Just as the long years of prosperity did not affect all capitalist countries equally, the onset of crisis has different effects in different countries. But everywhere the change from prosperity to stagnation is already visible, and to the fear of further inflation is joined the fear of a new crisis. Whether the spreading crisis can once again be halted by state interventions, which will combat today's difficulties at the cost of capital's life expectancy, cannot be theoretically determined. Without a doubt it will be attempted, but the result may very well lead to no more than the temporary consolidation of the given precarious circumstances—and with this to a prolonged decay of the capitalist system. Sooner or later we will daily find before our eyes the empirical confirmation of Marx's theory of accumulation: capitalism's susceptibility to crisis and decay.

Notes

1. See Paul Mattick, *Marx & Keynes. The Limits of the Mixed Economy*, Boston, 1969, ch. 1 and passim.

2. A. H. Hansen, *Fiscal Policy and Business Cycles*, New York, 1941, pp. 150-51.

3. *Essays in Dynamic Theory*, 1939.

4. *Essays in the Theory of Growth*, 1957.

5. *Economics*, New York, 1973, p. 757.

6. Ibid., p. 266.

7. H. Rittershausen, in *Das Fischer Lexikon: Wirtschaft*, Frankfurt, 1958, p. 259.

8. Notably J. M. Gilman, *The Falling Rate of Profit* (1958) and *Prosperity in Crisis* (1965), and P. A. Baran and P. M. Sweezy, *Monopoly Capital* (1966).

9. They are explored in, *inter alia*, U. Rödel, *Forschungsprioritäten und technologische Entwicklung*, Frankfurt, 1972; Braunmühl, Funken, Cogoy, Hirsch, *Probleme einer materialistischen Staatstheorie*, Frankfurt, 1973; R. Schmiede, *Grundprobleme der Marxschen Akkumulations und Krisentheorie*, Frankfurt, 1973; C. Deutschmann, *Der linke Keynesianismus*, Frankfurt 1973; Hermanin, Lauer, Schurmann, *Drei Beiträge zur Methode und Krisentheorie bei Marx*, Frankfurt, 1973; P. Mattick, "Value Theory and Capital Accumulation," in *Science and Society*, 23:1 (Winter 1959), pp. 27-51, and "Monopoly Capital," in P. Mattick, *Anti-Bolshevik Communism*, New York, 1978, pp. 187-209.

10. *Monthly Economic Letter*, First National City Bank, February 1974, pp. 12, 13, 15.

11. P. Samuelson, *Economics*, 9th ed., New York, 1973, p. 619.

12. A. P. Lerner, *Flation*, Baltimore, 1973, p. 12.

13. P. A. Samuelson, "Inflation—der Preis des Wohlstandes," *Der Spiegel*, 35 (1971), p. 104.

14. Ibid.

15. Ibid.

16. Ibid.

17. Ibid.

18. K. J. Arrow, "Somehow, It Has Overcome," *New York Times* March 26, 1973.

19. In a remarkable article Oskar Morgenstern discusses the main errors which, in his opinion, prevent modern economic theory from contributing

anything to the solution of economic problems. After demonstrating the theory's lack of connection with reality, he turns to an immanent critique of its central ideas, furnishing overwhelming proof that its premises do not lead to the conclusions economists have drawn from them. Of course, Morgenstern limits himself to a critique of neoclassical theory, without being able to propose any other alternative than the game theory invented by himself and von Neumann, which has exactly as little to do with reality. See O. Morgenstern, "Thirteen Critical Points in Contemporary Economic Theory. An Interpretation," in *Journal of Economic Literature*, 10:4 (December 1972).

20. "Left-wing" Keynesianism and its successor, "post-Keynesian economics," are most notably represented by Joan Robinson and the late Michael Kalecki.

Part II

5

Ernest Mandel's
Late Capitalism

I

In the field of present-day Marxism, Ernest Mandel occupies a leading position. His industry and ambition have produced a small library of Marxism to which even bourgeois economists pay some respect. In his book *Late Capitalism*,[1] Mandel practices a sort of self-criticism with respect to his earlier works. In particular he criticizes his *Marxist Economic Theory*,[2] first, for its "exaggeratedly descriptive character," and then for its "too small effort to explain the contemporary history of capitalism by its immanent laws of motion" (p. 7, German ed.).[3] Since the later book contains Mandel's corrections of his earlier works, *Late Capitalism* must be seen as representing, if not Mandel's final conception, at least his ideas of the moment, which makes a look back at his *Economic Theory* largely superfluous.

In the course of his various works, Mandel came to the conclusion, which should have been obvious from the beginning, "that our explanation of the history of the capitalist mode of production is only possible through a mediation between the laws of motion of 'capital in general' and the concrete forms of appearance of the 'many capitals'" (p. 7, German ed.; see English ed., pp. 8-9). The contemporary concrete form of appearance Mandel condenses into the concept of "late capitalism," although this does not feel quite right to him, since this term is not intended to suggest "that capitalism has changed in essence," although its purely chronological significance is also "unsatisfactory." In any case, calling the present state of the system "late capitalism" can in no way make "the analytic findings of Marx's *Capital* and Lenin's *Imperialism* out of date" (p. 10).

Since Lenin also claimed to hold to the analytical findings of Marx's *Capital,* one cannot speak of the analytical findings of Lenin's *Imperialism*: it only represents Lenin's interpretation of a particular situation, namely the First World War, on the basis of the —incorrectly understood, to be sure—Marxian laws of motion of capital. Thus Mandel can make but little appeal to Lenin, even when his political position compels him to place Lenin next to Marx, although, as Mandel himself points out, Lenin "does not provide a systematic theory of the contradictions of capitalist development" (p. 38, n.).

Up to now, according to Mandel, the relationship between the laws of motion and the history of capitalism has not been satisfactorily explained. He wants to fill this gap, which necessarily brings him into opposition with nearly every previous interpretation of capitalist development. Mandel nevertheless devotes the customary introductory pages to the "dialectical analysis"—now become a "commonplace"—which traditionally precedes every explanation of development, in order to emphasize that "to *reduce* Marx's method to a 'progression from the abstract to the concrete' . . . is to ignore its full richness" (p. 14). The concrete is the real starting point, as it is the goal, of the process of knowledge. The truth of the laws of development produced by theory must be empirically proven. Although there is nothing to object to here, the question remains whence the empirical proof will come.

Mandel attacks those who think that the capitalist mode of production stands in the way of a direct empirical verification of the Marxian theory, and who therefore restrict themselves to the abstract analysis of developmental tendencies. In opposition to them, he wants to describe not only the "tendencies" discovered by the abstract analysis but also the development of capitalism as a concrete, historical process, since Marx "categorically and resolutely rejected this quasi-total rift between theoretical analysis and empirical data" (p. 20). In this respect there is certainly little to be found in Marx, unless one sees empirical proof of his theory of capitalism in the fact that the production process, examined in the first volume of *Capital* in isolation from the rest of the system, is represented in the third volume as the process of production as a whole in the concrete forms in which it is experienced. But even in terms of the process as a whole, and despite the many illustrations taken from reality, one cannot speak of quantitative and empirical proof of the validity of Marx's developmental theory, since the data necessary for such a proof are in capitalism neither available nor to be expected.

But, Mandel objects, "In the first volume of *Capital* Marx calculated the mass and rate of surplus value for an English spinning mill, basing himself on exact data (declarations) from a Manchester manufacturer, as they had been given him by Engels . . ." (p. 21 n.). Now it goes without saying that one can represent the process of *surplus-value extraction* on the basis of the data, given in prices, for each capitalist enterprise. These data can also illustrate the degree of exploitation of the workers by the capitalists, and similar data on investments can be used to illustrate the organic composition of various capitals. In none of these cases, however, is any light shed on the developmental tendencies of capital. But this is the point of Marx's theory, not proving that capitalist production is the production of surplus value and is based on the exploitation of labor power—something known long before Marx and felt by every worker in his own life. It is impossible to prove the detrimental consequences of value and surplus value production by empirical statistics as long as capitalism's internal contradictions can be overcome by accelerated accumulation. What Mandel claims to show, namely how "the real history of the past hundred years" can be represented "as the history of the unfolding development of the internal contradictions of this mode of production" (p. 22), comes down, for him as for everyone else, to the concentration and related centralization of capital and to capitalism's susceptibility to crisis. The tendency to crisis arises from the valorization requirements of capital under the conditions of blind market processes. The "regulation" of the capitalist economy by the law of value means that the contradictory movement of capital cannot be continuously known and followed directly in its concrete manifestations. If this could be done, there would be no need for the theory of value to understand the history of the last hundred years.

For Mandel the law of value is not a key to the understanding of capitalist development but a sort of law of nature that must also apply to the precapitalist period. In this connection he cites Engels, who in a letter to Werner Sombart (and also in other places) declared that in precapitalist times, at the "beginning of exchange," commodities were evaluated by reference to their labor-time content, so that value had "a directly real existence." Only in capitalism is labor-time value so thoroughly modified that it can no longer be recognized in prices.[4] Both Engels and Mandel, however, are laboring under a misconception that is not alleviated by Marx's suggestion that the value concept has historical as well as theoretical significance. It makes no difference whatsoever whether commodities were exchanged in precapitalist times in accordance with their labor-time contents or not. In capitalism, in any case, this possibility is excluded, since here we find the *special* commodity labor power that produces a surplus value in addition to its value. The production of value and surplus value obviously had roots in precapitalist exchange, and in this sense these social categories have a historically factual aspect arising from the general necessity of taking the labor time involved in production into account. But labor time and value are not the same thing. Whether or not the exchange of labor-time equivalents takes place, it has nothing to do with the value character of capitalist production, which reflects the social relations of production peculiar to this system.

Capitalism is ruled by value not because production is regulated by labor time but because the exploitation of the workers is accomplished by means of exchange. To say that the value of the commodity labor power is determined like that of every other commodity is to explain the origin of surplus value (that is, extra labor for the capitalists). While the commodity market is constituted by the exchange of the products of the total labor time employed, there is no exchange of labor-time equivalents, since the capitalists have nothing to exchange but only appropriate a portion of the workers' total product. Thus the law of value can have neither a "directly" nor an "indirectly" *real existence* in exchange.

The law of value does not operate in reality as in the theoretical model developed to understand reality. It is based on the dual character of labor as a process both of production and of capital expansion, which appears in the dual character of the commodity, including the commodity labor power, as use value and exchange value. Capitalist production is the production of exchange value, and the use value of commodities is only a means to this end. With the increasing productivity of labor the quantity of goods produced increases while their exchange value falls, the one change counteracting the other. In this way the increasing productivity of labor results in the accumulation of capital, and the opposite movements of use value and exchange value have no visible detrimental effect on capitalist development.

The accumulation of capital thus expresses the growing productivity of labor, while the growth of productive capital in turn improves the productivity of labor. This process indicates that expansion of capital is tied to changes in labor-time relations. More total labor time expressed in products, or more products expressed in labor time, is needed if the goal of capitalist production, the growth of capital, is to be attained. Every capitalist firm attempts to expand production in order to make the maximum profit, and the general result of these attempts is the accelerating accumulation that overcomes the decline of exchange values by the more rapid growth of the mass of use values.

The increase in the productivity of labor implies that the use value—for the capitalists—of the commodity labor power rises more rapidly than its exchange value. In other words, productivity races ahead of wages. Expressed in terms of labor time, this means that a growing part of the total labor time—in any particular enterprise or in the society as a whole—must serve the ends of accumulation, while a decreasing part appears as the exchange value of labor power. In practical terms this implies that less labor must valorize (expand) a greater capital, i.e., that the organic composition of capital changes in favor of constant relative to variable capital. In this sense capital is only continuing the general development of society, insofar as this can be described as the improvement of the forces of production and the increase of production with less labor, although on the basis of a set of social relations compelling accumulation this is occuring at a previously unknown tempo and to a previously unknown extent.

In the change of the organic composition of capital, which is only another expression for the growing productivity of labor, the contradictory movement of exchange value and use value manifests itself as a contradictory movement of accumulation and profit. The increasing use value of labor power, or the rise in the rate of surplus value, confronts the tendency of the rate of profit to fall or the tendency of exchange value to decline relative to use value. But this too is a matter, at first, of mutually counteracting tendencies. So long as the rate of surplus value can be increased more rapidly than the rate of profit falls, these tendencies are factors stimulating accumulation without being distinguishably visible in it.

Aside from the fact that the price mechanism of the market economy, together with the competition-enforced tendency to the formation of an average rate of profit, makes exact observation of changes in the labor-time relations underlying this process impossible, capitalism's economic data are produced from the viewpoint of capital, not from that of Marx's theory of value. These data cannot be translated directly into Marxian categories, although the latter are embodied in market events and find in such phenomena as the fall of prices of production and of the level of the average rate of profit in the course of capitalist accumulation some confirmation of their relevance. Even if it were possible to transform all the available data into the terms of the labor theory of value, however, this would still lead only to the discovery that with sufficient surplus value, capital accumulates, and that with less it does not— a piece of knowledge that can be ascertained directly from the data of the bourgeoisie and of which everyone becomes aware in the course of the actual crisis cycle, without any need of further investigation.

The demonstration that commodity prices must be derived from labor-time values is not the goal of Marx's theory of value but its starting point. The aim of the value theory is rather to gain insight into capital's laws of motion. All price relationships only mirror the exchange relations, not the production relations which underlie them. In a system like the capitalist one, continuous and accelerating accumulation is the prerequisite for progressive development. If the level of exploitation cannot be increased more than the rate of profit falls, the capitalist dynamic turns to stasis, thus destroying the essence of the capitalist mode of production, the production of capital.

The exchange value of labor power is necessarily the equivalent of the labor time, embodied in products, required to produce and reproduce it; this is not contradicted by occasional and partial departures from the norm. The use value of labor power yields profit, the capitalist share of the total labor time, likewise in the form of products. Given a constant number of workers, the process of accumulation would require a continuous increase in their exploitation, which can be accomplished either by lengthening the absolute labor time or by shortening the labor time necessary to secure the workers' existence. If the possibilities of the first method are exhausted in the course of accumulation, those of the second will also be exhausted, since the necessary labor time is not reducible to zero. If exploitation can no longer be increased, accumulation will come to an end. The number of workers must therefore increase absolutely if the process of accumulation is to continue. And of course the accumulating capital requires further growth in the number of workers, while at the same time the potential for exploitation of these workers is progressively diminished.

This narrowing of the basis of accumulation appears in the changing organic composition of capital. While more and more workers are involved in the production process, the number of workers falls relative to the growing mass of capital (which is only another way of saying that less labor is used to produce more commodities). As a result the production of surplus value tends to decline, as the use value of labor power—its production for capital—cannot be extended to fill the total labor time but must stop at the point where the exchange value of labor power would fall below its reproduction requirements. The contradiction of capitalist accumulation, then, lies in the fact that the very process that increases the number of workers exploited, and with this the mass of profit, at the same time calls the continuation of accumulation into question. The increasing productivity of labor decreases the quantity of labor time employed, and therefore the surplus value produced, in relation to the growing mass of capital. This is manifested in the fall in the rate of profit (which is the ratio of surplus value to the total capital).

The rate of accumulation at any moment determines both

the growth of labor power and its displacement by the extension of production and the increase of exploitation. The increase of exploitation, however, is the prerequisite for the extension of production; and so long as the latter does not come up against objective limits, the former has an unobstructed path. These objective limits are set by labor-time relations, specifically by the relation between value and surplus value, between wages and profits. If the surplus value produced by a given quantity of labor power cannot be increased, it becomes impossible to exploit additional labor power, since this would require additional means of production, made available by accumulation.

The complex interrelationship of all these factors should be enough to show that the consequences of the process of capitalist accumulation can only be represented abstractly, by an analogical model based on the fundamental capitalist social relations. Although, according to the logic of the theory of value, the whole development of capitalism is to be explained in terms of the capital-labor relation, the incredible complexity of the real capitalist world forms an impenetrable agglomeration of apparently unconnected factors, which in practice cannot be made use of to provide empirical proof for the abstract theory. (It should be noted that if this is a "deficiency," Marx's theory shares it with bourgeois "economic science," which, despite its exclusive concern with prices, is also compelled to construct models if it is to become comprehensible—a state of affairs in no way altered by either the theoretical or the practical use of the modern apparatus of econometrics.)

It is thus an essential feature of capitalism that the quantitative linking of market phenomena to Marx's basic categories, which Mandel claims he is attempting (p. 21), is quite impossible to achieve. Even apart from this, what data there are for market phenomena are quite inaccurate. Although economic statistics has come a long way, it is still largely a matter of unreliable and inadequate indices that can hardly be taken seriously as a basis for conclusions about the laws of motion of capital. What partial notice has been taken of the development of production prices and commodity prices, of investment and employment, of income and its distribution, of trade relations, etc., provides no understanding of capitalist accumulation that can be correlated with Marx's basic categories.

Capital produces for the market, to which it abandons the regulation of social production within the framework of the production of surplus value. Its representatives can therefore understand neither the allocation of the total labor time necessary for the satisfaction of the social needs peculiar to capitalism nor the valorization difficulties that arise from the accumulation process. Without regard for social consequences, unknowable in any case, each firm seeks to maximize the profit it can realize on the market, and in accordance with this goal it seeks to reduce its costs of production to the minimum. This general effort alters the relation of social surplus value to the mass of the existing capital, influencing the continuation of the accumulation process in a positive or negative way. This influence is negative when the organic composition of capital does not permit an increase in profits sufficient to continue accumulation under the given conditions of production. The slowdown in accumulation itself indicates that not enough surplus value is being produced or, to put the same thing in other words, that too much capital has been accumulated in relation to the going rate of exploitation.

This state of affairs, engendered by changes in labor-time relations, appears from the capitalist viewpoint not as a problem of surplus-value production but as a phenomenon of the market, since the latter is not only viewed as the regulator of the economy but actually is its only regulator. It must be demonstrated in the market whether or not the preceding production was adequate to "social needs," and whether or not this production has yielded a surplus value sufficient for a profitable expansion of capital. Were it possible to explain market processes in terms of the law of value, it could be shown, in the negative case, that the relationship of labor to surplus labor does not meet the valorization requirements of capital, and (since the needs of society in general are defined within the framework set by these valorization requirements) that the discrepancy between surplus value and capital's need to expand affects all economic relations.

Since the market is the actual regulator of the capitalist economy, the changes in labor-time relations occuring in the sphere of production work their way through the system in the form of market processes, although in truth it is the value relations at the point of production that govern the market. The power of the law of value over social production manifests itself above all in economic crisis, which is experienced in the market, not directly as the overaccumulation of capital but in the form of insufficient demand and the overproduction of commodities. The fact that the reality of the law of value is demonstrated in the capitalist crisis indicates that this law had been infringed throughout the previous production period, to the point where the labor-time relations governing the production of surplus value and so the process of capital's self-expansion, together with the allocation of the total social labor time bound up with it, objectively excluded an unlimited continuation of accumulation. Just as the law of value works its way through crisis, the overcoming of crisis is nothing but the restoration—realized in the market but essentially concerning the sphere of production—of labor-time relations yielding a mass of profit adequate for further accumulation.

II

Instead of explaining the crisis cycle and capitalist development as governed by the law of value, Mandel does the reverse: he seeks confirmation of the law of value in the surface appearances of capitalist accumulation. He bases this attempt on the idea that history cannot be reduced to theory. Although there is without a doubt more to the history of capitalism than is covered by the theory of value, the latter is nonetheless necessary if the general developmental trend of the history is to be recognized. According to Mandel, however, all previous Marxist theories of capitalist development led to no useful result, since they illegitimately attempted "to reduce this problem *to a single factor*" (p. 34), while in his view, reference to "the interplay of *all* the laws of motion of capital" is necessary in order to explain a particular result of this development (p. 42). His understanding of this leads Mandel to oppose, to begin with, Rosa Luxemburg,[5] Henryk Grossmann,[6] Nikolai Bukharin,[7] and Rudolf Hilferding,[8] all of whom are supposed to have derived their theories of accumulation exclusively from the reproduction schemas of the second volume of *Capital*, thanks to which their work must be judged a failure.

While this criticism may tell against Luxemburg, Bukharin, and Hilferding, it does not bear on Grossmann, who explained capitalism's tendency to breakdown on the basis of the law of value and accumulation. Although Mandel's rejection of the theories of development based on the reproduction schemas must be seconded, his performance in this regard indicates insufficient knowledge of the material, something that cannot be made up for by appealing to the writings of Roman Rosdolsky.[9] It did not occur to Marx, as Mandel peculiarly maintains it did, to prove by means of the reproduction schemas *"that it is possible* for the capitalist mode of production to exist at all" (p. 25). (It could not have occurred to him simply because no one doubted the existence of capitalism.) According to Mandel Marx saw capitalism's existence as dependent on an equilibrium of the relations of exchange between the production of producer goods and that of consumer goods, although the reality of capitalism is "a dialectical unity of periods of equilibrium and periods of disequilibrium" (p. 26). Thus for Mandel Marx's reproduction schemas represent a one-sided, undialectical view of capitalist reproduction, incapable of yielding insight into capital's laws of motion.

Mandel would like to correct this by proposing an outline—which of course remains unrealized—of "other schemes which incorporate from the start this tendency for the two Departments [of production] and all that corresponds to them to develop unevenly." Of these schemes "Marx's reproduction schemas will only constitute a special case—just as economic equilibrium is only a special case . . ." (p. 27). Now Rosa Luxemburg, unlike Bukharin and Hilferding, had, to be sure, seen Marx's reproduction schemas as implying a perpetual disturbance of equilibrium; but this, according to Mandel, is also wrong, since capitalism is really a dialectical unity of equilibrium and disequilibrium. For Mandel the one arises from the other, both concepts referring to actual states of the economy.

For Marx, in contrast, any equilibrium, whether in the relations between departments of production or in the market generally, was a pure accident, obstructed as a rule by disproportionality. This did not prevent him from starting from the *assumption* of equilibrium in order to expose the essential traits of capitalist production and accumulation. Thus, for example, he used the assumption of an equilibrium of supply and demand in order to lay bare the laws of motion underlying competition. In the same way the reproduction schemas represent assumptions that certainly contradict reality but can nevertheless help in explaining it. The production process is at the same time a process of reproduction that requires circulation for its completion. For the *demonstration* of this process it is sufficient to analyze total social production into two departments in order to represent the conditions of an imaginary frictionless exchange. Although capitalist production is essentially the creation of exchange value, it nevertheless remains tied to use value. While the individual capitalist strives only to enlarge his capital as accumulated surplus value, he can do this only within the framework of social metabolism, which is also a social metabolism operating on use values. In the social context the theoretically conceivable equilibrium of capitalist exchange presupposes an equilibrium of the use values necessary for reproduction.

Just as competition cannot be explained by competition, the circulation process cannot be explained in terms of circulation. The possibility of reproduction, simple or expanded, depends on the circulation of goods containing definite quantities of labor time, represented in the form of values and use values and distributed in a definite way. To show this is the sole task of the reproduction schemas. They are depictions not of the real process of reproduction but of the necessities underlying this process. Since they make themselves felt only through capitalist categories, these necessities are unnoticed, but nevertheless must be respected, behind the backs of the producers if the accumulation of capital is to be possible. The reproduction schemas are a further *illustration* of the working of the law of value in the capitalist production and reproduction process. This means that the process represented abstractly in the schemas is in reality shot through with disproportionalities and crises.

The reproduction schemas constitute neither an equilibrium nor a disequilibrium model but simply the demonstration that accumulation depends on a certain proportionality between the departments of production, which must be established in the market but is determined by the law of value. For Mandel, however, the reproduction schemas are a method of equilibrium analysis to which he wants to add an apparatus of disequilibrium analysis. In this he follows in the footsteps of Rosdolsky, for whom the reproduction schemas on the one hand represent a "heuristic device" but on the other picture a real state of the economy. Thus Rosdolsky writes, for example, that in the capitalist mode of production,

> the proportional development of the various branches of production, and the equilibrium between production and consumption, can only be obtained . . . in the midst of continuous difficulty and disturbances. Naturally, this equilibrium must at least be attained for short periods of time, or else the capitalist system would not function at all. In this sense, however, Marx's schemes of reproduction are in no way a mere abstraction, but a piece of economic reality, although the proportionality of the branches of production postulated by these schemes can only be temporary, and "spring as a continual process from disproportionalIty."[10]

There are thus, according to Rosdolsky and Mandel, periods of equilibrium and periods of disequilibrium, without the first of which capital cannot survive. The contradictions intrinsic to capital thus only appear from time to time, which suggests the question, why they are sometimes there and at other times not. Rosdolsky answers, citing Marx, with the observation that accumulation is broken by "pauses," namely "periods of rest, during which there is a mere quantitative extension . . . on the existing technical basis," for which the reproduction schemas are valid, since they show "the possibility of extended reproduction through the mutual adjustment of the production-goods and consumption-goods industries, and hence also the possibility of the realisation of surplus-value."[11] This of course implies that the capitalist system can only function when accumulation is very slow and that any quickening of the pace must lead to crisis. And Rosdolsky actually explains that with the introduction of technological progress into the reproduction schemas, "the conditions for equilibrium of production turn into conditions for the disturbance of equilibrium,"[12] so that the equilibrium schemas must be supplemented by Marx's theory of crisis and collapse.

Of course, it is correct that capital can accumulate even without technological progress simply by the expansion of production. Only then it reaches the limits of accumulation more quickly, since under such circumstances it has only the resources of absolute surplus value (derived from lengthening the working day) to draw on. But apart from this it is obvious, according to Marx— and also aside from him—that the capitalist mode of production, under the compulsion of accumulation, increases the productive forces to an extent undreamed of earlier by concentrating on relative surplus value and only in this way develops its full potential. It is the acceleration of the rate of accumulation, not its retardation, that keeps capitalism viable by allowing it temporarily to overcome its immanent contradictions, only to bring them forth again at a higher level of accumulation.

Rosdolsky's, and so Mandel's, strange conception of the reproduction schemas can be accounted for by reference to their theory of crisis. Although Mandel is of the opinion that no crisis theory can be derived from equilibrium analysis, the reverse seems possible to him. Both, Rosdolsky and latterly also Mandel,[13] are adherents of an underconsumption theory of crisis, namely the primitive idea that the realization of the surplus value is difficult because the workers cannot buy back their surplus product. Given this idea it is understandable, if incorrect, to hypothesize that capital accumulates best when it accumulates least, and that when accumulation is restricted, it approaches a state of equilibrium in which consumption equals production; for, says Rosdolsky, "as long as accumulation progresses, and a portion of accumulated surplus-value is used to employ additional labor-power, i.e., workers, then these will help to realise the surplus-value created in the previous period of production by spending their wages."[14] And Rosdolsky says this even though he also sees that the surplus value is the part of the social product that is taken from the workers and whose value can therefore only be realized through accumulation and capitalists' consumption. How the realization of the surplus value through accumulation can decrease the gap between production and consumption remains his secret.

Although capitalism's susceptibility to crisis can be neither denied nor affirmed by reference to the reproduction schemas, the latter are still based on the law of value, which represents the contradiction intrinsic to capitalist production and accumulation. The schemas are not needed to prove the contradictory movements of capital, for they are already given in the theory of value. On the basis of this theory it is quite the same if accumulation proceeds quickly or slowly, if capital finds itself in a "period of rest" or in a state of hectic expansion, since under all circumstances an adequate part of the total product must be claimed as surplus value if accumulation is to take place. Otherwise there would be only simple reproduction, which is contrary to the capitalist mode of production and implies a state of crisis. It is of course true that accumulation requires additional labor power and thus additional consumption, without thereby affecting the realization of surplus value. The absolute increase in consumption through accumulation is at the same time its decrease relative to the expanded production.

What Mandel and Rosdolsky have in mind is of course the rapid rise in the organic composition of capital attendant on technological change, which, together with the displacement of workers by machinery, decreases consumption. But since accumulation can take place only with a relative reduction of consumption, this has nothing to do with the problem of the realization of surplus value but is simply the condition that has characterized capitalism from the start and from which it cannot escape without abolishing itself. Thus it is Rosdolsky's and Mandel's underconsumption theory that lead them to project a provisional theoretical assumption, used by Marx to analyze the process of reproduction, onto the real process of circulation. This misunderstanding would have been spared them had they analyzed accumulation with the help of the theory of value.

III

While Marx explained all the fundamental phenomena of capitalism on the basis of the law of value, Mandel takes as his starting point six distinct developmental tendencies, or "basic variables," of the capitalist system. He emphasizes "that up to a certain point *all* the basic variables of this mode of production can partially and periodically perform the role of autonomous variables—naturally not to the point of complete independence but in an interplay constantly articulated through the laws of development of the whole capitalist mode of production" (p. 39). By "basic variables" Mandel means: the organic composition of capital in general and of the two departments (of producer goods and of consumer goods, as in the reproduction schema) in particular; the division of constant capital between fixed and circulating capital, again in general and for the two departments separately; the development of the rate of surplus value; the development of the rate of accumulation; the development of the turnover time of capital; and the exchange relations linking the two departments of production.

The history of capitalism, and its law-governed regularity, can, according to Mandel, "only be explained and understood as a function of the interplay of these six variables" (p. 39). It does not occur to him that with this he is saying that the history and inner regularity of capital can only be understood by reference to the history and inner regularity of capital. The consequences of the production of value and surplus value show themselves, among other ways, in the phenomena of accumulation picked out by Mandel, all of which are governed by the law of value and in accordance with it are manifested by fluctuations in the rate of profit. For Mandel, however, these fluctuations "are only *results* which must themselves be explained by the interplay of the variables" (p. 39). Again, it does not occur to him that he is explaining the profit rate by the rate of profit when he explains the history and inner regularity of capital by its history and inner regularity.

It is in this way that Mandel wishes to bridge the gap between theory and reality. Abstractly considered, all the fundamental phenomena of capital follow from the postulates of the value theory. But in reality, Mandel assumes, the various aspects of capitalist accumulation resulting from the law of value have autonomous functions, at least at times, and independently influence the process as a whole. Therefore special attention must be devoted to these aspects, and their effects must be empirically investigated. This naturally presupposes a criterion by which the empirically determined facts can be made comprehensible and their connections with other such facts exhibited. For capitalism the theory of value is this criterion, as it deals with the basic production relations of this system. The value analysis makes it possible to discover the general tendency of capitalist development from any particular set of changes in Mandel's variables, while the observation of these variables, without application of the value analysis, permits no conclusion about the trend of development but remains the mere description of given circumstances.

Mandel gives a few examples to demonstrate the correctness of his thesis. He shows that the rate of surplus value is at all times a function of the class struggle. "To see it as a mechanical function of the rate of accumulation, . . . is to confuse objective conditions which *can* lead to a particular result . . . with the result itself. Whether or not the rate of surplus-value does in actual fact rise depends among other things on the degree of resistance displayed by the working class to capital's efforts to increase it" (p. 40). "Other things" refers to the influence on the rate of surplus value of the industrial reserve army of the unemployed. Thus for Mandel there are "numerous variations" in the determination of the rate of surplus value, as "can readily be seen from the history of the working class and the labor movement over the past 150 years." But this history also shows that accumulation, despite its interruption by crisis, was a continuous process that presupposed an adequate rate of surplus value and thus confirmed Marx's dictum that "the rate of accumulation is the independent, not the dependent variable; the rate of wages is the dependent, not the independent variable."[15]

Since capitalism still exists today, the "numerous variations" in the determination of surplus value have done it no apparent harm during the last 150 years, in any case not with respect to its developmental tendency. Despite all class struggles the rate of surplus value has remained sufficient for accumulation. As a "partially autonomous basic variable," the development of the rate of surplus value has had no effect. All that Mandel's approach allows him is to follow the history of the class struggle in the context of surplus-value production—a history that points not to the limits of accumulation but to the limits of the class struggle *within* the capitalist system.

It was not only because the opacity of the market economy makes it impossible to follow the quantitative changes in the rate of surplus value and their empirical consequences for the process of accumulation that Marx developed his theory of accumulation on the assumption that the value of labor power is always determined by its costs of production and reproduction. While in reality the wage can lie above or below the value of labor power, it can never—without calling capitalist society itself into question —depress the surplus value below the level required for capital accumulation. This limit of wage formation is not only determined by the supply and demand of labor power, and thus regulated by accumulation, but is also determined by the fact of capitalist control of the means of production. Thus the "numerous variations" in the formation of surplus value produced by the class struggle can be abstracted from in describing the accumulation process without the description thereby losing its realism.

To go into one more of the examples Mandel offers, "the rate of growth of the organic composition of capital" cannot, according to Mandel,

> be regarded simply as a function of technological progress arising from competition. This technical progress does admittedly cause living labor to be replaced by dead labor in order to reduce costs. . . . But . . . constant capital is comprised of two parts: a fixed part . . . and a circulating part. . . . The rapid growth of fixed capital and the rapid increase in the social productivity of labor that results from it, still tell us nothing definite about the tendencies of the development of the organic composition of capital. For if the productivity of labor grows more rapidly in the sector that produces raw materials than in the sector producing consumer goods, then circulating constant capital will become relatively cheaper than variable capital, and this will ultimately lead to a situation in which *the organic composition of capital, despite accelerated technological progress and despite accelerated accumulation of surplus-value in fixed capital, will grow more slowly and not more rapidly than before* (p. 41, translation corrected).

What, really, is Mandel saying here? "Constant capital" includes both fixed and circulating capital. The organic composition of capital, according to Marx, is "the value-composition of capital, in so far as it is determined by its technical composition and mirrors the changes in the latter."[16] It is clear that the cheapening of the raw materials entering into constant capital, accomplished by an increase in the productivity of labor, can alter the value relation between constant and variable capital and thereby slow down the growth of the organic composition. This, however, does not make the organic composition a "partially autonomous variable" but only means that capital can accumulate with a more advantageous organic composition. Since this is the case in general whenever capital is accumulating, Mandel in reality is saying nothing at all.

IV

These meaningless exercises are necessary, according to Mandel, to deal adequately with the "third phase" of capitalist development, or "late capitalism." Only study of the "independent variations of the major variables of Marx's system" (p. 42, translation corrected) will make it possible to understand the successive phases of the history of capitalism.

For Mandel "the capitalist world system is to a significant degree precisely a *function* of the universal validity of the law of unequal and combined development" (p. 23). It is true, of course, that capitalism developed first in certain countries and that this subjected the world economy to an unequal development. The capitalist "international division of labor," together with the concentration and centralization of capital that accompany accumulation, have divided the world into capitalistically developed and underdeveloped countries. But to say this is only to say that the "law of unequal and combined development" signifies no more than the development of capitalism.

Following a survey of the earlier development of world capital, which was consecrated to the blocking of capitalist development in the dominated countries and to the satisfaction of the profit and accumulation needs of the imperialist countries, Mandel concludes that present-day capitalism has seen "a change in the forms of juxtaposition of development and underdevelopment," and that "new differential levels of capital accumulation, productivity, and surplus extraction are emerging, which although not of the same nature, are still more pronounced than those of the 'classical' imperialist epoch" (p. 65). In late capitalism the share of the underdeveloped countries in world trade is declining, so that they are becoming poorer in comparison with the imperialist nations. As Mandel explains it, the imperialist countries depend on the raw materials of the underdeveloped countries and on the decline in their prices, which leads to a relative decline in the *value* of those raw materials. But since, according to Mandel, the share of the underdeveloped countries in world trade is diminishing, this must express imperialism's decreasing dependence on the raw materials of the poor nations, which leads to the drop in their prices. Mandel is however not satisfied with this observation; he wants to bring it into connection with the workings of the law of value on the world market, particularly because Marx "did not analyze it systematically in *Capital*" (p. 71).

On the basis of the logic of Marx's theory, as Mandel enlarges on it, "under the conditions of the capitalist relations of production, uniform prices of production (i.e., a wide-ranging equalization of rates of profit) only emerge within national markets. . . ." And "the law of value would only lead to uniform prices all over the world if there had been a general international equilization of the rate of profit as a result of the complete international mobility of capital and the distribution of capital over all parts of the world . . ." (p. 71). Now Marx's theoretical transformation of values into prices of production concerns not an actual market, whether national or international, but his abstract model of a closed capitalist economy. It represents his solution to the question of how the law of value operates despite the fact that goods are not exchanged in ratios determined by their values. Capitalists confront not values but cost prices, which refer to the unknown labor-time quantities contained in them. The price of production deviates from the value, since it is determined only by the paid labor, thus by the cost price, plus the socially average rate of profit. A further complication—the fact that the cost prices contain already realized profit, so that the price of production of one branch of industry enters into the cost price of another branch—has the result that the determination of price by value is even more obscured.

If we nevertheless want to prove that price is governed by value, this requires a mental experiment reducing the tangle of price relations to the division of total production into value and surplus value. For the analysis of social production as a whole, the different organic compositions, rates of surplus value, and profit rates of the individual capitals and branches of industry are irrelevant. Total production has a definite magnitude that is determined by the total labor time. It has reproduced the value it has consumed and has yielded a certain quantity of surplus value. The distribution of this surplus value among the different capitals can neither enlarge nor diminish it. The level of the rate of profit depends on the ratio of the total surplus value to the total capital and thus depends on the organic composition of the total capital. This in turn is equal to the average of the various organic compositions of the different capitals. If the organic composition of a particular capital is the same as the average composition of the total capital, its profit will be equivalent to its surplus value. Where this is not the case, profit and surplus value must differ from each other.

Since profit governs the movement of capital, capitalist competition effects the migration of capital from branches of industry poor in profit to those rich in profit (whence arises the tendency to the formation of an average rate of profit). This means in practice that some commodities are sold at prices over and others at prices under the value they contain. This in no way alters the determination of the value of every commodity by the labor time socially necessary for its production. But the distribution of the total value effected by the market mechanism, which produces the average profit rate, changes these labor-time values into prices of production. Without going more deeply into the complicated question of the formation of an average profit rate,[17] it should nonetheless be said that in the real world the process depicted in

Marx's model "acts as the prevailing tendency only in a very complicated and approximate manner, as a never ascertainable average of ceaseless fluctuations."[18]

The deviations from value expressed in the production prices cancel each other, so that for the total capital the sum of the production prices equals the total value. The intermixture of prices of production with the cost prices can also not affect this equality of the aggregates. The conceptual separation of the cost prices from the prices of production that have entered into them yields the total cost price, which can then be compared with the total profit. While this is in practice impossible, it is a theoretical possibility, just because the prices of production are constituted of two distinct elements, the cost prices plus the average rate of profit. In any case, however the total surplus value produced by the total social capital may be divided up, it can be dissociated no more from the labor-time relations of surplus-value production than from the process of production governed by labor time in general.

Capital, in Marx's words,

> is in and for itself indifferent to the *particular* nature of every sphere of production. Where it is invested, how it is invested, and to what extent it is transferred from one sphere of production to another or redistributed among the various sphere of production—all this is determined only by the greater ease or difficulty of selling the commodities manufactured.[19]

Through these migrations the average rate of profit is formed behind the backs of the capitalists, as a function of the total production, of which they are ignorant, and of the total surplus value they have produced. Although the law of value does not operate directly on the level of individual commodities, it nevertheless continues to govern production and exchange, if in an indirect manner, through the social character of surplus-value production. Capital experiences its reality in the fall in the average rate of profit, when the social surplus value no longer meets the requirements of accumulation. It is manifested in the fall and rise in the general level of the prices of production due to the increasing or decreasing productivity of labor. It appears, furthermore, on the terrain of the market in the superficial form of the interplay of supply and demand, and capitalist reactions to these market phenomena must, however blindly, reduce this interplay to the value relations underlying it in order to have any effect on the world of appearance.

Although Marx's model of the formation of the general rate of profit corresponds to reality, this is only because every capital must strive to increase its capital in order to maintain it; to this end it must seek to reach at least the average profit rate. The average rate of profit presupposes the existence of different rates of profit, which appear *in practice* as excess profits or as below-average profits. In the course of development the excess profits are lost through competition, and capitals that prove to be unprofitable disappear, only to leave the field to capitals with new differential rates of profit, which in turn succumb to the tendency to their equalization. There are also "pauses" during which the average profit rates stabilize, more or less, and appear to have definite magnitude.

The foregoing should be enough to indicate that the formation of the average rate of profit and production prices are not processes specific to the "national" or the "international" market but are features of the capitalist mode of production as such. For Mandel, however, it is a "fact that no equalization of the rates of profit occurs on the world market, where different national prices of production (average rates of profit) exist side by side and are articulated with one another by means of the world market in a particular manner..." (p. 351, translation corrected). These prices of production, uniform only within "national" markets, represent, according to Mandel, the "specific effect of the law of value on the international level," as "it is based on nationally differentiated levels of the productivity or intensity of labor...,nationally differentiated organic compositions of capital, nationally differentiated rates of surplus-value, and so on" (p. 71).

Since the capitalist market is the world market, it is incomprehensible why the formation of the average rate of profit should call a halt at national borders, with every nation forming its own average rate of profit. The fact that the national compositions of capital, their rates of exploitation, etc., are different in no way alters the fact that the surplus value of world production is divided up through world market relations exactly like that of the national economy, namely by way of the competitively determined formation of prices, which are ultimately regulated by the unknown quantity of total surplus value produced. And exactly as in the national framework it is possible for a while to avoid a low or falling average rate of profit by a monopolistic withdrawal from competition, it is also possible in the international context to take steps against the determination of prices by competition by bailing out of international competition. Both cases, however, involve measures that in themselves indicate the tendency to formation of an international average rate of profit.

In his critique of the classical theory of value, Marx asked how it is possible to make profits despite the exchange of equal values. He answered this question by pointing to the double character of labor power as having at once use value and exchange value. Given this he could show that profit arises not from circulation or trade but from production on the basis of capitalist relations of production. This must hold for the world market as well. The profits won here must objectively be derived from labor-time relations. Just as in the "national" framework profit arises from surplus value, the profit of world trade can only arise from the surplus value of world production. But how is it possible, despite the lower productivity of labor in the capitalistically underdeveloped countries, to extract from them the same or a larger surplus value than is created in the capitalistically developed countries, with their higher productivity of labor?

The answer is that in this case more labor is exchanged for less, the developed country handing over a smaller value for a greater one from the underdeveloped nation. This is Mandel's explanation also, but he writes as though the unequal exchange operates directly on the level of labor time. In reality, of course, it can only be accomplished by the detour of the market and is thereby subordinated to international competition and the formation of an international average rate of profit. The average rate of profit, into which all profits enter, regulates the prices of production formed by competition. In this way the total surplus value is distributed without regard for particular spheres of production in the "national" framework or within the world economy, not in the proportions in which it has been produced by the individual capitals but in proportions determined by the existence and accumulation of capital as a whole. Just because the tendency to the formation of an average rate of profit operates on the world market, the unequal distribution of surplus value, or unequal exchange, arises *within* each national economy *and* on the global level.

According to Mandel the law of value is modified on the world market because of the difference in commodity values resulting from the differential productivity of labor. Countries with lower labor productivity yield other commodity values and other average rates of profit than countries with higher labor productivity and allow the latter to win surplus profits in trade with the former. This particular form of exploitation, to follow Mandel, is based on the difference in commodity values, as a result of which the product of a day's work in a developed nation "is exchanged for the product of more than a day's work in an underdeveloped country" (p. 72). But since the productivity is different in the two countries, it is obvious that if a working day of one were exchanged against a working day of the other, the less productive country would exploit the more productive. If capital penetrates capitalistically backward countries, then products of lower labor productivity will be exchanged for products of higher labor productivity, which can only mean that more living labor must be given up in exchange for less living labor, if the exchange is to be equitable to both parties. But such an exchange does not mean that the developed country has exploited the underdeveloped one.

It means only that relative surplus value is not the same as absolute surplus value, since it permits the production of a greater surplus value with less direct labor time. This higher surplus value is precipitated in the prices of production and determines the labor-time equivalents, expressed in absolute surplus value, against which they must be exchanged. But since the productivity of the developed countries is many times greater than that of the underdeveloped countries, the former can use the channels of trade to crush any attempt of the latter to compete against them, which can be seen in the destruction of the minor industries and artisanry existing in the underdeveloped world. Even this does not imply exploitation of the underdeveloped by the developed countries but heightened exploitation within the developed countries, whose high rates of surplus value allow their capitalists to push aside the competition of the underdeveloped countries, or prevent it from arising, and thus create additional markets for themselves.

Since the determination of value by *socially necessary* labor time operates on the world market, the underdeveloped countries must, when they exchange with the developed countries, give more use value for less exchange value, more products for fewer products, or more labor time for less labor time. The commodities of the countries with a lower productiviy of labor contain labor time in excess of that socially necessary, but which nonetheless enters into exchange. To explain unequal commodity exchange, therefore, does not require reference to "national commodity values, average rates of profit, and prices of production," since on the basis of the law of value no other sort of exchange can take place.

Because the backward countries possessed no industries, their exchange with each other and with the industrial nations of the West was limited from the start to foodstuffs and raw materials. The entrance of developed industry into the underdeveloped countries excluded for the latter the development of their own industries and thus preserved their precapitalist social relations. The competition between capitalist nations is pursued by reducing production costs, so that they are all interested in cheap raw materials and foodstuffs. Although agricultural productivity in the backward countries is also lower than in the capitalist countries, the "price scissors" between finished goods and raw materials still makes it profitable for the capitalist countries to obtain a large part of the food and raw material they need from their colonies or semicolonies. Insofar as the imported raw materials and foodstuffs lower the developed countries' costs of production, this situation contributes to the accumulation of capital.

Since the use-value aspect of production cannot be ignored, capital will go to the backward countries for foodstuffs and raw materials even when they are more expensive than those produced in its own country. With the growth of industry agricultural production declines, and there are countries that could not exist without imports of raw materials and food. Since capitalist demand can raise the prices for these commodities, the extension of the world market appears also as a process of colonization pursued in order to subject price formation to monopolistic control. The colonizing nations seek not only to protect their own export markets from international competition, but also to accommodate the formation of the prices of colonial export goods to their own accumulation requirements. Thus they must on the one hand hinder the industrial development of the colonies and on the other seek to make the monopolistic exchange as profitable as possible by cheapening the goods produced in the colonies.

They thus interfere in the capitalist market mechanism in order to keep a portion of the total surplus value out of competition. But the surplus value extracted from the colonies enters into the profit rates of the imperialistic countries and there becomes a factor in the formation of the average rate of profit. It is only by this detour through the economic relations of the developed countries that the underdeveloped lands are drawn into the world market and thereby into capitalist competition. This is already apparent in the fact that the greater part of production in the underdeveloped countries was done outside of the capitalist system and was directly consumed. This subsistence economy had little to do with the market and money economy. But where no surplus value is produced, we cannot speak of the formation of an average rate of profit. These countries are only slowly drawn by imperialism into the machinery of the world market; but insofar as they are, they also submit to the conditions of the development of capital as a whole and to capitalist competition.

Apart from the imperialist countries' plundering of the colonies, accomplished by simple robbery, the proceeds of which entered into capitalist accumulation, the transfer of value, bewailed by Mandel, from the colonies to the capitalist countries was of necessity very limited due to the low productivity of labor prevailing in the colonies. Capital sought to remedy this by introducing capitalistic methods of production, developing the plantation economy, introducing wage labor, and modernizing the extraction of raw materials, all of which required the export of capital to the colonies. But such enterprises remained enclaves within the colonial economy as a whole and thereby demonstrated that it was not worth capital's while to carry out a thorough capitalization of its colonial possessions, and that investments in one's own or other capitalist countries were more profitable. This fact also shows that the surplus value available for capitalization was insufficient to extend accumulation beyond the limits reached at any particular time.

On the other hand, "small animals also produce manure," as the proverb says, and the lower rate of exploitation in the backward countries did not prevent capital from exploiting them too. While this reduced the limited accumulation possibilities in the dominant countries, it also made possible a slowing of the decline of the rate of profit by raising the productivity of the world economy. Since the fall in the rate of profit is a consequence of the higher organic composition of capital, the inclusion in the world market of capitals with lower organic compositions arrests this fall. In practical terms this means that insofar as surplus value can be transferred from spheres of production with lower organic compositions to those with higher compositions, the composition of the total capital will allow for a more favorable rate of profit. Whether this better rate will be sufficient to valorize the total capital cannot be calculated but can be seen in the actual accumulation of capital. A fall in the rate of accumulation shows that the organic composition of the total capital—despite the different compositions of the capitals entering into it—permits only a rate of profit unfavorable to further accumulation. This situation can only be remedied, in a contradictory way, by a further rise in the organic composition of capital—or, in other words, by a further rise in the productivity of labor—not only in the developed but also in the underdeveloped countries, and also by the destruction of capital within the world economy as a whole, which reduces the total capital within which the given mass of surplus value is distributed. Although neither of these processes can be consciously organized, they are nonetheless carried out by means of the peaceful and military competition between individual capitals and between capitalist nations. In this sense the law of value governs the capitalist world economy, since the extension of the economy depends on what happens in the spheres of production and this, in turn, on the relation of value to surplus value and of surplus value to the total capital.

Capital thus has a direct interest in the enlargement of the total surplus value; at the same time, this need can only be satisfied through the expansion of the individual capitals. Each capital strives for the lowest cost price and the highest profit, without concern for the social consequences on the national or the international scale. That the accumulation of one capital hinders that of another, or that the expansion of one capitalist nation limits that of another, in no way alters the fact that capital, *in the sense of capital as a whole*, nevertheless continues to develop with an increasing productivity of labor. The expansion of capital confirms the existence of the average rate of profit through which the capitalist economy reproduces itself in conformity to its needs by means of the market mechanism; but at the same time, it increasingly destroys the necessary prerequisites of this process.

While capital was able to accelerate its accumulation somewhat by means of the surplus value extracted from the backward countries, and while this additional surplus value was made possible by the formation of prices favorable to the industrial nations, this was only at the cost of a slow destruction of this already meager source of surplus value. To keep the source flowing it would be necessary to raise the productivity of labor in the backward countries through their industrialization, which would require a corresponding restriction of accumulation in the developed countries. But this contradicts the principle of capitalism. The falling profit rate of the countries with a higher organic composition goes hand in hand with falling profits in the countries with a lower organic composition. But what in the developed countries leads to the relative stagnation of capital, in the underdeveloped nations induces a runaway process of absolute pauperization.

Although this pauperization is a fact, this does not mean that there is a simultaneous enrichment of the capitalist nations, as Mandel wishes us to believe. Without any proof at his disposal, he maintains that "the average rate of surplus-value in the colonies often exceeds that of the metropolitan countries, especially since the production of *absolute* surplus-value in colonial territories can be extended beyond the limits encountered in metropolitan countries," and since as a result of a gigantic industrial reserve army, "the value of labor-power in the colonies falls, in the long run, not only relatively, but even absolutely" (pp. 343-44, translation corrected). Now, the value of labor power in the backward countries has for a long time been so low that a "long-run fall" is excluded, since this would lead to the extinction of the work force, and the productivity of labor is so limited that even lengthening the working day would not enlarge the *absolute* surplus value. The lengthening of the working day in itself yields no additional surplus value when the physical limit of exploitation has already been reached. Without a doubt great extra profits are made in the countries of the "Third World," but they derive from the extraction of particular raw materials that enter into the production of the capitalist nations and whose value is realized in them. But to conclude from these particular sources of profit that there is a higher "average rate of surplus value in the colonies" is so obviously wrong that there is no need to deplore the absence of relevant data.

The idea that the transfer of surplus value from the underdeveloped to the capitalist countries, achieved by unequal exchange, is destined to disappear and cannot be maintained by the increase of *absolute* surplus value also occurs to Mandel, who perceives this as a change in the form of imperialist exploitation. This transformation has two aspects:

> in the first place the share of colonial surplus profits has undergone a decline relative to the ttansfer of value via "unequal exchange;" in the second place, the international division of labor is slowly moving towards the exchange of light industrial goods for machines, equipment, and vehicles, in addition to the "classical" unequal exchange of foodstuffs and raw materials for industrial consumer goods (p. 368).

But since the transfer of value is not tied to a particular form of material production, "but to a difference in the respective levels of capital accumulation, labor productivity, and the rate of surplus-value," only the form of underdevelopment is changing and not its content, and "the sources of metropolitan imperialist exploitation of the semi-colonies today flow more abundantly than ever" (p. 368).

This change of form means that many "Third World" countries are beginning to industrialize, to produce additional surplus value, and to have more to exchange than just foodstuffs and raw materials, if also less of the latter. Since this changes the compositions of their capitals, their condition comes somewhat closer to that of the developed countries. To the extent that this happens, however, it influences the transfer of value to the imperialist countries, since a growing part of the surplus value must be capitalized, which had not previously been the case. Through the simultaneous diminution of the production of raw materials and foodstuffs, the "unequal exchange" is reduced by way of price formation under conditions of international competition and leads the developed countries to export capital to the underdeveloped countries in order to share in their surplus value. That this directly invested surplus value is still of relatively little importance can be seen in the fact that the great mass of capital exports still goes to the capitalistically developed countries.

According to Mandel, the head start made by the imperialist nations cannot be overcome, so that despite the slow industrialization of the "Third World" countries, the difference between the rates of surplus value in the two groups remains, which makes it possible for imperialism to continue to extract surplus value, in even greater amounts, from the backward countries and to accumulate at their expense. "Only if there were a *general homogenization* of capitalist production on a world scale," he writes, "would the sources of surplus-profit dry up" (p. 368). Since this "general homogenization," the total worldwide mobility of capital and labor, is not really conceivable, Mandel comes to the conclusion that capitalism cannot eliminate its combination of development and underdevelopment, and with it the exploitation of the "Third World." The only solution to this dilemma remains a social revolution that would put an end to the domination of the capitalist world market by socializing the means of production. In this way Mandel believes he has used the theory of value to explain both imperialism and the social revolutions expectable in the underdeveloped countries.

Since value relations are concealed behind price relations, unequal exchange is the normal case both nationally and internationally, but must have different effects due to the differences between the countries included in the world market. These differences with respect to commodity values and rates of surplus value lead, for Mandel, to nationally differentiated average rates of profit and prices of production, which first make unequal exchange possible. But Mandel's abstraction from the world market leads him to no conclusion that he could not have drawn without abstracting from it. Not only is Mandel's explanation of unequal exchange and value transfer incorrect, even if it were correct it would be superfluous. In every country the capitalists deal only with cost prices and market prices, which they experience as givens. The difference between these prices is the profit. The cost price consists of what the capitalist must pay his workers plus the cost of the means of production and raw materials they use. The price of production consists of these outlays plus the profit won on the market. It is all the same to the capitalists whether they make this profit at home or on the world market. This holds both for the capitalists in the underdeveloped and for those in the developed countries. The difference between them consists in the fact that for one the cost price includes less for means of production and more in wages, while for the other these proportions are reversed. But a higher rate of profit with a lower organic composition may yield a lower mass of surplus value than the lower profit that goes with a high organic composition. The productivity of capitals of higher organic composition is greater by far than that of capitals of lower composition, so that the loss of value that results for the total capital from the relative decrease in living labor is compensated for. This is the point of accumulation and the difference between developed and underdeveloped countries. Surplus value grows with accumulation, while it stagnates without accumulation and so makes extended reproduction impossible. As a result, the difference between countries with a higher and those with a lower organic composition must, as the former accumulate, continually increase to the disadvantage of the latter—so long, that is, as accumulation leads to an increase in the mass of profit more rapid than the fall in the profit rate due to the increase in the organic composition of capital.

The increasing mass of profit is embodied in products that individually contain less value and less surplus value, but the increased quantity of which compensates for this decline in individual value. The commodity produced with a higher productivity is cheaper than that requiring a great expenditure of labor. This cheapening is manifested in falling prices of production, something which at first sight appears to confirm Mandel's conception of the different average profit rates and prices of production. This cheapening, however, extends more or less to all commodities. Since foodstuffs and raw materials are produced not only in the colonies and semicolonies but also in the developed countries, the world market price of these products is affected by the general rise in productivity. In connection with the world's requirements for these products, their prices are determined not by national value relations but by the relationship between world supply and world demand. Thus the world market price for these products rises as soon as the demand for them rises, as for instance in a period of rapid accumulation in the capitalist countries or in the case of war. On the other hand, the world market price falls with capitalist stagnation and any reduction of production. The prices of the products of the "Third World" are formed in a context determined by the movement of the total capital on the global level.

The production prices of products of the underdeveloped countries are constituted by their cost prices and the profit determined by world market conditions. As far as their own production goes, their rates of profit result neither from the organic composition of their own capitals nor from those of the developed countries but from the supply-and-demand relations of the world market. They are thus subordinate to the movements of the total capital, which determine the formation of the average rate of profit and its magnitude. In other words, because the world market exists there can be no national average profit rates and no price relations reflecting national value relations. With respect to production in general, price formation in the underdeveloped countries is from the start determined by that in the developed nations, since the absence of modern industry rules out any ability to compete. Thus they must restrict themselves to the production of raw materials and foodstuffs in order to realize their profits in the prices of production dictated by the world market.

The introduction of industry into the underdeveloped countries cannot eliminate unequal exchange so long as the productivity in these countries is lower than the worldwide average socially necessary labor time. This disadvantage is to an extent offset by the low valuation of labor power, which at the same time hinders their further development. Of course, the lack of capital can be somewhat mitigated by investments from the developed countries. However, since most of the profits on these investments flow back to the capital-exporting countries, this has only a minor influence on the accumulation process in the underdeveloped countries. Since the export of capital is determined by profitability, it goes to those industries and countries that appear to yield the greatest return, and not only from some developed countries to others of higher productivity but also *from* the countries with lower productivity into those with a higher one. Surplus value flows not just under pressure but also freely from the backward to the developed countries. From this, however, it cannot be concluded that the exploitation of underdeveloped countries is what keeps the imperialist nations on their feet.

The end of colonialism was brought about not only by the revolutionary nationalist movements growing out of impoverishment but also by the dwindling profitability of the colonies, which made it easier for their possessors to give them up. It was also influenced by the appearance of new imperialist powers, in the world market or outside of the monopolistically controlled world market, with their own claims on the "Third World," either in the form of their own imperialistic conquests or in that of neocolonialism, which understood how to combine national self-determination with economic imperialist control. This process, which has already involved two world wars and many local wars, has not yet come to an end and cannot do so, as this would presuppose the abolition of competition and thus that of the capitalist relations of production. But all these endeavors reflect the desire to break the fetters of a low productivity of labor. The greatest efforts of both the bourgeoisie and the state-capitalist authorities are dedicated to economic development, i.e., to the increase of surplus value—an effort that is not completely without success.

It is the desire for additional surplus value that leads to the attempt to hasten the palpable though slow capitalization of the backward countries, of which even Mandel is aware. And it is this same creeping capitalization that gives the revolutionary nationalist movement its incentive to achieve the same goal by political methods that transcend the limited framework of private capitalist initiative. Whether the combination of these methods will suffice to squeeze out of the workers the mass of surplus value necessary for a simultaneous expansion and geographical extension of capital cannot be theoretically determined, although it is of decisive importance for the near future. What is evident from all efforts, however, is the continuing force of the tendency, inherent in capitalist production, of the rate of profit to fall, which leads to frantic exertions to raise the productivity of labor throughout the world.

Even Mandel realizes that the exploitation of the "Third World" cannot go on forever but must eventually come to an end. What is so remarkable about Mandel's economic theory is precisely that it is couched in such terms that everything and nothing can be drawn from it, which makes it easy for Mandel to evade any embarrassing difficulty. Through his principled rejection of any "monocausal" explanation of capitalist development he is in a position to appropriate all existing theories and use them for his own purposes; at the same time, by means of the "monocausal" theory of value he can demonstrate their inadequacy. Hardly has he done this than he rearranges the insights won with the help of the theory of value in a series of relatively independent variables in order to dispute the "monocausal" account of the course of history by reference to one or another of the developmental tendencies that follow from the value theory. Thus he finally succeeds, in his own estimation, in showing the inadequacy of bourgeois *and* all Marxist theories, and so in presenting himself as the man who, because of his correct understanding of Marxism, has for the first time explained "late capitalism" on the basis of the law of value.

V

We can agree with Mandel on one thing: it is certainly true that capital exploits the world and nevertheless has no future.

However, according to Mandel, the abolition of the capitalist system cannot be deduced from the capitalist relations of production alone, for there is also the problem of the *realization* of surplus value to consider. In this way Mandel adheres to two distinct theories of crisis at once: the overaccumulation theory, which is based on the relations of production, and the overproduction theory, which is based on the difficulties of realizing surplus value due to an insufficient demand for consumer goods. Now, the overaccumulation theory includes the overproduction theory, since the difficulties of realization arise directly from an insufficient accumulation of capital. The realization-problem theory, in contrast, cannot include the overaccumulation approach, as it implies a barrier to the appearance of this state of affairs.

The disproportionality between production and consumption is a *constant* feature of the system, being no more or less than surplus-value production itself, while overaccumulation, as a discrepancy between exploitation and the organic composition of capital, appears only from time to time. The rising organic composition of capital presupposes a growing disproportionality between social production and consumption, and by itself—that is to say, by accumulation—overcomes the realization problem. This problem only arises again with the suspension of accumulation, appearing then as insufficient demand, including the demand for consumer goods. "We mean by the concept of overaccumulation," writes Mandel, "a situation in which a portion of the accumulated capital can only be invested at an inadequate *rate of profit* . . ." (p. 109, translation corrected). Since it is not invested under these circumstances, the interruption of accumulation appears on the market as a lack of demand for producer goods and thus for consumer goods, in other words, as a crisis of overproduction. This is how it appears to Mandel, too, but he would nevertheless like to adhere "in the long-run" to the idea of overaccumulation in order to prove the necessary decline of capitalism. However, he does not want to do this in so "mechanical" a way as, for instance, Grossmann did; overaccumulation is to be shown to follow not from the assumption of a constantly rising organic composition of capital but from the continuous automatization of production and the displacement of living labor. Against Grossmann Mandel argues that the rise in the organic composition of capital can always be counter-acted by equivalent depreciation of capital. It does not occur to him that by the same logic, automatization could also be halted as soon as it affects profits. He is also not aware that he is only repeating Grossmann, although in different words. Continuous automatization is of course identical with a continuous growth of the organic composition of capital. But hardly has Mandel the "dialectician" pronounced his withering judgement on Grossmann the "mechanist" than he immediately takes it back, with the further insight that capital cannot automate for long without destroying itself.

Slippery as eels, the contradictions in Mandel's writing cannot easily be turned against him, since he calls attention to them himself, perhaps hoping in this way to disarm all possible adversaries. Thus he readily concedes "that the difficulty of simultaneously realizing surplus-value and raising the rate of surplus-value, is anchored in the capitalist mode of production as such . . ." (p. 272). But anchors can be raised and the voyage can continue as soon as one of the variables declares its independence. On the one hand, capital accumulates, according to Mandel, at the expense of the underdeveloped countries; on the other, in the course of this process "capital itself creates an insuperable limit to its own extension" (p. 85). Since meanwhile the problem of surplus profits, national and international,

> can be reduced to the question of the transfer of value or of surplus-value, there is no limit whatsoever in purely economic terms to this *process of the growth of capital accumulation at the expense of other capitals, the extension of capital through the combination of accumulation and devaluation of capitals, through the dialectical unity and contradiction of competition and concentration.* Limits to the process of capitalist growth are—from a purely economic point of view—in this sense always merely temporary, because while they proceed out of the very conditions of a difference in the level of productivity, they can reverse these conditions (p. 104, translation corrected).

In short, it is like this but also different; it depends entirely on with whomever Mandel is arguing at the moment.

It would take a new book to trace Mandel's inanities in detail if one wanted to show that his work represents not dialectics but ordinary inconsistencies. Perceptive readers of his book will see this for themselves. We therefore prefer to turn—after a look at Mandel's apologetic renovation of Lenin's theory of imperialism —to his analysis of "late capitalism." But since according to Mandel the current phase of capitalism must be explained not only theoretically but also in terms of history, we must take another look at the past.

Mandel distinguishes three main phases of capitalist development. "The early capitalist era of free competition" was "characterized by a relative international immobility of capital . . . above all because there were not as yet any critical limits to the expansion of capital accumulation on the home market . . ." (pp. 312-13). Then followed "the classical era of imperialism," in which "the concentration of capital became increasingly international in character" (p. 313). This was replaced by "late capitalism," in which "the multinational company becomes the determinant organizational form of big capital" (p. 316). In this we see "that contemporary forces of production are bursting through the framework of the nation state, for the minimum threshold of profitability . . . involves output series commensurate with the markets of several countries" (p. 316).

Now, it is a fact that the growth of the productive forces coincided from the start with the formation of the world market, which led to imperialism and the international concentration of capital as an expression of imperialist competition. According to Mandel, abstractly put, "in the final analysis the manifestations of imperialism are to be explained by the *lack of homogeneity* of the capitalist world economy" (p. 84). From this it should follow that the increasing homogenization of the world economy must weaken imperialism. But, Mandel says, this is simply not possible because "the accumulation of capital itself produces development and underdevelopment as mutually determining moments of the uneven and combined movement of capital" (p. 85).

According to Hilferding and Lenin, the competition-induced concentration and centralization of capital lead to an organized capitalism tending toward a single world trust—a development that can be prevented only by a prior proletarian revolution. Mandel still accepts this theory today and concludes from it "that en route to the 'single world trust,' the postponement of the proletarian revolution in the imperialist metropolitan countries has rendered possible, if not actually probable, the simplification of the pattern of multiple imperialist powers into three 'super powers'" (p. 334, translation corrected). In opposition to Kautsky, the originator of this idea, Mandel sees in this development not a weakening but "an *intensification* in the age of late capitalism of all the contradictions inherent in imperialism" (p. 334), since "the main tendency of the intensifying competitive struggle today is not for big capital to merge on a world scale but for several imperialist formations to harden in their mutual antagonism" (p. 338). Thus the "determinant organizational form of big capital" in "late capitalism" is in the final analysis only a secondary tendency, which is in turn overruled by the "main tendency."

But the secondary tendency, the international centralization of capital, must according to Mandel be understood as "capital's attempt to break through the historical barriers of the nation-state, just as national (and tomorrow perhaps supra-national) economic programming represents an attempt partially to overcome the barriers of private ownership and private appropriation for the further development of the forces of production" (p. 342). The true character of "late capitalism" here revealed has not been previously recognized either on the bourgeois or on the Marxist side. With respect to the latter, this lack is due to previous Marxists' neglect of "the interlinkage between 'organized capitalism' and generalized commodity production" (p. 523). Thus they have failed to comprehend "the famous formula applied to joint-stock companies by Marx in *Capital*" that describes them as representing "the abolition of the capitalist mode of production within the capitalist mode of production itself" (p. 532). Since Marx wrote this more than a hundred years ago, it seems that without knowing it, we have been in the era of late capitalism for a very long time. The appearance of joint-stock companies, which even preceded capitalism, was described by Marx as "private production without the control of private property," as capitalist production that is subjected to collective control. Far from seeing in this an "organizing" element of capitalism, Marx saw this type of capital as leading to the system's further disorganization and collapse.

> It establishes monopoly in certain spheres and thereby requires state interference. It reproduces a new financial aristocracy, a new variety of parasites in the shape of promoters, speculators, and purely nominal directors; a whole system of swindling and cheating by means of corporation promotion, stock issuance, and stock speculation.[20]

Marx was clearly not concerned here with the question later raised by Engels, whether there was not also a positive side to the creation of joint-stock companies, since they can be seen also as a sort of "reaction of the productive forces, in their mighty upgrowth, against their character as capital."[21] Marx viewed the stock companies rather as one more sign of the contradictions developing within capitalism, which engender both its rise and its decline. The material forces of production that can develop in capitalism are governed and limited by its accumulation; they cannot become independent of it and turn against their character as capital. The only force of production that can do this is the working class. It is therefore nonsense to suppose that capital is attempting to break through the barriers of the nation-state and private property for the further development of the productive forces. On the contrary, its "internationalism" exclusively serves the national capitals and private property, with or without private control.

The world market is also a capital market, and it goes without saying that with capitalist expansion, national firms become international ones. Two world wars have in addition demonstrated that the fronts on which imperialist competition is fought out are structured not by nation-states but by supranational imperialist combines. The world economy makes every crisis a world crisis and every war a world war. Even where war remains localized as a result of the momentarily superior strength of a particular state or combination of states, it nevertheless involves the whole world economy. Supranational combinations of capitalist powers have existed for a long time on the level of power politics as well as on the economic level, and they did not wait for the advent of "late capitalism."

The Second World War created favorable conditions not only

for an accelerating accumulation but, in connection with this, for the multinational growth of large corporations. The adaptation of the market to growing production and the new capital relations made the realization of profits easier, and the whole process led to an unequally distributed but general increase in profit production. This process, which can be understood as the internationalization of capital and of production, is, however, like every previous phase of capitalist development, limited in its evolution. It can collapse with any new world crisis or even with a decline in the rate of accumulation. Just as the world market fell apart at an earlier time as a result of sharpening competition, multinational capitalism too can come to an end in new competitive conflicts. But even at this point the increasing internationalization of capital cannot be construed as a growing susceptibility to organization but only as the present-day form of the disorganized capitalist competition that results from value and surplus-value relations. Now as before, it is the law of value that defines the possible organizational forms of capital, and therefore also the impossibility of an "organized capitalism."

The multinational corporations have not violated the national, and therefore imperialist, character of capital. Despite all their complex interrelations, the control of these corporations lies in the hands of definite national capitals, often directly connected with the national state, and the profits they make flow back to the nations from which the corporations start out. Stateless multinational concerns, as a true internationalization of capitalist production, may be a dream of the capitalists; this dream has no chance to become reality in the context of capital accumulation. Deeply influenced by the "multinational form of big capital" and alarmed by the "apparent" formation of three big imperialist powers grappling for control of the world economy, Mandel first evokes the gruesome perspectives this opens up, only to end with the more sober statement that "the survival of the national state is inseparable from capitalist or imperialist competition . . ." (p. 589, translation corrected).

But the "interlinkage between 'organized capitalism' and generalized commodity production" is for Mandel at once an international and a national phenomenon. On the national level it takes the form of state intervention in the economic mechanism to aid capitalist accumulation. Here it is to Mandel's advantage that he distinguishes the production of profit from its realization, since state intervention enlarges production by way of the realization of surplus value. From this it follows for Mandel that capital is attempting to break through the limits set to capitalist production by private property. This is accomplished by means of the arms industry and the war economy. However,

> in the long run an arms economy is functional for the accumulation of capital only if it absorbs surplus capitals without also deflecting into the armaments industry capitals needed for the extended reproduction of Departments I and II [of the reproduction schemas]. An arms and war economy carried beyond this point increasingly annihilates the material conditions for extended reproduction and thus in the long term hampers the accumulation of capital instead of promoting it (p. 168).

In other words, armaments are good for accumulation but bad when overdone. If the rate of accumulation falls despite the arms industry, this does not contradict Mandel's theory, for it only indicates that arms production has been pushed too far.

To demonstrate his theory Mandel offers a reproduction schema of his own, with three departments, including one for the arms industry (along with those for producer and consumer goods) whose production does not enter into the material process of reproduction but nevertheless, as a part of total production, promotes accumulation. We can easily ignore these little games, as they only say in numbers what has already been said in words. All three departments in Mandel's schema produce commodities and therefore surplus value. Armaments are financed out of surplus value, "which serves neither for the maintenance of the capitalist class nor for that of the working class, and in which capital finds new opportunities for creating and realizing surplus-value" (p. 282, translation amended).

It is necessary at this point to examine Mandel's conception of the law of value. For him "it has the function of regulating, through the exchange of medium-term equivalent quantities of labor, the distribution of the economic resources at the disposal of society into the various spheres of production, according to the fluctuations of socially effective demand, i.e., according to the structure of consumption" (p. 70). It is thus an equilibrium mechanism, which brings production and consumption into harmony. Accordingly, Mandel maintains, following Rosdolsky and citing Marx, that "the production of constant capital never occurs for its own sake but only because more of it is needed in the spheres of production whose products enter individual consumption" (p. 279 n.). Since the rising organic composition of capital means that always relatively fewer workers are newly hired, social consumption cannot increase sufficiently to absorb all the commodities produced for consumption. Thus the growing organic composition of capital engenders the realization problem, although it is not easy to see how the law of value, which is supposedly adjusting production to consumption, can permit such a growth of the organic composition of capital. When the constant capital can only grow provided that it is invested in the spheres of production serving consumption, then not the valorization of capital but social consumption is governing production. Still, there is the quotation from Marx—only it has been incorrectly understood.

VI

To produce capital the capitalist must have commodities produced that have exchange value for him and use value for others. The use value is realized in consumption. Just as the capitalist productively consumes the use value of labor power, the resulting commodities enter in one form or another into social consumption and there disappear. What does not disappear is the part of the surplus value, or surplus product, which serves as constant capital in the expanded reproduction of the relations of exploitation.

For capital to be accumulated, use values must be produced and find a corresponding demand on the part of those whom Mandel calls the "final consumers." It should not be concluded from this, however, that the "final consumer" actually determines the movement of capital. In other words, the "final consumer" has nothing to do with the "too slowly growing sum of wages for consumer goods," as Mandel imagines. For each capitalist, regardless of the kind of goods he produces, the exchange value of his workers is a cost price that he attempts to keep as far as possible below its use value. But for the capitalists producing consumer goods, all workers are also consumers to whose demand they are responding. The higher the wages paid to other capitalists' workers, and the lower those he pays his own employees, the better can his profit be realized on the market. But as this holds for every capitalist, the workers as a class receive only their exchange value, which is the equivalent of a smaller or greater quantity of commodities, while the capitalists receive the share of production, also represented in products, that corresponds to surplus value, which certainly also requires a "final consumer" but cannot find him in the working class. The realization of surplus value thus has nothing to do with working-class consumers but must be accomplished by capital itself.

If the workers produced no surplus value, there would be no capitalist economy; if the capitalists ate up the entire surplus value, we would indeed have capitalist production, but not the production of capital. The latter presupposes the accumulation of a portion of the surplus value. This portion must from the start have the form of new means of production, even if they are used in turn to produce commodities entering into consumption. Capital produces in principle neither means of production for the production of means of production nor means of production for the production of consumer goods. Both are only means to the end of transforming a given capital into a larger one. Since the production of consumer goods is tied to that of producer goods and *vice versa*, the demand for either depends on the general movement of capital. With accelerating accumulation the demand for means of production will increase relative to that for consumer goods, since the mass of surplus value at any given moment has a fixed magnitude. What is accumulated cannot be consumed, although accumulation, through the growth and improvement of the means of production, throws more consumer goods into circulation. The process of accumulation must therefore be at the same time a process extending the capitalist mode of production; the world market is from the start the condition of capitalist expansion. The growth of the means of production through accumulation and the higher productivity of labor leads to the production of a constantly growing mass of commodities, and the accumulation of capital proceeds via the realization of this mass of commodities.

The increase in labor productivity has in itself nothing to do with capitalism. Productivity grew in precapitalist times, although very slowly, and will also grow after the abolition of capitalism. The whole development of society is based on the increasing productivity of labor. This general process is accomplished under the capitalist relations of production in the specific form of capitalist competition. It is however not competition that engenders the development of the productive forces but the development of the productive forces that leads to capitalist competition. Once this process has begun, capitalist competition enormously stimulates the growth of the productivity of labor. Every capital, if it is to remain a capital, must increase its productivity and thus accumulate capital. This requires an increasing share of the surplus value and leaves a relatively diminishing share for capitalist consumption. Although the quantity of consumer goods to be realized increases and allows the capitalist an ever more luxurious existence, an increasing part of the surplus value, its quantity determined by the previous level of accumulation, is capitalized. More means of production and fewer articles of consumption are required. The production of commodities shifts in response to the changed demand. With respect to the realization of surplus value—and from the standpoint of the total capital the realization problem concerns only the surplus value—this is accomplished through capitalists' consumption and the accumulation of capital.

Supply and demand adapt themselves to the accumulation needs of capital. It is of course true that in the final analysis, the increased means of production are used to produce consumer goods and that these must find a market if they are to be transformed back again into capital. But this market arises from the dynamic of capital, from its continuing and broadening accumulation in the course of which a growing quantity of surplus value is invested in means of production. Capital thus creates its own market and realizes its profit in accumulation and in growing capitalist consumption. This process is only possible because the workers are excluded from the realization process of capital. If the realization of surplus value were to hinge on its increasing consumption, this would mean a corresponding loss of profit for capital and would therefore be accompanied by a lower rate of accumulation and decreased capitalist consumption. But the value character of labor power excludes this possibility and reserves the surplus value for capital as its "final consumer."

The idea that capital could be unable to use its surplus value and so realize it is hard to understand. Even aside from the compulsion to accumulate, the desire to accumulate is generally unlimited. No capitalist ever finds himself "too rich," and his wealth represents capital for him. Accumulation brings him a larger mass of profit, which makes possible his continued accumulation. The use of additional labor power, his own increased consumption, and the extension of the world market make it possible for the capitalist to transform the unconsumed portion of surplus value directly into additional capital in the expectation of further expansion and irrespective of the actual market situation. Since production must precede consumption in any case, the production of means of production is not limited by the current market demand for consumer goods. So long as the rate of surplus value keeps step with accumulation or exceeds it, the accumulation of capital means no more than the extension of the capitalist mode of production itself: capital's conquest of the world. It continuously creates new prerequisites for capitalist production, long before the old ones have completed the metamorphosis from the commodity form of capital into the capital form, so that the accumulation of capital always outstrips consumption and determines its extent.

Capital would have had a different history if its accumulation had really depended on the realization of surplus value by those whom Mandel calls the "final consumers." In reality accumulation has always proceeded at the cost of consumption, which, while growing, lagged behind the expansion of captail. While the production of constant capital must ultimately lead to the production of consumer goods, this does not mean that it is *only* employed when there is a corresponding demand for consumer goods. "Since the aim of capital is not to minister to certain wants, but to produce profit, and since it accomplishes this purpose by methods which adapt the mass of production to the scale of production, not vice versa, a rift must continually ensue between the limited dimensions of production under capitalism and a production which forever tends to exceed this immanent barrier."[22] Thus, according to Marx, actually

> too many means of labor and necessities of life are produced at times to permit of their serving as means for the exploitation of laborers at a certain rate of profit. Too many commodities are produced to permit of a realization and conversion into new capital of the value and surplus value contained in them under the conditions of distribution and consumption peculiar to capitalist production, i.e., too many to permit of the consummation of this process without constantly recurring explosions.[23]

But these contradictions and the explosions fueled by them are always the consequence of a successful period of accumulation during which *the same contradictions* have provided an impetus for accumulation. The limit of the capitalist mode of production is, according to Marx, to be seen in the fact that

> the development of the productivity of labor creates in the falling rate of profit a law which at a certain point comes into antagonistic conflict with this development and must be overcome constantly through crises . . . [and] that the expansion or contraction of production are determined by the appropriation of unpaid labor and the proportion of this unpaid labor to materialized labor in general, or, to speak the language of capital, by profit and the proportion of this profit to the employed capital, thus by a definite rate of profit. . . .[24]

Only at the point where the organic composition of capital, rising as a result of accumulation, lowers the rate of profit is this overaccumulation accompanied by the overproduction of commodities, the discrepancy between production and consumption, and the realization problem. These difficulties are *always immanent* in capitalist production, without thereby being an obstacle to accumulation, until the latter itself becomes an obstacle.

The cessation of accumulation indicates that it was dependent not only on the profitability of capital but also on the restriction of consumption this involves, which appears on the market as a problem of realization. This does not mean that the capitalist crisis that appears as overproduction can be overcome by an increase in consumption. The difficulties of realization of surplus value must be overcome by the continuation of the accumulation process. The solution must be found in production and not in the market. Surplus value must be increased so that the mass of profit can be adjusted to capitalist expansion despite the *continuing* relative decline of social consumption. The crisis of overproduction itself becomes a means to this end, on the one hand through the devaluation of capital, and on the other through the continuing concentration of capital and the alteration of the capital structure connected with it, which lead to a rise in the rate of profit.

It is therefore possible to show abstractly, without introducing the realization problem, that the limits of capitalist production are a direct consequence of value production. Even on the assumption that capital can sell all its commodities and realize their full surplus value, while the worker receives the value of his labor power, with the rising organic composition of capital profit must dry up at that point of accumulation at which the rate of exploitation of the labor force employed by capital can no longer be increased. In reality this *decisive contradiction* of capitalist production appears in the form of a series of contradictions flowing from it, such as the actual difficulty of realizing surplus value, the difference between production and consumption, and the various disproportionalities of the economy, which are all specific to this system and cannot be overcome within it. Thus the realization problem appears in reality not in the form in which it arises from the capitalist relations of production—namely as a problem exclusively of the realization of surplus value—but as a problem of the realization of commodity values, including both value and surplus value. If a part of the surplus value cannot be realized as profit, a part of the value can also not be realized, so that the problem of realization appears as general overproduction.

If it were true that, as Mandel says, "the difficulty of realization can ultimately be resolved only by increasing the monetarily effective demand for *consumer goods*" (p. 281), it could never be resolved, but at most hidden temporarily by an acceleration of accumulation. Mandel also knows this. This "ultimate" case cannot be realized, since "this runs counter to the whole logic of the capitalist mode of production" (p. 281). But this "ultimate" case contains the key to Mandel's theory of the realization of surplus value by the armaments industry. What cannot be accomplished by the "final consumers" appears to him to be taken care of by the arms industry.

VII

According to Mandel, it makes no difference with respect to the creation of value whether a commodity is produced for the consumption of the workers, the capitalists, or the state. "For Marx," Mandel explains, "it is abstract labor that creates value, i.e., labor which as a part of the total social labor capacity, produces a commodity which, irrespective of its use-value, finds its equivalent on the market because it fulfills a social need" (p. 292, translation corrected). Thus the domain of value production is the same as that of commodity production, so that the rate of profit depends on the mass of surplus labor "set in motion in the production of commodities by social capital, *irrespective of the sector*"—including, e.g., the armaments sector—"in which this occurs" (p. 292).

We can ignore Mandel's reflections on whether the arms sector, as the third department of his reproduction schema, has a higher or lower organic composition of capital and on the positive or negative influence of this on the average rate of profit. For in reality the arms industry does not represent a particular sector but exists within capitalist production in general. What is important to us are the questions of whether the armaments industry is really a case of commodity production, whether these commodities are exchanged for others, and whether their putative value enters into the total value.

Mandel answers these questions in the affirmative, but with the qualification that this holds only under certain conditions, from which it actually would follow that the arms industry is not an ordinary case of commodity trafficking at all. The qualification asserts that Mandel's answer holds only "so long as there are unused reserves available in the economy," and since "this is the starting point of the 'permanent arms industry' no particular problems are created by the specific use-value of the additional production . . ." (p. 294, translation corrected). Then follows a further qualification, namely that the acceleration of capital accumulation made possible by arms production is only successful when the entire surplus capital (the unused reserves) is switched into weapons production "gradually rather than suddenly" (p. 295). When this is the case, previously idle capital can be valorized by the arms industry.

The concept of "abstract labor" refers to the total social labor time, into which all particular labor times enter and in which they are dissolved. It does not refer to the distribution of value or surplus value, which depends on the concrete relations of capitalist production, determined by the use values of the commodities. Under the *assumption* that all labor produces value, the total labor time equals the total value, which is divided into value and surplus value. Since the value of a commodity must be realized on the market, every commodity must find a buyer, so that—in constantly changing foms—labor-time quantities can exchange against labor-time quantities. The "commodities" produced in the arms industry, however, are exchanged neither against the labor-time values of the working class nor against the surplus value of the capitalists. Apart from the insignificant portion of weapons production that enters into private consumption, the state is the buyer of these commodities. Of course, the state cannot exchange its own "abstract labor" for the "abstract labor" contained in armaments because it produces nothing at all. Its income is derived from taxation of the social income yielded by the production of value and surplus value.

Even Mandel knows that state spending (including the purchase of weaponry) represents a deduction from wages and profits for which there is no value counterpart, and that it thus diminishes wages and profits and therefore cannot change the total value. But in his eyes this is true only in the case of full employment and the utilization of all productive resources. So long as some of them are idle, value and surplus value will be enlarged and accumulation encouraged by the additional production for military purposes. The additional "commodity value" will be realized by state purchases. But then as before the state has only taxes and borrowed funds at its disposal, which gives rise to a growing national debt, which in turn can be financed and paid off only through taxes. Although production is increased by military spending, the total "newly created value" must be counted as a deduction from the proceeds of capitalist commodity production, as there is no market for the products of the armaments industry. In opposition to this Mandel speaks of "the growing significance of the arms traffic in world trade—a business which, incidentally, shows how nonsensical it is not to treat the production of weapons as commodity production and not to see the investments in this sector as accumulation of capital" (p. 308). It escapes him that this alters nothing in the case: in international trade too it is governments who buy the weapons, paying for them out of taxes, so that here too for capital as a whole arms production is not matched by revenue created in production.

Mandel imagines that production, just because it is carried on in capitalism, must be capitalist production and the production of surplus value. It is certainly true that the arms industry makes profits and accumulates capital and appears in no way different from other businesses. But its profits and new investments derive not from commodity circulation but from state expenditures, which are drawn from a part of the realized value and surplus value of other capitals. This is not obvious, since a larger part of weapons production is financed by loans rather than directly by taxation, so that the burden on private capital is spread over a long period of time. Capital gives the government credit, which can indeed enlarge production but can yield no additional surplus value, since the goods of the arms industry must be paid for out of the surplus value of the creditors.

If, according to Mandel, the arms industry means a deduction from wages and profits under conditions of full employment and the full utilization of productive resources, this is only to say that it produces no value and surplus value of its own and so cannot be described as commodity production. This cannot change just because a portion of capital is idle. Just as the capitalist valorization and realization problem cannot be overcome by the increase in consumption, it can also not be vanquished by means of the arms industry, whose products, exactly as in the case of increased consumption, are not transformed into new capital but simply disappear. The arms industry, like all other state expenditures that are not covered by the state's own production, falls, from the social point of view, exclusively into the sphere of consumption and not into that of accumulation.[25]

Notwithstanding the "value and surplus-value-producing" character of the armaments industry as "one of the most important levers for the solution of the problem of surplus capital," Mandel comes most amazingly to the conclusion that "the more the development of the arms economy threatens to reduce the gross profit of the major corporations (in other words, the higher the tax rate it determines) the stronger will be the resistance of these companies to any further extension of it" (p. 303). Now it is no longer true that it is all the same from the viewpoint of value formation which kind of commodity is produced, that arms production involves "abstract labor" which creates value and accumulates capital. If it were so, then it would be all the same to capital how far the arms business developed, since this would be equivalent to the development of value production. But we can conclude discussion of this theme here, since Mandel, as is proper for a revolutionary, explains after all that the arms industry, like capitalism in general, has objective social limits.

VIII

And since according to Mandel the long period of prosperity, for which the arms industry is partly responsible is nearing an end, the problem can in any case be left aside as a matter of the past. What is important today is the crisis cycle, which must work itself out in "late capitalism," as at any previous time. In his earlier book, *Marxist Economic Theory*, Mandel was still strongly under the influence of Keynes's theory of capitalist economic management and under the spell of the long postwar period of prosperity.

It seemed to him then that capital had succeeded, in comparison with the past, in bridging the great contradiction between surplus capital and effective demand in such a way as to stabilize the system. In his new book this holds only for the recent past but not for its future development. But a Marxist explanation of the unexpectedly long phase of prosperity must nonetheless be furnished, and Mandel believes that he has found it in the theory of "long waves."

As for everybody else so also for Mandel the industrial cycle represents "the successive acceleration and deceleration of accumulation" (p. 109). He asks, however, whether there is "a peculiar inner dynamic to the succession of industrial cycles over longer periods of time" (p. 110). According to Marx, Mandel explains, the "renewal of fixed capital explains not only the length of the business cycle but also the decisive moment underlying *extended reproduction* as a whole, the upswing and acceleration of capital accumulation" (p. 110). Now it is true that Marx attempted to bring the business cycle into connection with the turnover time of capital, which, just like the cycle, had an average span of ten years. Of course, the lifetime of capital can lengthen or shorten. However, according to Marx, what is important is not a particular number of years. This seemed evident to him:

> the cycles of interconnected turnovers embracing a number of years, in which capital is held fast by its fixed constituent part, furnish a material basis for the periodic crises. During this cycle business undergoes successive periods of depression, medium activity, precipitancy, crisis. True, periods in which capital is invested differ greatly and far from coincide in time. But a crisis always forms the starting point of large new investments. Therefore, from the point of view of society as a whole, more or less, a new material basis for the next turnover cycle.[26]

Marx never followed up this vague hypothesis, if only because the lifetimes of different capitals are different, and because they are renewed not at the same time but according to their individual starting points, while the business cycle is a matter affecting the whole society at one particular moment. Certainly crisis leads to a concentration of new investments at one time and thus to a sort of "material basis for the next turnover cycle." And doubtless capital finds itself "under the spell of its fixed component," since the latter, in accordance with its reproduction time, must be renewed in order to be a basis for new investments. The shorter the turnover time, the sooner the renewals and new investments participate in the improved productivity due to the "perpetual revolutionizing of the means of production," and the lower are the costs of the "moral depreciation" that precedes the physical end of capital. But in the final analysis all of this only means that "the crisis always forms the starting point of large new investments," i.e., that the productivity of capital is sufficiently improved to recommence the process of accumulation.

But according to Mandel it must be explained "why at a particular point in time this additional capital is expended on a massive scale, after lying idle for a long period." For him "the answer is obvious: only a *sudden increase in the rate of profit* can explain the massive investment of surplus capitals—just as a prolonged fall in the rate of profit . . . can explain the idleness of the same capital over many years" (p. 114). According to Mandel the rate of profit grows as the result of a sudden fall in the average organic composition of capital; a sudden rise in the rate of surplus value; a sudden cheapening of elements of constant capital; and a sudden shortening of the turnover time of the circulating capital (p. 115). In this way arises the possibility of achieving "not only a partial and moderate, but a massive and general revolution in production technology," particularly "if *several factors are simultaneously and cumulatively* contributing to a rise in the average rate of profit" (pp. 115-16). In short, it is absolutely clear that accumulation is a consequence of the sudden rise in profitability.

These new investments revolutionizing production techniques, which are at once results and causes of the sudden rise of the rate of profit, lead to further growth of the organic composition of capital, which leads in a "second phase" of development to new valorization difficulties and new idle capital. "Only if a combination of specific conditions generates a sudden rise in the average rate of profit," continues Mandel, "will this idle capital, which has slowly gathered over several decades, be drawn on a massive scale into the new spheres of production capable of developing the new basic technology" (p. 120). On the basis of this "development of basic production technology," "the history of capitalism on the international plane" must be understood "not only as a succession of cyclical movements every seven or ten years, but also as a succession of long periods, of approximately fifty years . . ." (p. 120). These "long waves," although noted by a number of people, were most notably discussed by Kondratiev, who attempted to prove their existence statistically.[27] They impressed Mandel's mentor, Leon Trotsky, strongly enough for him to investigate them critically but sympathetically. The moment was particularly opportune, as the New Course announced at the Third World Congress of the Communist International was based on the hypothesis of a stabilization of the capitalist system postponing the world revolution. Trotsky's argument was directed against so-called "economism" and against "the purely mechanical conception of capitalist breakdown," which was attributed to those who still maintained a world-revolutionary perspective. The theory of the "long waves" was a godsend in this connection, since it could not be foreseen whether an end or a beginning of one of these waves had been reached.

According to Kondratiev and Trotsky, the economic curves have different characteristics at different times. In order for capitalist development to take place, the new prosperity released by the crisis must surpass the prosperity preceding the crisis. One can identify epochs of capitalist development that, apart from their economic curves, exhibit a general upswing tendency and other epochs that have a more static character. But these long, epochal waves of slower or more rapid accumulation should, according to Trotsky, be viewed not in the same way as the phenomena of crisis Marx brought to light, which are inherent in capitalism, but as the results of the influence of external causes on capital accumulation, such as "the capitalist conquest of other lands, the discovery of new sources of raw materials, and the accompanying superstructural phenomena, like war and revolution, which determine the character and change of rising, stagnating, or collapsing epochs of capitalist development."[28]

Mandel goes farther than Trotsky, who obviously has said only that capitalism exists not in a vacuum but in the real world. While Trotsky attacked any "monocausal" or "purely economic" explanation of capitalist development, Mandel's "long waves" are again seen as "monocausal" and "purely economic" phenomena, since, although the average rate of profit "must be explained by a series of social changes" (p. 129), it is nevertheless the movement of the profit rate that determines both short and long waves. Since this whole discussion turns more or less around a pseudo problem, Mandel can also rest undisturbed by the fact that the existence of "long waves" cannot be convincingly proved by statistics; he regards "the main problem *not* as one of statistical verification, but of theoretical explanation, although it goes without saying that, if the theory of 'long waves' could not be confirmed empirically, it would be an unfounded working hypothesis and ultimately a mystification" (p. 140).

Mandel nonetheless believes that his own contribution has been to explain the "long waves" in terms of "the inner logic of the process of long-term accumulation and valorization of capital" (p. 145), and thus he refers without further ceremony to the existence of the "long waves" in order to shed light upon the previous history of capitalism as well as on "late capitalism." This is what he comes up with: Accumulation leads to the fall in the rate of profit; the profit rate can be raised in order to continue accumulation. As the world changes, this is at one time easier and at another time harder to do, not only in relation to a particular reproduction cycle but also historically. By linking theory with history we can distinguish between different but overlapping epochs of capitalist production. In an extended period of depression, in which a series of cyclical movements takes place without leading to a noticeable upswing, we are dealing with a declining long wave of capitalist production, while in an epoch of capitalist development in which shorter cyclical movements do not counteract a generally upward trend, we can speak of a long wave of prosperity. Thus for Mandel the accelerated accumulation, without serious crisis situations, characteristic of "late capitalism" is explained as a "long wave with an undertone of expansion" (p. 194), made possible not only by the arms industry but also, and more importantly, by structural changes in capital and new conditions of production.

The "long wave with an undertone of expansion" that lasted

from 1940 to 1965 and formed the basis for a "third technological revolution" was, however, according to Mandel,

> by no means "purely" the product of economic development, proof of the alleged vitality of the capitalist mode of production or a justification for its existence. All it proved was that in the imperialist countries, given existing technology and forces of production, there are no "absolutely hopeless situations" in a purely economic sense for capital, and that the long-term failure to accomplish a socialist revolution can ultimately give the capitalist mode of production a new lease on life, which the latter will then exploit in accordance with its inherent logic . . . (p. 221).

Thus capital succeeded once more in enlarging the productive forces. But the "third technological revolution" indicates also the historical limits of capital, for "who is supposed to buy a doubled volume of durable consumer goods if, with a constant selling price, the nominal income of the population is reduced by half?" (p. 205). Here we have arrived with Mandel "at the absolute inner limit of the capitalist mode of production. . . . It lies in the fact that the *mass of surplus-value itself necessarily diminishes as a result of the elimination of living labor from the production process in the course of the final stage of mechanization-automation*" (p. 207).

The "absolute inner limit" of the capitalist mode of production, however, according to Mandel, confronts the fact that "there are no absolutely hopeless situations" for capital, since it depends exclusively on the proletariat whether it can muddle on further even without "a justification for its existence." It does not exist on the basis of its own "vitality" but because of the proletariat's readiness to give it a new "lease on life," thus because of the vitality of the nonrevolutionary working class. If we therefore have the working class or, more precisely, its incorrect leadership to thank for the "long wave with an undertone of expansion," the new "long wave with an undertone of stagnation" (p. 459) will demonstrate "the increasing liability of the social system to explosive social crises" that compel capital to give precedence to the task of "the destruction of proletarian class consciousness—particularly in its socialist form" (p. 437, German edition; compare English translation, pp. 485-86). Meanwhile, and despite the lack of vitality, it has turned out that "far from representing a 'post-industrial society,' late capitalism thus constitutes *generalized universal industrialization* for the first time in history. Mechanization, standardization, overspecialization and parcellization of labor . . . now penetrate into all sectors of social life" (p. 387). By this its abolition is assured.

The characteristics of "late capitalism" appear for Mandel to be the shortening of the turnover time of fixed capital; the cheapening of constant capital; the increase in the rate of surplus value; capital's entry into the circulation and service sectors; and economic programming in order "to bridge over, at least partially, the contradiction between the anarchy of capitalist production inherent in the private ownership of the means of production and the growing objective pressure to plan amortization and investments" (p. 231). All these properties, which have characterized capital from time immemorial, lead in "late capitalism" to a "permanent inflation," which is at the service of the "long-term protection of the expanded reproduction" of capital.

The permanent inflation is in Mandel's eyes a permanent credit inflation or the specific accommodation of the banking system and money creation to the interests of monopoly capital. Through the expansion of credit demand is increased, which leads to the employment of surplus capital in additional production. In view of the underutilization of productive forces, the inflationary creation of money and credit are able to push the development of the productive forces beyond the limits set by private property. Behind the inflation lies the "conversion of idle capital into productive capital" (p. 443). Like the arms industry, credit inflation leads to an increased production of value and surplus value. It slows down the decline in sales of consumer goods. The expansion of credit can stimulate prosperity "up to the point beyond which it risks jeopardizing the share of the world market controlled by the country in question" (p. 455). The "long-term diminution of the industrial reserve army, which was the corollary of the substantial growth in the accumulation of capital, enabled the working class periodically to chip away at the rate of surplus-value somewhat" (p. 457). Thus according to Mandel everything indicates "a decline in the relative autonomy of the credit cycle, and hence the ability of creeping inflation to restrict the cumulative effect of crises of over-production" (p. 459).

Why the extension of private credit should have inflationary consequences is hard to see in light of unused productive capacity and accumulated surplus capital; and this all the more since, according to Mandel, the increase in demand is closely connected with a corresponding production of value and surplus value. With respect to manufacturing industry, he himself says that "if substantial over-capacity already exists, even the most abundant injections of credit money . . . will not lead to a stimulation of private investments . . ." (pp. 457-58). But was it not the function of credit injections to overcome overcapacity by means of increased demand? The "stimulating impact of inflationary creation of credit ceases to be effective," according to Mandel, "when a rising debt-burden begins to restrict current purchasing power" (p. 459). But why should the debt burden rise when the process released by "credit inflation" leads to new additional value and surplus value? It makes little sense to go into Mandel's theory of inflation seriously, since it consists of no more than the assertion, pulled out of thin air, that credit must in itself lead to permanent inflation.

Mandel comes somewhat closer to the heart of the matter as soon as he deals with the credit-supported interventions of the state into the economy. "If such state outlays," he writes,

> are wholly financed by taxation, then once again there will be no change in global demand. . . . Only if these investments at least to some extent result in a direct nominal increase in purchasing power—i.e., bring additional means of payment into circulation—will they have a stimulating effect of the economy. . . . But since such investments do not increase the quantity of commodities in circulation to the same extent as they create additional means of payment, they inevitably contain an inflationary bias (p. 552).

The state's creation of credit by way of deficit financing is here a means to induce an additional production not achieved through the private credit mechanism. It becomes a necessity just because the expansion of private credit does not increase demand, and thus production, sufficiently to keep unemployment and overcapacity in socially manageable proportions.

The policy of inflation, which according to Mandel does "not increase the quantity of commodities in circulation to the same extent as it creates additional means of payment" and thereby drives up prices, expresses the simple fact that the production thereby made possible is not production of commodities in the usual sense of the term. It does not yield value and surplus value but must nevertheless yield profit for the capitals participating in this production. The quantity of commodities has not really increased along with the expansion of production, since the final products of the state-induced production do not enter the market. Production has increased, but without a corresponding increase in profit. The "profit" made in state-induced production must be taken in the form of taxes from the unenlarged mass of profit of capital as a whole. This pressure on capitalist revenue is fought by price increases, so that the costs of unprofitable production are paid by Mandel's "final consumers."

The demand determined by the "final consumers"—which, to believe Mandel, in the final analysis determines the movement of capital and thereby denies it a secure future—continues to be reduced, relative to increasing production, in order to avoid social upheavals. With this is connected the insubstantial hope that it represents a transitory situation that will sooner or later be overcome by a general upswing of capitalist production. In accordance with this goal capital now, as before, continues down the one-way street of profit expansion. The fate of the "final consumers" appears first as the fate of the working class: increased exploitation through inflation. With the more rapid increase in commodity prices relative to wages, a profit can be made in circulation whose extraction at the point of production would lead to greater opposition. Inflation is above all a wages policy meant to secure capitalist surplus value and, when possible, to increase it; it is also a method of decreasing the expenses of the noncapitalist but also unproductive strata of society. But since steadily increasing inflation can also damage the interests of capital, it represents a policy forced on capital that it would gladly be done with but cannot do without.

Mandel's "long wave with an undertone of expansion" differs

from his "long wave with an undertone of stagnation" only in the circumstance that the instruments used by the state to combat crisis, "discovered" during the last great world crisis, are on the point of losing their effectiveness. They encounter definite limits in capitalist production that cannot be infringed without destroying the system. The long period of prosperity after the Second World War encompassed only the great capitalist powers. But despite the enormous destruction of capital, despite the further extension of the concentration of capital on an international scale, despite the "third technological revolution" and all the other structural changes in capital, even these nations remained tied to the contradictory pursuit of unprofitable production. Even the economic programming so emphasized by Mandel remains a matter of blind reactions to the still uncontrollable laws of motion of capital. The crisis, always latent, is becoming acute again, and it is no longer possible to counteract it by the state interventions used in the past. Inflation, which was supposed to combat unemployment, becomes inflation with growing unemployment; the international planning of investments becomes the ruthless competitive struggle of national capitals; "late capitalism" shows itself to be the same capitalism that all along moved only in one direction, that of its final abolition.

Notes

1. Frankfurt, 1972. English translation, London, 1975.
2. London, 1968.
3. Page numbers in parenthesis refer to *Late Capitalism*. This passage does not appear in the translation, so it is cited from the German original.
4. Marx-Engels, *Werke* (MEW), vol. 39, p. 428.
5. *Die Akkumulation des Kapitals*, Leipzig, 1912.
6. *Das Akkumulations- und Zusammenbruchsgesetz des kapitalistischen Systems*, Leipzig, 1929.
7. *Der Imperialismus und die Akkumulation des Kapitals*, Vienna, 1926.
8. *Das Finanzkapital*, Vienna, 1910.
9. R. Rosdolsky, *The Making of Marx's "Capital,"* London, 1977.
10. Ibid., p. 496.
11. Ibid., p. 504.
12. Ibid., p. 505.

13. In his *Marxist Economic Theory* Mandel explained crisis as due to a lack of profit caused by a rise in the value of labor power, thus as due not to underconsumption but to the too great consumption of the workers.

14. Rosdolsky, op. cit., p. 462.

15. K. Marx, *Capital*, vol. 1, Harmondsworth, 1976, p. 770.

16. Ibid., p. 762.

17. A detailed discussion will be found in chaps. 9 and 10 of *Capital*, vol. 3.

18. Marx, *Capital*, vol. 3, Moscow, 1962, p. 159.

19. Marx, "Results of the Immediate Process of Production," in *Capital*, vol. 1, pp. 1012-3 [translation corrected].

20. Marx, *Capital*, vol. 3, p. 429 [translation corrected].

21. F. Engels, *Herr Eugen Dühring's Revolution in Science*, New York, 1939, p. 303 [translation corrected].

22. Marx, *Capital*, vol. 3, p. 251.

23. Ibid., p. 253.

24. Ibid. [translation corrected].

25. Mandel reproaches me for wavering to and fro between different interpretations of the effects of war production. "At one point," says Mandel, Mattick "claims that 'production which the government commands, whether in the form of public works, welfare, or armaments, falls in the sphere of consumption' and not of capital accumulation. Elsewhere, however, he states that war production is not simply 'waste production' but helps to step up the process of accumulation again" (p. 300 n., translation and quotation corrected). But these are not two different interpretations, since the war economy—exactly like the capitalist crisis—can be and up to now has been a means to restore the broken process of accumulation by means of the destruction of capital and structural transformation of the world economy.

26. *Capital*, vol. 2, Moscow, 1961, p. 186.

27. N. D. Kondratiev, "Die Langen Wellen der Konjuktur," in *Archiv für Sozialwissenschaft und Sozialpolitik*, 56:3 (December 1926).

28. *The Fourth International*, May 1941.

About the Author

Paul Mattick was born in Germany in 1904 and came to the United States in 1926. From 1934 to 1943 he edited the journals *Living Marxism* and *New Essays*. He has contributed numerous articles to scholarly and political journals in Europe, South America, and the United States and is the author of *Marx and Keynes, Economics, Politics, and the Age of Inflation, The Neo-Marxists, Anti-Bolshevik Communism*, and *Unemployment in the United States.*